Consuming Mission

Consuming Mission

Towards a Theology of Short-Term Mission
and Pilgrimage

ROBERT ELLIS HAYNES

Foreword by Laceye C. Warner

PICKWICK *Publications* · Eugene, Oregon

CONSUMING MISSION
Towards a Theology of Short-Term Mission and Pilgrimage

Pickwick Publications
An Imprint of Wipf and Stock Publishers
199 W. 8th Ave., Suite 3
Eugene, OR 97401

www.wipfandstock.com

PAPERBACK ISBN: 978-1-5326-3919-7
HARDCOVER ISBN: 978-1-5326-3920-3
EBOOK ISBN: 978-1-5326-3921-0

Cataloguing-in-Publication data:

Names: Haynes, Robert Ellis, author. | Warner, Laceye C., foreword.

Title: Consuming mission : towards a theology of short-term mission and pilgrimage / Robert Ellis Haynes ; foreword by Laceye C. Warner.

Description: Eugene, OR : Pickwick Publications, 2018 | Includes bibliographical references and index.

Identifiers: ISBN 978-1-5326-3919-7 (paperback) | ISBN 978-1-5326-3920-3 (hardcover) | ISBN 978-1-5326-3921-0 (ebook)

Subjects: LCSH: Discipling (Christianity). | Spiritual formation. | Mission of the church. | Missional church movement.

Classification: BV4520 .H38 2018 (paperback) | BV4520 .H38 (ebook)

Manufactured in the U.S.A.   11/07/18

For Elizabeth, Joshua, and Megan.
Your work made this possible.

Contents

Foreword by Laceye C. Warner | ix
Preface | xi
Acknowledgments | xv

Section I: The Landscape of Mission Theology

1   The Biblical Mandate for Mission | 3
2   The Mission of God and Its Church | 16
3   A Wesleyan Theology of Mission | 47
4   Short-Term Mission and a Theology of Mission | 65

Section II: The Practice of Short-Term Missions

5   Hearing from United Methodist Short-Term Missioners | 85

Section III: Short-Term Mission, Tourism, and Pilgrimage

6   Influences on the Practice of Short-Term Mission | 159
7   Pilgrimage, Tourism, and Mission | 181
8   Consuming Mission: Towards a Theology of Short-Term Mission and Pilgrimage | 205

Appendix: Participating churches/ministries | 219

Bibliography | 221
Index | 231

Foreword

In the pages that follow Rev. Dr. Robert Haynes offers a treasure of original research featuring insightful questions and intriguing findings regarding short-term missions. Dr. Haynes, Director of Education and Leadership for World Methodist Evangelism, shares the results of his study to illumine the profound impact and, at times, unintended consequence of this beloved local church practice. Trained by years of pastoral leadership and scholarly work, Dr. Haynes frames the study with biblical and theological themes to inform original field research data gleaned from participants in short-term mission trips.

The results of this study reveal hopeful as well as troubling results gathered from the implicit and explicit theologies of lay and clergy participants in short-term missions. Short-term mission trips represent a seemingly ubiquitous Christian experience that has spread rampantly among U.S. evangelical Christians. Dr. Haynes explores the many layers of participation from the costly economics of time and money by those traveling and hosting, to the perceptions and desire for ministry service and impact, alongside personal growth and edification. Dr. Haynes articulates the tensions created from mixing mission, pilgrimage, and tourism—and offers important steps to move the practice away from using mission only for personal edification.

This project is a rare gift of original field research and interdisciplinary expertise reflecting upon a widespread and influential practice. With gratitude to Dr. Haynes for unpacking the cultural influences and critical tensions, may this work inspire careful and attentive Christian practices of evangelism to share the gospel of Jesus Christ with those near and far.

Laceye C. Warner
Royce and Jane Reynolds Associate Professor
of the Practice of Evangelism and Methodist Studies,
Duke University Divinity School
August 21, 2018
Durham, North Carolina

Preface

From my first days of ministerial service, my peers and mentors advised me to get involved in short-term mission (hereafter STM) trips. These trips would, they assured me, have profound effects on my ministry. Such trips would lead to a deeply moving experience for those who served on the team. These team members would then begin to serve in the church in new ways, and this would lead to more fruitful ministries in my local congregation. Who would not want those sorts of outcomes in the local church? As a bonus, the people of the other country would be helped along the way. It seemed like an easy decision to make. I set about establishing these service trips to strengthen existing and to establish new domestic and international relationships and to generate excitement among key people in the church. As both a lay youth worker and an ordained minister, I led several STMs.

However, they did not always seem to manifest the sort of change that I was told to expect. When talking about their trips later, some people in my churches did talk of the life-changing experience they had. Their accounts were inspiring. I heard stories of the great things happening "over there": vibrant worship experiences, pastors who made great sacrifices to serve their people, and children saved from the clutches of abject poverty. Team members, who were complete strangers before the trip, were behaving like life-long friends just a week later. Several people spoke of the need to do more things like that at home. Yet, much like a sapling tree, my team members could be sent into place for a week or so during the trip, but when released back home, they quickly returned to their previous state.[1] Few significant, lasting lifestyle changes were made, it seemed, in the mission participants. That is, until it was time to prepare for the trip again. The drive to recapture something lost since the last trip seemed to fuel their preparations for the next one. They were ready to be bent again "over there." Others

1. I am grateful to Kurt Ver Beek for this imagery. Ver Beek, "The Impact of Short-Term Missions."

seemed to experience less of a seismic shift in their lives on the trip. They spoke of it being nice to see the beauty of the land and to meet the people, but since they had now seen that country, they wanted to visit somewhere new. Others spoke of some things that they enjoyed about the trip, but still felt the North Americans could teach "those people" a thing or two about how to run their country.

Over the years, I grew increasingly curious as to why there was such a wide range of responses among people who were from the same church and participated in the same trip. I wondered why similar people who experienced similar things could be affected in such different ways. Investigating the phenomenon further, I discovered that my experience was not unique. Throughout this inquiry process, I found that many of the conversations I had about STM trips, whether they were mostly negative or mostly positive, were highly emotive. Many long-term missionaries expressed disdain for the practice. I heard stories of short-term teams who unconsciously undermined years of work with their ethnocentrism. People who repeatedly took STM trips talked as though the location of their trips was the only place where God was at work in the world and they were counting the days until they could go back. One day I received a phone call that generated a mixture of emotions. A congregant called me to register her fourteen-year-old daughter for an upcoming trip to Central America. She wanted the teen to go, she told me, because she wanted her daughter to "know just how good she's got it here in America."

I thus began a period of careful reflection. As I considered the conventional wisdom, questions grew around all that it purported. Why would people spend their money, vacation time, and hard work for people they had never met? What compelled comfortable Americans to put themselves amongst the hardships of poverty and natural disasters? As a Wesleyan, I understand service to another to be a means of grace: a way in which we grow closer to God. But that leads to the question: For whom is the service done? Does one serve in order to grow in faith? Or does one grow in faith and then serve because of it? Or is the relationship more complicated than that? In fact, the question is much more complicated than that.

We live in a world where the vitality of the church in the West is in question. At the same time, the church is seeing significant growth in the Global South, which is often the destination of such mission trips. What does this mean for the exchanges of theology that are likely to happen on a short-term trip? Could it be that the mission hosts will be the primary ministers, rather than the short-term missioners?

STM is widely practiced throughout the United States and involves millions of people and billions of dollars. The influence of those who participate in the practice can be felt far and wide. The question is, just what is that influence and how is it being used? For this study, I chose to interact with teams from United Methodist congregations and/or parachurch ministries. This was not done with a sense of superiority for United Methodist mission. Rather, I am a United Methodist minister and, as such, I can speak about that expression better than others. In addition, United Methodist international mission is prevalent in churches in the Southeastern United States where I am based.

As I began preliminary studies of the practice of STM, I noticed plenty of advice on the practice but not much development on the theology that should motivate such practice. My initial hunch was that this could explain the wide range of emotions, negative and positive, around the practice. I wanted to know if there is a relationship between one's theological understanding and one's actions. In what way does theology relate to practical application?

This is a project about mission theology. While it is important to hear directly from those who are participating in STM today, we will first need to examine a theology of mission. We will take an overview of the contemporary landscape of missiology to better understand the dynamics of the mission practices observed. In chapter 1, we will examine the biblical basis for mission. The discussion of the biblical texts will focus upon the New Testament teachings around mission and the primitive church's expression thereof.

To move towards an articulation of current missional expression in the Wesleyan tradition, it is necessary to acknowledge significant contributions to the field of mission theology and history. In chapter 2, we will briefly examine the landscape of historical mission though and the development of the concept of the *missio Dei*. While there have been several important movements in mission, we will examine some of the outcroppings on the missiological landscape important to our discussion: Fresh Expressions, the Emerging Church Movement, and the Third Wave Mission movement.

Having established that portion of the landscape of missiology, I will use chapter 3 to illustrate five essential points of Wesleyan mission theology and discuss them in light of such a landscape. I examine the formulation of Wesleyan mission as currently expressed by The United Methodist Church. I will show where such a theology resonates and where dissonance remains in the larger terrain of missiology.

One of the most widely practiced and least understood areas of contemporary mission is the wide-spread phenomenon of STM. In chapter 4, I examine some of the implications for mission of this grassroots movement. I consider issues such as globalization, World Christianity, and the use of social capital in ecclesial efforts. Through these first chapters, I will establish a Wesleyan theology of mission and the place of STM in contemporary Methodist church life.

Once established, we will then be prepared to examine the practice of STM directly from its practitioners. Chapter 5 is an account of the implicit and explicit theology in the narratives of the transnational STM team members. My goal was to hear the theologies and related motivations of STM participants in a broader context than my own limited ones. I know of no other studies that seek to do so in the same manner. I attempt to faithfully represent their stories while connecting them to some important points of the theology of mission I established.

In chapter 6 I provide some framework for discussion of the implications of these narratives in relation to contemporary culture and the theological expressions found in the field data. Using sociological and economic models, I provide dialogue partners for the issues of missiology found in my discussion with the field research participants. I interpret the field data considering these sociological and economic models in chapter 7.

Having synthesized the data from the field research, I examine it in light of the essential points of a Wesleyan theology of mission in chapter 8. I will affirm the current efforts of STM that align with such a theology and provide suggestions for necessary correction in others.

Acknowledgments

I owe a debt of gratitude to many people for their contributions to this project. I am thankful to all who have helped shape my thinking about these topics, chief among these are Prof. David Wilkinson and Dr. Mathew Guest of Durham University. Dr. Calvin Samuel, thank you for the most interesting conversations in front of the fireplace, or any other place. I am indebted to Dr. Robert Tuttle for seeing this project long before I could. I am grateful to those who participated in the field research portion of the data collection. I have attempted to faithfully represent you and your answers. May they be used for mutual edification. I must express my thanks to my dear colleagues, the members of PG5. Our conversations on the Bailey were a welcome companion.

I deeply appreciate the support of friends and the churches who have encouraged our family through this journey. Catherine Watterson, your skill and your red pen were helpful tutors throughout the revision process. Rev. James Cook, thank you for helping me do the difficult things that had to be done. Gabriel Holloway, I am grateful to have you as a dialogue partner in writing and ministry. Daniel Nance, I appreciate you sharing your expertise in the Economy of Experience. To Murray and Zoe, your companionship throughout the revision process was a gift. Chiefly, it is to my family that I owe the deepest thanks. Your sacrifices, encouragement, and confidence kept me going. Thank you.

SECTION I

The Landscape of Mission Theology

1

The Biblical Mandate for Mission

To better understand the contemporary STM movement we must begin with a discussion of the biblical mandate for mission and the way the church has sought to practice mission thus far. This first section will help us see how mission theology drives mission practice. This first chapter will briefly explore the biblical mandate for mission. The subsequent chapters in this opening section will examine how the church has understood its role in mission practice. Chapter 2 will examine historical practices of mission and the development of an important mission concept for contemporary practice: the *missio Dei*. This discussion will help us map the landscape of mission theology and find our current place on that landscape. In chapter 3, we will narrow our focus to the missional work inside the Wesleyan movement before moving on to an examination of mission in the STM movement in chapter 4. But first it is important to offer a preliminary definition of "mission" to better understand our vantage point as we survey the terrain.

The way in which many use the term "mission" is a recent development, with an important shift in that usage coming in the mid-twentieth century. A dramatic rise in the use of the word coincided with this shift in meaning. Until the 1950s the term was often used to mean the sending of one to work in a distant place, the activities of those missionaries, the designated areas where the missionaries were at work, the agency that sent them, or the object of the Christian work of conversion. In ecclesial terms, it has come to include fresh connotations that could include nurturing fledging congregations in a new context or a concentration of evangelistic services. In theological conversations, both historical and contemporary, it has been used to describe, as missiologist David Bosch puts it, "(a) propagation of faith, (b) expansion of the reign of God, (c) conversion of the heathen, and (d) the founding of new churches."[1]

The term itself "presupposes a sender, a person, or persons sent by the sender, those to whom one is sent, and an assignment."[2] It supposes that those who participate in mission have a right to do so, or assume that they do. Historically, it is the church that said it had the right to do so. Until the sixteenth century, the term was used to describe God's action in the sending of his Son Jesus and the Father and the Son sending the Holy Spirit into the world. The Jesuits were the first to use the term in the sense of spreading of the Christian faith to others, including Protestants.[3] In the present day, as theologian Kirsteen Kim points out, "[m]ission has. . .become accepted by Christians of virtually all persuasions as 'a participation in the movement of God's love toward people shown in Christ.'"[4]

Martin Kähler says that mission is the "mother of all theology."[5] Theological expression finds its roots in an understanding of mission. The church's foundation is laid upon a missionary theology. The gospel writers sought to not merely give a historical impulse, but the account of a deep faith in Jesus Christ to their known world. The Evangelists' writings, and instructions and demonstrations for mission, were not "produced by historical impulses but as expressions of an ardent faith, written for the purpose of commending Jesus Christ to the Mediterranean world."[6] This mission would be expressed in various ways by the New Testament writers. So much, in fact, that there is no single, all-encompassing term for mission in the New Testament. Instead, there are at least "ninety-five Greek expressions which relate to essential but frequently different aspects of the New Testament perspective on mission."[7] The New Testament writers did not dwell on providing a definition of mission for their readers, but instead to emphasized the necessity of a missionary existence.[8]

For centuries, Christians have argued that the motivation for mission should be shaped and formed by Christian Scripture. Wesleyan theology's emphasis on concerted and thoughtful reflection on Scripture is helpful when developing a mission theology. Mission is the proclamation of Jesus'

1. Bosch, *Transforming Mission*, 1.
2. Bosch, *Transforming Mission*, 1.
3. Bosch, *Transforming Mission*, 1.
4. Kim, "Missiology as Global Conversation," 1.
5. Bosch, *Transforming Mission*, 16.
6. Bosch, *Transforming Mission*, 16.
7. Bosch, *Transforming Mission*, 16.
8. Bosch, *Transforming Mission*, 15–16.

message that is demonstrated in the biblical literature. Any understanding of biblical mission is, of course, dependent on a view of the nature of Scripture. For our purposes, I will outline two broad approaches to viewing Scripture to help distinguish the lens we will use in our discussion. One can see Scripture as religion-historical or salvation-historical. The religion-historical approach sees the biblical Scriptures as an evolutionary product. In this view, the Old Testament accounts of the history of Israel, the life and work of Jesus, and the beginnings of the church are all seen in terms of human evolutionary growth of religious understanding. This anthropocentric view of God, and the surrounding concepts of worship and ethics, are all human constructs. Likewise, mission is understood in a similar fashion. To this type of thinking, the act of mission is yet another development in the human invention of God and the idea of sharing religious convictions is centered in humankind's desire to meet the needs of another.[9] However, as Andreas Köstenberger correctly argues, to view Scripture as a solely human conception as a part of a growing religious consciousness has "devastating effects on one's view of Scripture,"[10] as well as one's understanding of the crucifixion, death and resurrection of Jesus, and the deity of Christ: "For where there is no inspiring, revealing, redeeming God who intervenes in human history, there is no unity of purpose, but only diversity of human religious views."[11]

A salvation-historical model, on the other hand, at its core, understands Scripture to be divine revelation. It is a record of God's disclosure of his very nature and his redemptive acts, both of which are offered to his people. The Scriptures, then, are not an attempt to codify human religious consciousness, but instead "the inspired record of God's revelation and redemptive acts in human history."[12] While there is progression, it is initiated by God rather than humans. While there is also diversity in the Scriptures, there is also an underlying unity and cohesiveness from the revealing, redeeming, and inspiring God. This same God is the God of mission. The Scriptures testify to his plan of mission and his redemptive purposes. It is this salvation-historical view that will guide our discussion of the use of Scripture in shaping our understanding of mission. Further, while both the Old and New Testament Scriptures point to the over-arching mission of God, the sharpest demonstration and instruction for mission come from the Gospels, the Acts of the Apostles, and the letters of the Apostle Paul.

---

9. Köstenberger, "The Place of Mission," 349.

10. Köstenberger, "The Place of Mission," 349.

11. Köstenberger, "The Place of Mission," 349.

12. Köstenberger, "The Place of Mission," 350.

For our purposes, I will limit the discussion to these works. In exploring a biblical treatment of mission theology, we begin in Matthew's Gospel.

MATTHEW

The key to understanding Matthew's missionary emphasis is found in Matt 28:16–20, what many have called "The Great Commission":

> Now the eleven disciples went to Galilee, to the mountain to which Jesus had directed them. When they saw him, they worshiped him; but some doubted. And Jesus came and said to them, "All authority in heaven and on earth has been given to me. Go therefore and make disciples of all nations, baptizing them in the name of the Father and of the Son and of the Holy Spirit, and teaching them to obey everything that I have commanded you. And remember, I am with you always, to the end of the age."

These verses must not be dismissed from the rest of the Gospel of Matthew as an isolated Missionary Manifesto, as some in the Protestant Church are apt to do. Instead, Jesus' call here should not be disconnected from the teachings, works, and commands of the rest of the Gospel. If they are separated, then Jesus' words here cannot be properly understood. The entirety of Matthew's Gospel leads up to this point and the Great Commission can be seen as the apex. Correctly understood, the Great Commission is a mandate to emulate Jesus' commands and actions that are illustrated in the preceding chapters.

To begin such an understanding, it is important to recognize Matthew's intended audience and his context and community. Matthew sought to keep a delicate balance in his mixed community of Jews and Gentiles. Matthew understood that this new group of Christians was a part of a renewal movement inside the Jewish nation. Jesus had come to call the people of Israel to live into the New Covenant that he embodies. In doing so, he proclaimed the Reign of God was breaking anew into the world. That meant false understandings of moral teachings must be put aside and that the correct understandings, such as those that were given in the Sermon on the Mount, should be embraced. Orthopraxy, Matthew emphasizes, is essential. Matthew's definition of such orthopraxy is, quite simply, Christian discipleship.[13]

---

13. Bosch, *Transforming Mission*, 57–71.

Discipleship is a key theme for Matthew, even more so than baptism or teaching. The noun "disciple" (*mathetes*) is commonplace in the four gospels and in Acts. Moreover, the term is far more important in Matthew than the other synoptic gospels. Matthew's Gospel is a lesson in Christian discipleship. This instruction culminates in the last command he mentions from Jesus: the aforementioned "Great Commission." The lesson is a command for "a commitment to God's reign, to justice and love, and to obedience to the entire will of God."[14] From this call to discipleship a call for Christian mission must flow. As Bosch puts it,

> Mission involves, from the beginning and as matter of course, making new believers sensitive to the needs of others, opening their eyes and hearts to recognize injustice, suffering, oppression, and the plight of those who have fallen by the wayside.[15]

The "Great Commission" cannot be primarily viewed as a charge for evangelism while other passages are relegated to instructions on social involvement. To fulfill Matthew's "Great Commission" Jesus' disciples must participate in God's call for justice for the poor.

LUKE AND ACTS

The combined books of Luke and Acts give us another important view of the landscape of the Bible's teaching on mission. In his two-volume work, Luke writes to a church which was facing three crisis points:

- Identity: who where they and what did their Jewish roots now mean in Jesus?

- Stagnation: this second-generation church didn't look like the vibrant one of the previous generation

- Hostility: from both Jews and Gentiles

Luke is concerned about extending Jesus' mission past these original ecclesial roots. Much as Matthew had a central pedagogical mission text (the Great Commission), Luke's central pedagogical mission text can be found in the scene of the Nazareth synagogue recorded in Luke 4:16–30 and, in particular, his declaration of his purpose found in verses 16–21:

> When he came to Nazareth, where he had been brought up, he went to the synagogue on the sabbath day, as was his custom.

14. Bosch, *Transforming Mission*, 83.
15. Bosch, *Transforming Mission*, 83.

He stood up to read, and the scroll of the prophet Isaiah was given to him. He unrolled the scroll and found the place where it was written:

> "The Spirit of the Lord is upon me,
>> because he has anointed me
>>> to bring good news to the poor.
>
> He has sent me to proclaim release to the captives
>> and recovery of sight to the blind,
>>> to let the oppressed go free,
>> to proclaim the year of the Lord's favor."

And he rolled up the scroll, gave it back to the attendant, and sat down. The eyes of all in the synagogue were fixed on him. Then he began to say to them, "Today this scripture has been fulfilled in your hearing."

This declaration of the centrality of Jesus' ministry to the poor, the setting aside of vengeance, and the mission to the Gentiles is primary. In this announcement of Good News to the poor he has in mind not just the financially disadvantaged, but also those deemed as pariahs by many in society, namely women, tax-collectors, and Samaritans. In a radical departure from the religious and societal barriers of the time, Jesus includes positive treatment for these otherwise shunned groups.[16] Such is the declaration of Jesus' mission. For Luke, the category of "poor" is not limited to financial position, but it is a social category that can be used to describe the disadvantaged, spiritually blind, oppressed, and captives as illustrated in the discourse in the synagogue in Nazareth.

While he emphasizes Jesus' ministry to the poor of all types, in a unique role from the other gospel writers, Luke is also an evangelist to the financially rich. He sees the rich as the *plousios*: the greedy, those who exploit the poor, those who worry more about money than the coming Kingdom of God, those who do not notice the poor in their midst, those who are choked with cares about money, and those who are slaves of and worshippers of money. In Luke, Jesus calls upon the rich to give up exploitation and the abuse of power and set aside their arrogance. He calls them to solidarity with the poor. Zacchaeus and Barnabas are examples of how wealthy Christians are to live. Zacchaeus is commended as a disciple, even if he doesn't physically follow Jesus.[17] Jesus' message of mission and kingdom in Luke is that the poor are not just those who are financially challenged and that

---

16. Goheen, "Bosch's Missional Reading of Luke," 239–42. See also Bosch, *Transforming Mission*, 89–90.

17. Bosch, *Transforming Mission*, 99–103.

rich and poor alike could and should participate in the mission of God to-gether. In other words, "we may conclude that Luke cannot really be called the evangelist of the poor; 'He can more correctly be called the "evangelist of the rich."'"[18]

Luke's missionary message is also a pneumatological one. In the Luke/ Acts writings we find that Jesus' mission starts with an outpouring of the Spirit (Luke 3:21–22); the church's mission begins with an outpouring of the Spirit (Acts 2:1–13); the Spirit is the "initiator, guide and power of the church's mission;" and he is the source of Jesus' power for his mission.[19] Luke establishes his message of kingdom and mission through Jesus' proc-lamation of the reign of a kingdom of peace and justice in the Nazareth synagogue, through his teachings, healings, and miracles, and in the move-ment of the Spirit through Jesus and his subsequent empowerment of the young church.

The declaration in the Nazareth Synagogue is a key event in under-standing Jesus' message of the mission of the Kingdom of God and the contemporary believer's role in that mission. To better understand the im-plications of this commandment at the *beginning* of Jesus' earthly ministry, we must look at another commandment near the *end* of Jesus' early minis-try. For that we turn to John's Gospel.

JOHN

Just as the end of Matthew's Gospel records an important command for those who would follow Jesus in mission, so too does the Gospel of John. John's Gospel records not only what the disciples are to do when demon-strating Jesus' teaching, but also how to do so. John records Jesus' post-res-urrection appearance to the disciples and his announcement to them about this new reality of life: "Jesus said to them again, 'Peace be with you. As the Father has sent me, so I send you.'" (John 20:21) The operative word in this commandment is "as." Everything hinges upon this. The essence of church lies in the realization of Jesus sending the disciples to operate in a particular manner: the same way he operated. Theologian Lesslie Newbigin says:

> [T]his "as" contains the whole crux of the matter. How did the Father send the Son? Well, one could go back to that basic text in Mark 1.14, where Jesus comes into Galilee preaching the Gospel of God, the good news of God, and saying: "The time is

---

18. Bosch, *Transforming Mission,* 104, quoting Schottroff and Stegemann.

19. Goheen, *Reading Luke,* 240.

fulfilled, the Kingdom of God is at hand, repent and believe the good news—believe the good news that I'm telling you". Now, that is the announcement of a fact. It is news in the strictest sense of the word.[20]

An understanding of what it means to be sent "as" the Father sent Jesus is a key for understanding the church's role in mission.[21] Missiologists often see three key points in this commissioning: 1) Jesus showed them the scars from his crucifixion wounds. As such, missioners, like all other Christian disciples, should not draw back from human suffering. Such suffering could not be as profound as the suffering Jesus endured. 2) It is significant that the disciples are sent "as" Jesus was sent by the Father. They are to go in the same way God sent Jesus. The disciples are now sent by Jesus. That means that his followers are to do the things he did, teach the way he taught, and to seek the people he sought. 3) Jesus breathed on the disciples as they received the Holy Spirit.[22] The Holy Spirit is the one who will empower them to teach, to suffer, and to serve as he has just commanded. From fulfilling the Old Testament admonishments in Micah to love mercy, do justly, and love God to the commission of Jesus to "go" and serve "as" the Father sent him, Christians must respond to the needs of others. This must be done not only in transnational contexts, but in local contexts as well.[23]

PAUL

Each of these unique emphases on mission can serve to help us see the much bigger picture of God's mission. Matthew's vision of mission is centered on the disciple. Luke's vision of mission is centered on removing boundaries between poor/rich, Jew/Gentile. John's vision is the manifestation of the Kingdom. We now turn to a discussion of Paul's vision of mission, which is centered on time. Paul is poignantly aware that Jesus of Nazareth has initiated a new cosmic age: an age of grace. Paul's message of mission is an urgent plea to his readers to: a) comprehend what this grace period means for them, b) take advantage of it for the purpose God intended, c) proclaim the same to all the nations. Paul felt it a privilege to proclaim the message of this grace period since he had experienced it firsthand. With deep gratitude, he

---

20. Newbigin, *Missionary Theologian*, 135.

21. Newbigin, *Missionary Theologian*, 135.

22. See Newbigin, *The Open Secret.*

23. Howell, *Short-Term Mission,* 230.

spread this news and calls others to do the same.[24] Paul traveled to proclaim this message to both Jew and Gentile. In doing so, he broke down racial barriers. At the same time, he destroyed other societal barriers between slave and free, and between men and women. The incorporation of the members of the local communities was essential to his mission and ministry which he saw as a function of the church.[25]

Paul's message of mission is that when one is reconciled to God, is justified, and is transformed, one cannot remain isolated from the larger Christian community. The Christ-event requires the believer to move into the community of other believers: the church. In this body, believers come together to celebrate a new life and to embody God's reign in the world. These communities, though small and weak, gather to celebrate the victory that Christ has already won and to pray for the *parousia*, the promised coming of the Lord. In doing so, members of the community become keenly aware of the tensions between what they believe and the empirical evidence at hand. Yet they, the church, look ahead to an "eschatological horizon" and come to an awareness that they are a "proleptic manifestation of God's reign, the beachhead of the new creation, the vanguard of God's new world, and the sign of the dawning new age in the midst of the old."[26] In Paul's theology the kingdom is real and present now, while there is an eager anticipation of the not yet. The Christian community is to take its comfort and its leadership from the Spirit in this time of missional tension.[27] Paul balances such tension of the ongoing mission of the kingdom with a gracious urgency, a strategic plan, and humble confidence.[28] These dichotomies are demonstrated in 2 Cor 4:7–10: Paul and his co-workers are "afflicted—not crushed; perplexed—not despairing; persecuted—not forsaken; struck down—not destroyed."[29] It was in this tenuous balance that the young church began spreading its message about the Kingdom of God.

At the close of this brief discussion of Scripture, to shape our understanding of mission, I wish to point out a few intersections with these treatments of the expressions of mission and a Wesleyan theology of mission. A correct view of Wesleyan missional theology is important to the discussion of Methodist STM that we will see later. Wesleyan missional theology affirms an understanding of mission firmly rooted in Scripture. It is vital that

24. Nussbaum, *Transforming Mission*, 33.

25. Bosch, *Transforming Mission,* 134–35.

26. Bosch, *Transforming Mission,* 146.

27. Cray, "Theology of the Kingdom," 49.

28. Nussbaum, *Transforming Mission,* 40.

29. Bosch, *Transforming Mission,* 180.

"any sound theology of mission, including any purportedly Wesleyan one, must be thoroughly biblical."[30] Wesleyan theology affirms the claim that an essential role of the church is to constantly assess its mission by the standard of Christ found in "the first witnesses. This implies, naturally, that we cannot, with integrity reflect upon what mission might mean today unless we turn to the Jesus of the New Testament, since our mission is 'moored to Jesus' person and ministry.'"[31] The theological source for mission can only be "the point of departure of our faith: God's self-communication in Christ as the basis which logically precedes and is fundamental to every other reflection."[32]

More specifically, Wesleyan theology embraces the all-encompassing focus of the Gospel of Matthew: that believers have a responsibility to share in the work of Christ in bringing a message of hope in this world, not just waiting for the next. The assertion that Luke's evangelism to the rich should be a part of the missionary message is another area of intersection. While Wesley was enthusiastic in service to the poor, he had strong messages for the rich to see their own deep needs as well.[33] The notion that the proleptic work of the church is "the beachhead of the new creation, the vanguard of God's new world" has strong resonance with Wesley's assertion that God is calling his people to work in the bringing about of this new creation. The Johannine proclamation of the work of the kingdom and the Pauline notion of the urgency of the timeliness of mission are both important premises for a Wesleyan mission theology. Such biblical motivations are foundational to Wesleyan mission.

EKKLESIA

At the conclusion of our examination the New Testament teaching on mission, there is one more point to consider as we transition to an examination of the ways the Christian witness has been practiced by the church. Before moving on, it is important to look at the transition period recorded in the New Testament works outside the gospels. The Pauline writings demonstrate the manner in which Jesus' followers understood the mandate to spread his message beyond his first hearers. However, the transitional period of the earliest days of the community of Christian believers requires

30. Snyder, "Wesleyan Theology of Mission," 21.

31. Bosch, *Transforming Mission*, 22, quoting Hahn.

32. Bosch, *Transforming Mission*, 23, quoting Kramm.

33. See Maddox, "'Visit the Poor.'"

further treatment. It is important to address some of the church's earliest understandings of itself that are relevant to our discussion of contemporary mission.

Scripture prescribes that the church is to bear God's mission. As Charles van Engen points out, the "New Testament gives no formal definition of the church."[34] Therefore, we must look to contextual clues for the church's own understanding of itself. In its origins, the church understood itself as a gathered group in and for the sake of the world. The term used in Acts to describe the gathering of Christians, the church, is *ekklesia*. This term was a secular term, and Luke does not use other terms with more religious connotations. In a secular sense, *ekklesia* was used as the gathering of the people of the city at the bidding of the municipal leaders. Lothar Coenen points out that

> centuries before the translation of the [Old Testament] and the time of the [New Testament, *ekklesia*] was clearly characterized as a political phenomenon, repeated according to certain rules and within a certain framework. It was the assembly of full citizens, functionally rooted in the constitution of the democracy, an assembly in which fundamental political and judicial decisions were made.[35]

By choosing to call themselves *ekklesia*, the earliest disciples desired to be a group gathered among the whole city and desired that they could, one day, be a gathering of the whole city.[36] To fulfill the mission to which they were called, Christians did not remain an insular body, rather "[t]he community which confesses that Jesus Christ is Lord has thus been, from the very beginning, a movement launched into the public life."[37]

What made the members of the early movements of Christianity distinct from the world was that they saw themselves as not just the *ekklesia*, but as the "*ekklesia tou Theou*," or the gathering of the people of God. *Ekklesia* is a term used in secular Greek for the assembly called by the town clerk. It was the role of this clerk to call the people to assemble for his purposes. In the same way, as the *ekklesia tou Theou*, the Christian community was proclaiming that God was calling all believers for his purposes. Such a bold proclamation said that Jesus' lordship is over all aspects of life. As such, they

34. Van Engen, "Church."
35. Coenen, "Church, Synagogue," 291.
36. Schmidt, "Ekklesia."
37. Newbigin, *The Open Secret*, 18.

were publicly declaring all other religions and societal structures as inferior to God as demonstrated in the person of Jesus of Nazareth.[38]

The leaders of the early church derived their authority for such a declaration from Jesus himself. Jesus instructed the apostles to share his message with the people in their immediate presence, the nearby places, and into all the earth. This missionary commandment was an instruction to continue the example of Jesus through the sharing of his teachings and the demonstration of the example he set. Such a command was not an isolated instruction, but a directive to continue what Jesus had inaugurated.[39]

Jesus' ascension and promise to return put the disciples in the unique role of carrying on the mission without him in their physical presence any longer. At Pentecost, the outpouring of the promised Holy Spirit demonstrated the depth and the consummation of the Easter event. The newly empowered disciples were to carry out Jesus' command by the Holy Spirit until his return. The *ekklesia*, both in the local gathering and the collective body of believers, now had the directive and the power to fulfill the mission. As such, the attention turns away from the isolated church and instead to the fulfillment of that mission in the proclamation of the Kingdom.[40]

Pentecost initiated an outward movement of the people of God. They were now to move "beyond the frontiers of faith, to share the gospel with those who have not yet heard it. Mission means movement from Christ by his Spirit to the world he reconciled."[41] Pentecost marked the dawning of a new era in which Christian disciples move in expectation of the consummation of the kingdom they are commanded to proclaim.[42] "The Spirit is the first-fruits of the harvest which will be reaped at the end of the age."[43] The completion of this harvest will come when Christ returns. As such, the Holy Spirit is, at present, the power for Christians in the proclamation of the Kingdom. Using the gifts given them by the Holy Spirit, Christians are to point to the kingdom that is of the present age and its completion in the age to come. The church, as the people of God, is to participate in the work of the Spirit in times of joy and of suffering. The Spirit-in-mission overlaps with the kingdom and its work. As such, the Spirit expands Christ's saving presence all over the earth. "The Spirit is the 'already', the presence of the

---

38. Newbigin, *The Open Secret* 18.

39. Bosch, *Transforming Mission,* 58.

40. Glasser et al., *Announcing the Kingdom,* 259–62. See also Ward, *Liquid Church,* 67.

41. Glasser et al., *Announcing the Kingdom,* 263.

42. Glasser et al., *Announcing the Kingdom,* 263.

43. Cray, "Theology of the Kingdom," 39.

Kingdom, and part of his ministry is to sustain us in both the hope and pain of waiting for the 'not yet.'"[44]

The issues of kingdom and church help us to begin to develop an appropriate ecclesiology, which requires an appropriate formulation of the theology of mission. Throughout history, the church was continually reformulating its ecclesiology in light of its understanding of mission.[45] Having now examined the biblical foundations of mission and some of the earliest efforts to be a church in mission, we turn now to a discussion of some of those understandings of the mission of God and its church.

44. Cray, "Theology of the Kingdom," 39–40.
45. Goheen, "Lesslie Newbigin's Missionary Ecclesiology," 354.

2

The Mission of God and Its Church

As we move towards a better understanding of contemporary mission practice, and specifically STM, it will be helpful to examine some of the ways the church has previously seen itself serving in mission. Having now examined the biblical underpinnings we are ready to do so. The title of this chapter gives us a hint of where we are headed: the mission has a church to use—as we shall see below. While it is beyond the scope of our discussion here to give a full treatment to all of the church's mission history, there are a few areas to emphasize for our purposes. To examine these understandings, we will discuss how the church has expressed mission from the era of primitive Christianity to contemporary emerging paradigms. Doing so will help us better locate ourselves on the mission terrain and thereby understand the ground on which we walk. Below, we will briefly touch upon historical expressions of mission important to our discussion. After doing so, we will need to spend a bit more time discussing the significance of the development of the theology of the *missio Dei* before finally addressing contemporary missiology. It is important to bring these areas into the discussion in order to see parts of missionary practice that the church should continue to emulate and parts that should be left behind. For our purposes, we will examine four important paradigms in the church's mission history:

1. The Early Church Paradigm

2. The Medieval Roman Catholic Paradigm

3. The Protestant (Reformation) Paradigm

4. The Modern Enlightenment Paradigm

I will briefly review each of these and then offer a more in-depth discussion of a contemporary one: the emerging ecumenical paradigm and its current expressions of kingdom and mission.

THE EARLY CHURCH PARADIGM

Recalling our discussion of *ekklesia* in the previous chapter, we begin our discussion of historical mission paradigms with the early church. The early Hebrew renewal movement that was the early church shifted into the Greek world in which it found itself in the second and third centuries. The Christian faith is incarnational and unless it chooses to remain a "foreign entity, it will always enter into the context in which it happens to find itself."[1] The early Christian church was no exception. The church grew in much of the Roman Empire in the first centuries. By some estimates, about half of city populations in some provinces of the Roman Empire professed a Christian faith. When the legalization of Christianity came, it was a pervasive faith system.

The "normalization" of Christianity eventually led to theological debates. These new church leaders were educated in Greek philosophical systems and, naturally, brought some of these same thoughts into Christian theology. However, the apostles' teachings were often at odds with Hellenistic thought. Much of the mission of the early church was to codify its beliefs into a workable theology in the various structures of Hellenistic life. What began as a movement slowly became an institution.[2]

THE MEDIEVAL ROMAN CATHOLIC PARADIGM

During the Middle Ages, the period AD 600–1500, the church continued to define itself in reaction to the heresies that developed in the course of further Christian thought and conversation. This also led to a centralization of theological and ecclesial power in the leadership of the Catholic church. To spread the mission of Christ, it was believed that the church must be the only authority in the matters of faith and life. The mission shifted from the individual to the institution. The initiator of mission was no longer seen in the Person of the Spirit, but in the institution of the church. This can be seen in the adoption of such thinking as *"extra eccleisam nulla salus"* or "There is no salvation outside the [Catholic] church."

---

1. Bosch, *Transforming Mission*, 195–96.
2. Bosch, *Transforming Mission*, 197–206.

As such, baptism became the goal, even over conversion. Church leaders and missionaries believed that to baptize was to make an indelible mark upon the person. They believed that those who were baptized, yet who were ignorant of Christianity, would grow in the knowledge of the church after baptism. Therefore, the goal of mission became to baptize as many as possible using the forces necessary to overcome resistance and compel the reluctant. The prevailing thought was to grow and propagate the church through baptism and do so by any means necessary, even if that meant war in which the apostates were killed.[3] "The killing of a heathen or apostate, it was now suggested, was exceptionally pleasing to God."[4] Such travesties were the foundations of the ideas of a "just war" to produce "converts" and colonialism of Christian ideas and culture. The damage of these travesties remains. It is in this period that we first see the idea of mission: a "missionary" sent as an "envoy" for the church. Previously, mission was the sending of the Son by the Father and the Holy Spirit by the Son and the Father. Here, the term changed to an idea of the church sending one to do its bidding.

Despite the damages being done on the institutional level, there was effective missionary action taking place in the monasticism of the age. Monastic communities, particularly the Benedictines, were thoroughly missionary. The monks lived among the people and worked to provide spiritual and physical improvements in the lives of their neighbors. Monasteries became centers of education and culture.[5] Additionally, monks would at times travel for personal spiritual growth. Since they had shunned most of their worldly goods they were dependent upon the kindness of others they met along the way. These monks returned such kindness with acts of service and love. As such the mutual influences of pilgrimage and mission[6] began to develop. As I point out later, similar influences remain in modern mission efforts.

THE PROTESTANT (REFORMATION) PARADIGM

Three movements that had an influence on the practice of mission during the Reformation period were the Anabaptists, the Puritans, and the Pietists. These three groups were, at times, in tension with one another and the principal Reformers. The Anabaptists staunchly disagreed with the judgment that the "Great Commission" was no longer applicable in this post-apostolic

3. Bosch, *Transforming Mission*, 220–30.

4. Bosch, *Transforming Mission*, 230.

5. Bosch, *Transforming Mission*, 231–40.

6. Nussbaum, *Transforming Mission*, 59.

age, a position that was held by some Reformers in the Lutheran orthodoxy. Additionally, the Anabaptists called for a clean separation between church and state. They could not accept that the state should participate in mission alongside the church. However, the mainline Reformers could not conceive of Christian mission in places where a Protestant government was not already established.

The Pietists resisted the idea of group conversions and instead preferred conversion by the decision of the individual. Additionally, the locus of mission was not on the church but on Christ, working through the Spirit. The Pietists emphasized the individual as the main instrument of mission over the institutions of church or state.[7] They did not wait for governmental authorities to send them into colonial missional settings, but established them where they felt God was calling them to proclaim his Kingdom.[8] The Puritans and the Second Reformation had a significant impact on the missionary development.

Puritan theology, rooted in Calvinism, emphasized a mission of the proclamation of the glory of God. Working within the boundaries of the ongoing colonial expansion, they saw that their mission would bring a "cultural uplift" and transform society and government. They envisioned a clean slate in the colonies where theocracies could be established. The Puritans did so with a foundation of the declaration of the sovereignty of God and, what was for them, the foundational attribute of predestination.[9] To many the doctrine of predestination is a hindrance to mission. "Why bother trying to persuade people to accept the gospel if God has already decided who will be saved?"[10] Yet, this served as a motivator for some Puritans to see themselves as predestined in another way: to proclaim God's kingdom in the new colonies.[11] In such an environment, ideas of church and mission were influenced by the subsequent Enlightenment period, to which we now turn our attention.

THE MODERN ENLIGHTENMENT PARADIGM

An assessment of all the impacts of the Enlightenment on Christian thought is beyond the scope of this work. However, we need to take a brief view of some of the important motifs and thoughts around mission for their

7. Bosch, *Transforming Mission*, 250–61.

8. Nussbaum, *Transforming Mission*, 67.

9. Nussbaum, *Transforming Mission*, 263–66.

10. Nussbaum, *Transforming Mission*, 66.

11. Nussbaum, *Transforming Mission*, 66.

influence on present-day mission. These motifs were at various times reactions, products, and rebuttals to Enlightenment teachings.

Mission for the glory of God. While early Calvinist missionary theology focused upon the Glory of God as a motive for mission, Enlightenment thinking emphasized humans in the center of life, rather than God. As a result, thinking shifted. It moved to an emphasis on sharing Christ's love, proclamation of salvation to the heathen, and later a social gospel.[12]

Mission to show Jesus' love. Following the Pietist movement and similar awakenings, there was an emphasis on personal religious experience. Thus, people began to make great personal sacrifices for others, even for those whom they had not yet met, in response to a sense of Jesus' love in their own lives. This was mixed with an Enlightenment thinking that considered the indigenous people of the newly colonized lands as "noble savages." They were viewed not with a compassion born out of Christian solidarity, but instead with condescending pity.[13]

The approaching millennium. In the mid-1800s evangelicals became increasingly divided on the doctrine of the millennium, a teaching which influenced mission efforts. A detailed discussion of the pre-, post-, and a-millennium views are beyond this discussion of mission, but suffice it to say that their effects were felt in the discussion of mission, if each for its own reason. Premillennialists laid the foundations of their mission of preaching in their understanding of an impending time of increasing tribulation and strife. They shunned a message of social concern in favor of preaching a message of the need for immediate salvation that would bring prosperity. The postmillennialists were in the majority through the beginning of the 19th century. They continued to hold that the great changes around them supported their view of the coming Kingdom. Events such as the American Civil War, technological advances that led to new societal problems, and new teachings of eschatology in academia were used as evidence of their theories. They were often at odds with the premillennialists and their increasingly widespread, influential teaching and preaching. Amillennialists were a product of Unitarianism and the Enlightenment that birthed it. They placed an emphasis on the Social gospel to bring about an evolution of humanity to do its part in making the Kingdom of God complete on earth.[14] They put forth "the new doctrine of the *fatherhood of God and the brotherhood of all people.*"[15] In the decades that followed, significant shifts

12. Bosch, *Transforming Mission,* 292.

13. Nussbaum, *Transforming Mission,* 75.

14. Bosch, *Transforming Mission,* 322–32.

15. Bosch, *Transforming Mission,* 329. Emphasis original.

in missional thinking were proposed: 1) not all other religions were entirely false, 2) mission activity was to focus on issues of human development, not just preaching, 3) salvation meant life in this world, not after death, 4) missional emphasis moved to a society rather than the individual.[16]

Mission as obedience to the "Great Commission." Another teaching emphasized about the same time was Jesus' command in Matt 28:18–20, often called "The Great Commission" which we examined in chapter 1. Several missionary leaders of the nineteenth and twentieth centuries used texts like Acts 16:9 (the vision of the Macedonian asking for Paul), Matt 24:14 (preaching before the impending end), and John 10:10 (a promise of abundant life) to motivate missioners to fulfill this understanding of commissioning. These have been powerful motivators, but at times were misappropriated while attacking ecumenism and championing biblical proof-texting.[17] At times there was a tendency to move the "church's involvement from the domain of *gospel* to that of *law*."[18]

Mission and the gospel as part of Western culture. As Western missionaries moved into other cultures, their impacts were both positive and negative. Improvements were made in the areas of the abolition of slavery, the status of women, agriculture, and medicine. However, in doing so, they ignored the positives of those cultures. They developed structures in which the indigenous churches were dependent upon the Western churches to a crippling degree.[19] We will return to this struggle for appropriate inculturation below.

Mission as a part of the "manifest destiny" of Western nations. In addition to these practices, the Enlightenment and its technological developments, the ever-increasing colonialism, and a sense of entitlement led the Puritans to believe that God had chosen the Anglo-Saxon race to "guide history to its end and usher in the new millennium."[20] This accompanied a strong sense that the North Americans would properly bring about God's kingdom in this world. To propagate this message, there was a strong push for overseas missionary activity, even to the neglect of service to people of their home nation.

Mission and Colonialism. As governments established themselves in new areas, they endeavored to use missionaries to assist in the conquering of people and cultures. There were, however, some who opposed the

16. Bosch, *Transforming Mission, 329.*

17. Bosch, *Transforming Mission, 348–49;* Nussbaum, *Transforming Mission, 78.*

18. Bosch, *Transforming Mission, 349.* Emphasis original.

19. Bosch, *Transforming Mission, 300–01.*

20. Bosch, *Transforming Mission, 301.*

attempts by the British, Spanish, Dutch, and Portuguese governments to enslave and take advantage of the new peoples they encountered. Bartolome de Las Casas, William Wilberforce, William Carey, and others attempted to tame the improper use of people for the colonizer's gain. At the same time, there was a move amongst educated individuals of these nations to be involved in overseas mission. These upper-class, educated missionaries had the means and desire to attempt to save the world. In doing so, they took charge wherever they went. This was a regression in the work of mission due to the misconception by colonial leaders and missionaries who saw their role as paternal guardians of the "less-developed races." Additionally, they tended to see other races as dependent upon white patrons to guide them into cultural maturity.[21]

There were many shortcomings of the colonial attitudes of mission that prevailed in much of the early twentieth century, when leaders understood the goal of mission to be the "Three C's: Christianity, commerce, and civilization."[22] Writing in 1950, Alex Berthoud was among those who believed that Europeans and Americans were to conduct their missionary efforts overseas.[23] In his understanding, mission was but a program that the church was to carry out. Such a program had one important goal: to preach the gospel into all the world so that the eschaton may be realized. "And only then the end will come, and the Church will disappear to make room for the kingdom so long expected."[24] Berthoud espoused the idea that the church has as its termination point the preaching of the gospel in the farthest reaches of the earth. This puts mission as a task of the church and therefore a work of the people who have within their power the steps necessary to bring about the parousia. Berthoud represents a common line of thinking in missionary theology for the first half of the twentieth century.[25]

This somewhat misguided conquering attitude continued to show an imperialistic mindset on the part of many in the sending churches.[26] The European and American missions had established several churches in the foreign mission field that were now in something of a parent/child relationship. The younger churches were established to be theological copies of the parent churches. These "three-self" churches were seen as successful when they were "self-governing," "self-supporting," and "self-propagating." The

---

21. Bosch, *Transforming Mission*, 307–14.

22. Bosch, *Transforming Mission*, 312.

23. Berthoud, "Church and Mission," 263.

24. Berthoud, 267.

25. Bosch, *Transforming Mission*, 299. Berthoud, "Church and Mission," 267.

26. Bosch, *Transforming Mission*, 311.

mission was deemed a "success" when such a church was achieved. Eventually the younger churches began to "self-theologize" and missionary thinking was reexamined.[27]

Mission as voluntarism. The Enlightenment period also saw a change in the way missionaries were sent into kingdom work. Volunteers began to take over the work that had previously been reserved only for leaders in the ecclesial structures. There was a move away from the hierarchy of the church authorizing and deploying emissaries to do its work. A key principle of the Reformation that allowed such a move was the idea of private judgment in matters of theology. As such a new way of thinking about mission developed, one in which "like-minded individuals could band together in order to promote a common cause."[28] Since people were encouraged to read Scripture, worship, and exercise religious disciplines individually, it naturally followed that they should take the same view of missional activity. Believers banded together in individual societies and mission organizations to serve in ministry far afield. With the lack of denominational guidance, there was tension on how the new churches should be organized. Rufus Anderson and Henry Venn were advocates of the aforementioned movement to make the new churches "self-governing," "self-supporting," and "self-propagating." As noble as this idea was, it became lost in the fights for denominational territories.[29]

Some of voluntarism's principles remain an important influence in missionary activity today. I will illustrate the STM's demonstration of some of these notions in later chapters. Additionally, STM finds its roots in an optimistic fervor that is combined with a certain pragmatism, a notion which I now elucidate.

Missionary fervor, optimism, pragmatism. By the end of the nineteenth century, these missional movements had prepared a new generation of leaders to see themselves as uniquely poised to bring the gospel to the entire world and see its conversion by the end of the current generation. The Student Volunteer Movement proclaimed that God's hand was opening the door for the church to reach every person on earth. Missioners saw scientific advancements as gifts to make possible this proclamation. This high enthusiasm reached its pinnacle in the Edinburgh Missionary Conference in 1910. In this missionary climate, a more ecumenical, yet militaristic, attitude developed. The meeting in Edinburgh was a ground-breaking opportunity for churches and missionary organizations to examine their

27. Bosch, *Transforming Mission*, 339, 462.

28. Bosch, *Transforming Mission*, 335.

29. Bosch, *Transforming Mission*, 339.

commonalities. The delegates intentionally moved away from problems of dogma and theology.[30] Embracing a more unified front and using language with militaristic overtones, optimism was high among the delegates that this was the decisive hour for the Christian movement to conquer the world.[31] Within just a few decades, much of this optimism was lost as world events forced a rethinking of missiology and its underpinning theologies. Two world wars, the independence of India, the Chinese communist revolution and subsequent expulsion of the missionaries, and the war in Korea all contributed to an environment where leaders re-evaluated the role of mission and how to judge their current successes and failures. Consequently, new ways of thinking about mission were developing.[32]

THE *MISSIO DEI* AS A SOURCE OF MISSION

As seen in this brief survey of historical mission development, the twentieth century missionary thinking was moving beyond an institutional, church-centered view to an examination of the source of missional foundations. We are beginning to see our place on the map and some of the historical influences that shape contemporary practice. Before moving to a discussion of some of some contemporary emerging paradigms, that will enhance our understanding of contemporary STM, it is important to spend more time examining a significant development in mission theology: the more recent, and ongoing, discussion of the *missio Dei*. Doing so will help us better understand the contemporary STM phenomenon. The development of the *missio Dei* mission theology remains among the most important contemporary conversations in mission theology today.

Missio Dei simply means "Mission of God." When we examine mission, we must ask: "Where does mission come from? Whose mission is it?"[33] Such are the questions the church has sought to answer in its pursuit of mission. Believe it or not, the idea of mission being *God's* mission, as we are discussing here, is a relatively recent development. In the twentieth century, under the influence of Karl Brath, Lesslie Newbigin and others, thinking around mission began to move away from the practice as a human agency or a church actively. Rather, Barth emphasized that mission was not merely "a human activity of witness and service" or a work of the church. Instead, it is God who engages in the work of mission "by sending of God's self in the

---

30. Ritschl, "Ecumenism."
31. Bosch, *Transforming Mission*, 346.
32. Bassham, "Theological Basis for Mission," 329.
33. Nussbaum, *Transforming Mission*, 95.

mission of the Son and the Spirit."[34] Barth was influential in developing the understanding of mission as something that God himself initiates. In the decades that followed much of his work, scholars developed the *missio Dei* concept. Speaking of this development, Bosch explains:

> In [this] image mission is not primarily an activity of the church, but an attribute of God. God is a missionary God. 'It is not the church that has a mission of salvation to fulfill in the world; it is the mission of the Son and the Spirit through the Father that includes the Church.'[35]

Newbigin's insistence that the mission of God be understood in Trinitarian terms is important. For example, he says of Peter's confession in Matt 16:17:

> It is the action of God by which he chooses and anoints the messengers of his reign. It is the work of the sovereign Spirit to enable men and women in new situations and in new cultural forms to find ways in which the confession of Jesus as Lord may be made in the language of their own culture. The mission of the church is in fact the church's obedient participation in the action of the Spirit by which the confession of Jesus as Lord becomes the authentic confession of ever new peoples, each in its own tongue.[36]

In the opening chapter, I noted that mission presupposes that one has a sender and has been, at least in some way, authorized to do what they are doing. In Christian mission, we understand that it is God who sends. However, what or who is God sending and where is he sending them? The Easter and Pentecost events initiated the people of God as Jesus' church in the "already" and in anticipation of the "not yet." Jesus told the disciples that he was sending them with a mission, just as the Father had sent him. They were to proclaim, as he did, that the Kingdom of God is at hand. The Kingdom of God is no longer removed nor at a distance. It is not a mere movement nor a cause to join. It is a reality that confronts all humanity. As such it requires a decision: what will one do with it? Jesus appears not just to his believers, but seeks even those who are hostile to him and his message. This is seen in the appearance to Paul on the road to Damascus (Acts 9:1–22). Mission, therefore, is faith in action. It takes place in the immediate

---

34. Bevans and Schroeder, *Constants in Context*, 290.
35. Bosch, *Transforming Mission*, 400.
36. Newbigin, *Missionary Theologian*, 21–22.

context. It is a movement to new lands and thereby new people.[37] It is "acting out by proclamation and by endurance, through all the events of history, of the faith that the Kingdom of God has drawn near."[38]

Mission, quite simply, is not a program nor an arm of the church. The church does not run a somewhat parallel course to God's mission, intersecting with it every now and again. Mission encompasses the entire church and the church must find itself wrapped in the mission of God, as demonstrated in Jesus, and carried forth by the Spirit. The most important element of this mission is the proclamation of the gospel and its "dawning kingdom." This kingdom is one that sets people free from slavery, poverty, sin, and death. As Jürgen Moltmann points out, "Evangelization is mission, but mission is not merely evangelization."[39] This means that acts of mercy and work to bring about liberty and preaching and ordering all have a place in the missionary church. Since Jesus sends the church just "as the Father sent" him, then the church too has a place and function with God's saving history. The *missio Dei* is from God and as such it is here that the church finds its foundation. It is also through the church that God continues his work and calls the church to spread that work worldwide and find "its goal in the consummation of all creation in God."[40] Engelsviken, in harmony with Newbigin's emphasis on the Johannine text as an impetus for mission, goes on to say,

> One draws especially on John 20:21, which one could call the "classical" way to refer to *missio Dei*, where God's mission is primarily carried out through the church. The other understanding is where God is seen as active in the secular political and social events of the world and where it is the role of the church to discern what God is doing in the world, and then participate in it.[41]

To correctly understand the *missio Dei*, it is important to emphasize that mission does not have its origin in the hearts of people or in the structure of the church. The source of mission is in the heart of God. Mission is bigger than the confines of the church. God may very well work outside the understood realms of "the church." The church is a product of mission, not vice versa. Therefore, mission cannot be an afterthought in the church, but must be the central concept of every aspect of the church. Mission cannot

---

37. Newbigin, *Missionary Theologian*, 37–39.

38. Newbigin, *Missionary Theologian*, 43.

39. Moltmann, *Power of the Spirit*, 10.

40. Moltmann, *Power of the Spirit*, 11.

41. Engelsviken, "Missio Dei," 490–91.

be measured by superficial enumerations of conversion or an increase in church membership. God has much greater purposes in mind.[42]

One must be careful not to misuse the *Dei* of the *missio Dei*. Other religions have taken the term Dei to mean something other than the "Father-Son-Spirit God of the New Testament."[43] This differentiation is essential to the understanding of Christian mission. When we speak of Christian theology, it is important to note that "theology has 'no reason to exist other than critically to accompany the *missio Dei*.'"[44] In the first chapter we saw that Christian mission must seek its source in the Christian Scripture. In the opening of this chapter we have seen how the church sought to interpret that impetus for mission in their time. This need to seek a biblical understanding of mission is an ongoing process. Good biblical scholarship protects missiology from a tendency to read preconceptions into the church without regard to its intended meaning. Meanwhile, missiology allows biblical studies a means for modern contextualization of ancient texts. Mission needs theology needs biblical criticism, in a triangular relationship.[45] By maintaining such a relationship of critical reflection, one can correctly understand the *missio Dei*.

With an understanding of mission finding its source in God himself, the church will find that it cannot compartmentalize mission as a program or as an activity, but instead must recognize it as the very source of everything the church does. This would also mean that hard denominational divisions must be reassessed and removed when possible. Moving the locus of mission from individuals or churches to God will begin to remove such barriers. Earlier in church history the clergy were the only ones who could be considered as emissaries for God's work in the world. In a *missio Dei* understanding of mission, the historically hard lines between laity and clergy are blurred. All Christians have a mission in which to participate: that of the mission of God himself.[46]

Before proceeding further, it is helpful to stop and scan the landscape we have covered so far. We have examined a biblical understanding of mission. We then saw some relevant paradigms in mission history. We have paid careful attention to the development of the *missio Dei*, a concept that will continue to be important throughout the rest of this work. Writers and teachers have attempted to use this concept in various ways since it was first

42. Bosch, *Transforming Mission*, 400–02.

43. Nussbaum, *Transforming Mission*, 97.

44. Bekele, "Missio Dei," 154.

45. Bekele, "Missio Dei," 154.

46. Nussbaum, *Transforming Mission*, 116–20.

introduced. In this summary, however, it is important to emphasize a point above: mission is now "accepted by Christians of virtually all persuasions as 'a participation in the movement of God's love toward people shown in Christ.'"[47] Now we focus on a nearby outcropping of the terrain in the form of emerging paradigms of mission.

EMERGING PARADIGMS

Since this is a work that addresses current mission practice (STM in particular), the discussion of emerging mission paradigm deserves more attention than some of the previous ones. This paradigm also deserves our further attention because some leaders have suggested considerable changes to the way the church should understand its role in mission and this has influenced the development and implementation of STM. Some have sought to make the message of the gospel more accessible and attractive to unbelievers to increase receptivity among their hearers. In doing so, these leaders have used tools like inculturation and contextualization to redefine the church in the name of mission and evangelism. Seeking to be a "missional church," some are imploring those inside the church to abandon the traditional ecclesiastical form for the sake of those outside the church community. Leaders in the Emerging Church Movement seek to rework the church into a model of what, they maintain, is more like the New Testament community of faith. Similarly, Fresh Expressions has sought to rework the Church of England in midst of a modern decline. The Fresh Expressions movement is also gaining influence in the United States. Both of these seek to provide contextual ministries that directly address the culture in which the ministry finds itself.

In our discussion of some emerging paradigms we will examine the role of contextualization and inculturation in a very general sense. Then we will examine specific efforts to do so in the United Kingdom, the United States, and Australia that involve Fresh Expressions and the Emerging Church Movement. The last portion of our discussion of these paradigms will attempt to interweave the roles of such efforts with the manifestations I mentioned previously, *ekkelsia* and *missio Dei*. These concepts will help us better understand the present day mission terrain for our later discussions of Wesleyan missional theology and STM.

---

47. Kim, "Missiology as Global Conversation," 1, quoting Bosch.

CONTEXTUALIZATION AND INCULTURATION IN MISSION

Contextualization of the gospel is the participation in the mission of God and his Kingdom. From the beginning, "the missionary message of the Christian church incarnated itself in the life and world of those who had embraced it."[48] Friedrich Schleiermacher took some of the first steps toward viewing the work of the Reformation as an attempt to engage Scripture, which reconstructed the past in a manner appropriate for the present time. Other theologians would advance these studies to further the understanding that the "text [of Scripture] is not only 'out there,' waiting to be interpreted; the text 'becomes' as we engage it. . . . Interpreting a text is not only a literary exercise; it is also a social, economic, and political exercise."[49] Theologians bring their context to bear when interpreting biblical texts. Therefore, we must admit that "all theology. . .is, by its very nature, contextual."[50]

Contextualized theology appropriately moves beyond theoretical questions of God and engages the practical questions of God's commitment to the poor and marginalized. Theologians should begin to ask questions of how a Christian should act in response to the structures and practices that impoverish, oppress, or abuse. In some ways, these questions are asked on a global level, but they are properly answered when asked in the local situation. In seeking such answers, the church moves from a place of theoretical discussion to a place of practical and meaningful action that embodies the gospel message.[51]

Western theology has often neglected the implementation of the theologies they discuss. In biblical teaching "it is the doers who are blessed."[52] Such meaningful actions include careful attention to the voices of those who experience the marginalization the Scriptures decry. When this occurs, the conversation properly includes both theory and praxis. "The relationship between theory and praxis is not one of subject to object, but one of inter-subjectivity. . . . 'Orthopraxis and orthodoxy need one another, and each is adversely affected when sight is lost of the other.'"[53]

Contextualized theology must be approached in a proper manner. Mission should always be contextualized and attempts to remove mission

---

48. Bosch, *Transforming Mission*, 431.

49. Bosch, *Transforming Mission*, 433.

50. Bosch, *Transforming Mission*, 433.

51. Nussbaum, *Transforming Mission*, 108.

52. Bosch, *Transforming Mission*, 435.

53. Bosch, *Transforming Mission*, 435, quoting Gutiérrez.

from its context should be resisted. God is interested and involved in the world he created. Theology should not become merely "other-worldly" to the point where it neglects the present needs of those who need the gospel's complete message. God is involved in the concerns of the victims and their oppressors. Robust theologies must do the same. Just as God incarnate became a part of the world, so must robust theologies. They must close the gap between humanity and God, just as Jesus came to do. Robust theologies must not remain detached from the real concerns of the captives, the poor, the blind, and the oppressed. The proclamation of the resurrected Jesus Christ must be central to orthodoxy and orthropraxy.[54] "The power of his resurrection propels human history toward the end" with a proclamation that Jesus is making all things are new.[55] Therefore, robust theology must keep the Messiah attached to history and to the future.[56]

There are a few cautions to mention around contextualization. While God is involved in human history, one must not focus too closely upon all the events of history and mistake them as God's doing. For example, some Christians saw the rise of Nazism as a divine intervention of God's favor. If theology becomes too localized, it can slip into relativism. Connection and accountability should be maintained with the global body of Christ lest we should trust ourselves and our localization too much. Missiologists and theologians must maintain a healthy balance between theory and practice.[57] "[P]raxis needs the critical control of theory."[58] Practice and theory must also be joined with beauty, awe, and mystery. "The best models of contextualized theology succeed in holding together in creative tension *theoria*, *praxis*, and *poiesis*—or, if one wishes, faith, hope and love."[59] This lays the foundation for the idea of inculturation.

As I have stated, theology is done in a context specific to those who are engaged in the work of theology. Inculturation is a move beyond a simple adaptation, accommodation, or indigenization of the gospel. In the twentieth century, church growth in the Global South—a key destination for STM—forced theologians and church leaders to reconsider how the kingdom was at work. They observed that the chief agents of change were the laity who were local converts, led by the Holy Spirit, and not the professional missionary leadership. They emphasized the needs of the local

---

54. Nussbaum, *Transforming Mission*, 108–9.

55. Bosch, *Transforming Mission*, 436.

56. Nussbaum, *Transforming Mission*, 109.

57. Bosch, *Transforming Mission*, 435–40; Nussbaum, *Transforming Mission*, 109.

58. Bosch, *Transforming Mission*, 441.

59. Bosch, *Transforming Mission*, 442.

communities in a holistic context, e.g. political, economic, educational. This holistic nature is important as it does not pick and choose certain features of the context to include or exclude. Inculturation is continuing Christ's example set forth in his incarnation. In a manner of speaking, the church is born anew in each new context, instead of the church expanding itself and the new context adopting it as necessary. It is akin to a seed being planted rather than a mature tree being transplanted.[60]

The gospel is, at least in some ways, foreign in every culture and has often been a point of contradiction. Yet, inculturation should not mean the destroying of a culture and a new one built upon the smoldering ruins.[61] How then should a mission of the kingdom be understood in regards to the principles of contextualization and inculturation? Recall that as the theology of mission began to move from an imperialistic view, mission leaders recognized that new churches and Christian communities were to become "self-supporting, self-governing, and self-propagating." They saw such indigenization as a sustainable model of growth.[62] Their efforts produced only limited results. In later developments, they affirmed a fourth self, "self-theologizing," for Asian, African, and Latin American churches.[63]

Modern theologians and church leaders have wrestled with contextualization, inculturation, and the "four selfs" in seeking effective ways of ministry. Movements such as the Emerging Church in North America and Europe have sought to express new forms of church that relate to a culture in which they currently find themselves. Emerging churches consider themselves "missional." Emerging church leaders seem to find their mission inextricably linked to context. With some success, these missional emerging churches see themselves as working in mission to a changing postmodern culture in their native countries.[64] We will examine these outcroppings as we develop an understanding of how they shape the terrain.

FRESH EXPRESSIONS

One such effort to explore a reformation of familiar church practices to connect to an emerging context in the West began in the United Kingdom and has influenced missional engagement there as well as in the United States. Written in 2009, *Mission-Shaped Church: Church Planting and Fresh*

---

60. Nussbaum, *Transforming Mission,* 112–13.

61. Bosch, *Transforming Mission,* 466.

62. Bailyes, "Understandings of Mission," 339.

63. Bosch, *Transforming Mission,* 462.

64. van Wyngaard, "The Emerging Church," 1–2.

Expressions of Church in a Changing Context sought to re-examine the role of the church amidst the changing culture of modern Britain. Facing the reality of a dynamic environment in which increasing numbers of people did not prioritize church activities, the writers of Fresh Expressions sought to respond to the problem of church participation reaching an all-time low. They addressed the fact that new ways of experiencing community continue to emerge. Thus, they contended, many in Britain increasingly considered the idea of gathering in traditional church environments for worship, community building, and socializing to be an outdated notion. Much in the same way that people select a shop on High Street for the perceived value they receive from the experience there, the predominately consumerist culture means that people "shop" for religious values that may or may not include traditional Anglican views. Additionally, Fresh Expressions aimed to address the belief that Britain is a post-Christendom society in which the mainstream culture may not have a basic biblical literacy. This lack of biblical literacy, they felt, was likely a result of these new cultural realities.[65] *Mission-Shaped Church* sought to answer these problems with a fresh contextualization of the established Church of England. It affirmed the *missio Dei* as still active in Britain. It put forth that this mission required the church to rethink and remodel most of its practices. It called for the church to re-work itself to remain effective: "Hence conversion ought not to involve the transfer of individuals from their native cultures to the Church, so much as the conversion of their culture enriching the cultural life of the Church."[66] The writers of *Mission-Shaped Church* recognized that such a transformation would not be easy, but they saw it as necessary. They did so with a supposedly strong sense of mission at the center of their theology.[67]

While it can be praised for beginning the discussion of the issues, *Mission-Shaped Church* is not without its critics. Some have rejected the idea that the church should shed all its traditions and practices for the accommodation of modern consumerism and individualism. Rather, they have offered a condemnation of current cultural practices to maintain what they see as the proper practice of ecclesiology.[68]

Mission-Shaped Church should be commended for its attempt to engage the church in mission to the world. The authors affirmed that "[i]t is not the Church of God that has a mission in the world, but the God of

65. Archbishop's Council on Mission, 1–11.

66. Archbishop's Council on Mission, 87.

67. Archbishop's Council on Mission, 93, 102.

68. Davison and Milbank, *For the Parish*, 131–32.

mission who has a Church in the world."[69] They were correct to reject the idea of planting churches merely for the inflation of numbers or to prop up the institution. However, they collapsed their argument by failing to properly explain the role of the church's relationship to the Kingdom of God. They demonstrate their misunderstanding of the role and relationship of the two in statements like, "The Son of God expressed this mission in terms of the Kingdom of God. The kingdom is a divine activity whereas the Church is a human community."[70] Further, they claim that God moves through the kingdom while the church is "always catching up with him."[71] Making such a bifurcation neglects the complimentary relationship of the two and mischaracterizes the church's role in mission and the Kingdom of God. While the Archbishop's Council responsible for Fresh Expressions should be commended for its efforts to engage the church with the culture, it failed to maintain an ecclesiology that appropriately understands *ekklesia*'s role in the *missio Dei*. We will look further into the role and relationship of mission, kingdom, and church later in this chapter.

THE EMERGING CHURCH MOVEMENT

Similar to the conversations of Fresh Expressions, others are encouraging new models of church though what has been termed the Emerging Church Movement (hereafter ECM). The movement is, in many ways, a reaction to a dissatisfaction with the Evangelical Megachurch movement and Mainline Protestantism. Many in the ECM equally reject both the seeker-friendly church model and the solemnity of mainline denominations. They say that these are moving away from a Christian expression by their devotion to rote expression, formal expectations, or performance experiences.[72]

At their best, ECM leaders express concern about the decline of the church in the West and seek to support strategies that would bring about something of a new Reformation. For example, some have advocated for a rejection of the Church of Christendom. Instead, leaders have insisted that the church has failed in its mission and that Emperor Constantine's declaration of Christianity as a legal religion in AD 313 was the beginning of the end for the true church. They asserted that over the past seventeen centuries, the church slowly marched to reach the present perceived crisis. They maintained that to make things right again, everything before now

69. Archbishop's Council on Mission, 86.
70. Archbishop's Council on Mission, 86.
71. Archbishop's Council on Mission, 86.
72. Marti and Ganiel, *Deconstructed Church*, 110–11.

must be abandoned. They proposed an abandoning of church buildings, and undoing of the church structures and hierarchies.[73] Though not all ECM congregations would shun the use of a traditional church structure, meetings are likely to occur in someone's home or a space repurposed for Christian worship. Such a repurposed space might be a coffee shop or other such business. The spaces for ECM gathering and worship vary greatly.

Just as ECM leaders often reject traditional worship spaces, so too do many reject traditional hierarchies of ecclesial leadership. They prefer the egalitarian forms of responsibility and leadership in these "flat" structures. Leaders often arise from the members of the group. Without formal training, group members may take on roles normally reserved for those who have been formally trained or ordained. For example, members of an ECM group may choose a presider at communion or the speaker for a sermon because they feel as though there are qualities in that person that are appropriate to the task. Contrast this to a historical understanding of ordination as a prerequisite to presiding in such leadership responsibilities. For those ECM leaders who are ordained it is not unusual to take only part-time employment with the local church and outside of a traditional denominational structure. In doing so they defer much of the work traditionally given to pastors to volunteers in the congregation. Some saw this as serving two functions. First, it forces ministry leaders to keep jobs in spaces outside of the church context. Some see such a posture as a reflection of the missionary spirit of the Apostle Paul who made tents as a way of supporting himself and his ministerial efforts. Second, it allows for a more agile governmental structure for the congregations. This is a way for leaders to free themselves from denominational rules and regulations, or from, what they see as, distant and disconnected church leaders who might be unaware of the particular needs of that congregation.[74]

Leaders in the ECM point to several problems in the church when calling for new forms of missional engagement. Many in the church would say that Christianity is in decline in the West and in the Orthodox East. Participation in the life of the community of Christians is rapidly dwindling in most parts of Europe and North America.[75] There are tensions in government agencies about the role of the values of the historical Church in the laws of those nations. Popular culture often makes Christianity the object of ridicule and scorn. The voices of the ECM should be commended for their

73. Frost and Hirsch, *Shaping of Things to Come*, 14. Frost and Hirsch, *ReJesus*, 243. Frost and Hirsch, *The Faith of Leap*, 24.

74. Marti and Ganiel, *Deconstructed Church*, 111. Bielo, *Emerging Evangelicals*, 118–37.

75. Effa, "Missional Voices Down Under," 64–66.

work in the church. However, there are a few points of caution that should be mentioned.

The discussion of renewal in the church must engage a broad context. The problems many ECM leaders tend to point out are largely the problems of the developed nations of the West. They failed to address the church and cultures in places without a historically Christian presence. Does the same hold true for contexts like Africa, Southeast Asia, Latin America, and the Middle East? These regions represent a larger portion of the world's population than the largely Western context. The mission of the church goes beyond the places where Christianity was historically entrenched. Such an omission of important principles is what can happen when one claims "hermeneutical and theological supremacy."[76]

Some ECM leaders propose a model that is too narrowly focused on what Allan Effa notes as the "relatively young, trendy, white, highly urban, somewhat marginalized and secularized people."[77] Though they do make attempts at discussions of multiculturalism, some of the models suggested do not always adequately deal with the increasing tensions around issues of race or nationality that many churches face. James Bielo points out that some in the ECM see themselves as missionaries when seeking to connect with people of other races and socioeconomic status, but often behave as colonists instead. He asserts, "As Emerging Evangelicals seek to 'have missional hearts' they construct an imagined missionized Other, the details of which are used to create institutions for fostering evangelistic efforts."[78]

Another point of caution is encourage ECM leaders to avoid establishing false dichotomies between "evangelistic-attractional" and "missional-incarnational" church models. Some tend to reject anything that looks "evangelistic-attractional" and for their preferred "missional-incarnational" model. Some would dismiss churches, communities, buildings, or programs that they consider attractional, going so far as to call this a departure from the biblical model. But, "the early church was certainly attractional, not in the sense of designing programs or special services to draw in seekers, but in the attractional force of its communal life and witness."[79] Artificial boundaries between the so-called "evangelistic-attractional" and "missional-incarnational" church models should be resisted. In actuality, the church engaged in mission will attract new people to be part of the community of

76. Bekele, "Missio Dei," 154.

77. Effa, "Missional Voices Down Under," 71.

78. Bielo, *Emerging Evangelicals*, 136.

79. Effa, "Missional Voices Down Under," 69.

believers.[80] When exercising mission, churches will be places where those who are exploring faith are welcome. Open and nonjudgmental, such communities welcome questions and explorations. These communities do so without compromising core values, or boundaries, to which newcomers are expected to adhere.[81] Such communities are what Bruce Bauer calls "bounded sets." Such bounded sets are, to some extent, natural and expected in the church. Bauer contrasts these to a "centered sets," which he defines as people coming together around a common ideal. In such a setting, boundaries are nebulous and fluid. It is the proximity of the center that defines the community members, rather than their placement inside a defined parameter. Though some ECM leaders emphasize centered sets as their preferred model,[82] as Jim Peterson points out, "It is not that bounded sets are always bad and centered sets are always good. Boundaries do exist. Salvation is a bounded set. One is either in Christ, or not in Christ."[83] In reality, the church often resembles one model, then another, and then back to the first. Keeping these ideas in constant discussion with one another is an important task for the church.[84]

A third area of caution is that any "new" mission movement should resist tendency to dismiss the contributions of the previous efforts, as some are apt to do. While it is important to point out that there are those in the church who have made mistakes in the past. However, this does not require a complete disregard of the church. It is presumptuous and reckless to disregard 1,700 years of church history because there is, at present, a perceived broken church system, while claiming that a single writer or group of writers will have the only answer.[85] That would require one to disregard all the things that went right in that timespan as well. Some leaders in the movement would say that not much, if anything, went right. They call for a complete rejection of Christian structures and that Christ's followers should rebuild the church in the manner they propose.[86] Modern theologians and ministry practitioners rely upon theological concepts and biblical interpretations that are not solely their own, standing on the shoulders of the theological giants that have come before. To dismiss all of Christendom requires the dismissal of all that it contributed to. Arguments to reform the church

80. Effa, "Missional Voices Down Under," 70.

81. Bauer, *Bounded and Centered Sets*, 11–12.

82. Frost and Hirsch, *Shaping of Things to Come*, 47. Hiebert, "The Mission Task."

83. Petersen, *Church without Walls*, 174.

84. Hiebert, "The Mission Task," 426.

85. Bekele, "Missio Dei," 154.

86. Frost and Hirsch, *ReJesus: A Wild Messiah for a Missional Church*, 225.

are strengthened by embracing the contributions of those who have shaped the ones making such arguments.

One area to emphasize in our discussion of the ECM in relation to modern Methodist STM is the role of the individual in the aforementioned structures. Just as traditional forms of worship and physical structures can be rejected, some would reject traditional roles of ministry leadership and accountability. Though historical Methodism places a high emphasis on accountability, we will see later that tensions remain in the contemporary Methodism between the role of the individual and the role of community in accountability. Such accountability is vital, yet the ECM, at times, reveals its post-Enlightenment thinking that runs the risk of building upon a "sacarlized self," and creates opportunities for the individuals to take on "sacred activities that might have once been assumed the preserve of God."[87] Joined with the flattening of structures, the determination of what is sacred can move from the beneficial accountability of vetting by religious leaders or historical premise and instead moves to the determination of the individual. Some ECM teaching risks misplacing the locus of God's activity in the world and instead places the locus of activity in people. In this understanding, God works through people by what Marti and Ganiel call "moral individualism."[88] An emphasis on the responsibility of the individual to act in response to God's precepts is affirmed in a healthy missionary theology. However, it is important to avoid putting more emphasis on the role of the individual versus the role of the one who prompts the individual to such action: God. Maren Freudenberg says that when individuals have such a great deal of influence on shaping the practice, "they usually shape them according to the group members' interest."[89] Without careful self-reflexivity, this can allow the group to over contextualize their thinking and subsequent practices at the expense of appropriately robust theologies. Pete Ward offers a helpful directive to balance new forms of church with historical connectivity. His proposed network-based "Liquid Church" possesses many of the qualities that ECM leaders would affirm. He was correct to insist that "liquid church will remain committed to an exacting orthodoxy and committed theology."[90] This is done when leaders are conscious that, "In developing a more fluid notion of church it is essential that we do not float away into a world of our own imagining."[91] Church leaders benefit from the inter-

---

87. Marti and Ganiel, *Deconstructed Church*, 185.

88. Marti and Ganiel, *Deconstructed Church*, 184–87.

89. Freudenberg, "The Emerging Church," 314.

90. Ward, *Liquid Church*, 56.

91. Ward, *Liquid Church*, 67.

connectivity of historical and contemporary accountability to avoid such a "floating away."

THE EMERGING CHURCH, *EKKLESIA*, AND *MISSIO DEI*

We have previously discussed the role of the *ekkleisa* and the *missio Dei* in mission theology. The work of the contemporary movements like Fresh Expressions and ECM should be affirmed where it embraces its place in the *ekklesia* and the *missio Dei*, both historic and contemporary. Mission should be understood in the context of Trinitarian history and God's dealings with the world and in view of salvation history and the eschatological hope. The church does not have a mission of salvation to fulfill in the world. That mission belongs to God. As part of that work, God has established the church as a piece of the mission of the Father, the Son and the Spirit. The church works in the Messianic mission of Christ. The church participates "in the creative mission of the Spirit."[92] The church participating in God's mission celebrates the liberation of people from all that enslaves. The church that participates in God's mission also participates in the suffering that love requires when necessary. Jesus demonstrated such love on the cross. The church likewise participates in the celebration of the joy of conversion and liberation as well as self-sacrificial love. It is here, in both the suffering and the celebration, that the church and mission are found.[93]

Such an understanding rules out three incorrect views of the church and mission. The first incorrect view is to see numerical growth as a criterion for its own sake. To make converts merely to make other converts is not why God sent Jesus and is an incorrect sense of the Reign of God. Second, the local church community cannot simply be an outlet for folk religion.[94] ithout a "sharp call for radical conversion. . . . [T]he New Testament is very clear that there is a radical repentance needed, a radical conversion, if one is to see the Kingdom of God."[95] Third, the church should not see itself as a mere function. Instead it should correctly see itself as a harbinger. It is a sign that the kingdom is the horizon to which all missional thinking looks. The church is entrusted with the message and should act as a sign that

---

92. Moltmann, *Power of the Spirit*, 65.

93. Moltmann, *Power of the Spirit*, 64–65.

94. "Folk religion" need not be considered only that which is outside of Western Christianity or some other "developed" faith structure. Even in predominately Christian contexts customs, traditions, and ways of thinking exist within communities that are beyond Scriptures' teachings.

95. Newbigin, *Missionary Theologian*, 137.

God reigns. The church should be a "sign, instrument, and foretaste" for the world in whatever setting the community of believers find themselves called to work.[96]

Until recently, "[t]he problem of contextualization in the West is that 'we still believe that the gospel had already been properly indigenized and contextualized in the West.'"[97] In such an attitude, the church has failed to recognize the dynamic nature of culture and therefore neglects the need for dynamic approaches to inculturation. Context is seldom static. Western culture has changed and so too has its relationship with the message of the church, in many ways. ECM churches, as with any church movement, must recognize the contextual nature of their own theology, while looking for movements of the mission of God in those contexts.[98]

Properly understood, the Kingdom of God is both the present and final salvation that God offers through Christ and by the power of the Holy Spirit. This salvation will include an ethical and social transformation. As such, the *missio Dei* is restricted to salvation history in Jesus and found through faith in him and in participation in the church he established. The *missio Dei* may use government or other agents to make a present, ethical change. However, as Tormod Englesviken correctly points out:

> it is through the church and its mission that the peace and justice of the kingdom are worked out. The church, seen as the people who belong to the kingdom, is God's main instrument to serve the world in all its needs, both through personal service and through social and political action.[99]

God has used the church to carry out his mission of the proclamation of the Kingdom of God in Jesus Christ. We have seen above that each mission paradigm is, at least in part, dependent upon the previous, and an influence upon the next as it serves as this instrument of God. However, the complex relationship of mission, church, and the Kingdom of God deserve further explanation. A robust theology of mission will seek to understand these interdependent concepts.

96. Newbigin, *Missionary Theologian*, 138.

97. van Wyngaard, "The Emerging Church," 4.

98. van Wyngaard, "The Emerging Church," 4–10; Bosch, *Transforming Mission*, 467.

99. Engelsviken, "Missio Dei," 483.

MISSION, CHURCH, AND KINGDOM

Thus far we have surveyed the landscape of contemporary mission theology. We have examined the outcroppings of two important developments in the theology of mission: the *missio Dei* and church movements like Fresh Expressions and the ECM. We have seen that mission, correctly understood, is couched within a scriptural, Trinitarian understanding. We have seen that the church exists because of the mission of God. Philip Wickeri provides a helpful summary of what we have discussed thus far: "[t]he church is missionary by its very nature. . . . 'The church exists by mission as a fire exists by burning.'"[100] And we have seen that it exists to proclaim the Kingdom of God. Yet, as we saw above, questions remain about mission, the church, and the Kingdom of God. We now turn to an exploration of some questions related to the complex relationship between those three.

As relevant to our discussion, leaders of church movements like Fresh Expressions, ECM, and others are to be commended for seeking to articulate an understanding of the relationship between kingdom, mission, and church. It is the deeply interconnected relationship between these three where each finds its full expression. None can stand on its own. All three are required. This examination also moves us closer to an articulation of Wesleyan mission theology. For its contribution to an understanding of mission, Wesley's theology remained largely underdeveloped in two important areas. The first such area is that of ecclesiology and the priesthood of all believers to use their spiritual gifts. The second is an understanding of the Kingdom of God.[101] Therefore, before we move towards a Wesleyan theology of mission, it is necessary to examine these important areas further.

MISSION, CHURCH, AND KINGDOM, IN RELATIONSHIP

Correctly understood, the relationship between Mission, Church, and Kingdom can be expressed this way:

1. Jesus inaugurated the Kingdom of God by his life, work, teaching, death, and resurrection.

2. As instituted by Jesus, the church carries forth the proclamation of this Kingdom.

---

100. Wickeri, "Mission from the Margins," 187. Quoting Brunner. See also Brunner, *The Word and the World*, 108.

101. Snyder, "Wesleyan Theology of Mission," 26. See 1 Peter 2:5.

3. The institutional church serves the larger movement of the church's mission.

4. Mission, therefore, must be conducted as a harbinger of the Kingdom of God (*missio Dei*).

Jesus inaugurated the Kingdom of God by his life, work, teaching, death, and resurrection

Jesus announced what Israel already knew: God reigns. However, Jesus brought new hope to those who had suffered generations of defeat and loss,[102] because God was fulfilling his promises in Jesus.[103] With the life, death, and resurrection of Jesus, God's reign broke into history in a new way, by the sending of his Son to bring life to all, to serve all, and to reveal himself to all.[104] Jesus' ministry was initiated by his baptism. He faced temptations. He provoked controversies in his teaching, healing, and actions. He dealt directly with religious misunderstandings and offered corrected teachings. He exposed the perceived security in money, prestige, and power as a falsity.[105]

In the gospels, the action and teaching of Jesus discloses that the kingdom itself is revealed by Jesus. In the person and presence of Jesus, one sees the kingdom. At the same time, Jesus' actions are signs that God is acting in a new way towards his people. Robert Harris says it well: "[T]he kingdom is both revealed by Jesus and revealed *to be Jesus*."[106]

In Luke 4 Jesus announced that he is the fulfillment of the prophecy from Isaiah 61. In doing so, he said that he is the one who has come to set things right among the poor, the outcast, and the displaced.[107] Jesus announced that the Kingdom of God is now at hand (see Luke 10, among others). Jesus' announcement of the Kingdom of God is his way of "expressing the meaning of his mission."[108] It is important that this remain central to missional thought. Yet, Jesus did not expressly define the "Kingdom of God." Therefore, it is necessary to look at the comprehensive scope of theme of kingdom. This must include his preaching, his priorities, and his example. As Donald Senior and Carroll Stuhlmueller say "Jesus' parables about

---

102. Newbigin, *The Open Secret*, 23.

103. See Luke 4:14–30.

104. Newbigin, *The Open Secret*, 24.

105. Kirk, *What Is Mission?*, 49–50.

106. Harris, *Mission in the Gospels*, 77. Emphasis original.

107. Bosch, *Transforming Mission*, 85.

108. Senior and Stuhlmueller, *Biblical Foundations for Mission*, 145.

a gracious God, his fellowship with outcasts and women, his healing and exorcisms, his conflicts over interpretation of the law—all of these become a cumulative definition of what the Kingdom of God meant."[109]

This teaching culminated in the work on the cross. Jesus showed that the kingdom must be demonstrated in peace, in love, and ultimately in the cross. The battle must not be fought with the weapons of the enemy, e.g. power, prestige, or wealth.[110] Rather, all of Jesus' teaching, miracles, demonstrations, and death on the cross are empty of power without the resurrection and its eschatological implications. The resurrection shows Jesus exalted as *Kyrios*, Lord. All Christological titles have their meaning in Easter. The resurrection disallows isolating Jesus as merely a historical person. It is in the resurrection that the Kingdom of God, church, and mission find their ongoing power.[111]

As Instituted by Jesus, the Church Carries Forth the Proclamation of This Kingdom

To illustrate this point, it is helpful to recap our discussion on the scriptural basis for mission earlier in this chapter. The gospels record that soon after the resurrection, Jesus put his followers to work. He commissioned them to carry on the kingdom that he inaugurated. Recall that writers often use Matt 28:18–20 (the "Great Commission") in contextual isolation. However, to correctly understand this command, it must be seen as a culmination of all of Matthew's message. The Gospel of Matthew is a missionary work. The work is not merely a record of Jesus' life, but to teach the first Christians, and subsequently all followers, how to understand their calling and mission.[112]

Luke through Acts teaches that Jesus instituted the work of his followers by the power of the Holy Spirit. They are to carry on the proclamation to those immediately around them and eventually to all the world. They do not receive their power from themselves but from on high. Luke ties the work to "the Jewish roots of the church, [and] also affirms the boundary-breaking nature of the church's universal mission."[113] Luke assures the young church that the Spirit will sustain them in their work.[114]

---

109. Senior and Stuhlmueller, *Biblical Foundations for Mission*, 146.

110. Wright, "Imagining the Kingdom," 359.

111. Moltmann, *Power of the Spirit*, 73–75.

112. Bosch, *Transforming Mission*, 57–58.

113. Senior and Stuhlmueller, *Biblical Foundations for Mission*, 259.

114. Senior and Stuhlmueller, *Biblical Foundations for Mission*, 259.

While these are important paradigms to understand the church's proclamation, the Johannine version is key to our discussion. It is John's gospel that records the sending of the disciples in the same manner that Jesus was sent. This, Newbigin says, "is the launching of the church. The church is a movement launched into the world in the same sense in which Jesus is sent into the world by the Father."[115]

The Institutional Church Serves the Larger Movement of the Church's Mission

The question must be asked, then, "What is the church?" Again, a summary of the work earlier in this chapter is helpful. Newbigin touches on it in the above quote: it is a movement. It is not a movement in the sense that one must sign up enough followers for its validity. It is a movement in the sense that it is a dynamic at work around the world.[116] The first Christians saw themselves as a gathering of people and as part of a movement. As noted above, the New Testament term *ekklesia* was a gathering of the people at the behest of the leader. They were a group gathered, called out for a purpose, yet among the community.[117] The first community of those who confessed Jesus Christ as Lord sought to maintain their movement in the public sphere.[118]

Sociology teaches that any movement must eventually find some level of organization to persist. So it was with the church. From the fledgling organizations that Paul began (as recorded in Acts and his letters) to local independent churches to multinational institutions, the church has continued to systematize itself. In their history, these institutions and systems have, at times, served as instruments of the Kingdom of God. In their history, they have, at times, denied God's leading and required reform and renewal. In their history, they have, at times, incorrectly seen themselves as the only initiator of mission. Such misguided thinking around an institutional-centered model of mission was seen in Western theologies as a means of propagating the institution in numbers of churches and members.[119]

Since God is on the move, the church as an institution must serve the movement of the broader church.[120] This means that the church will continue to be renewed by expressions of biblical Christianity in new contexts.

---

115. Newbigin, *Missionary Theologian*, 134.
116. Nussbaum, "Missiology as the Queen of Theology?," 64.
117. Schmidt, "Ekklesia," 515.
118. Newbigin, *Missionary Theologian*, 18.
119. Bosch, "Evangelism: Theological Currents," 168, 206.
120. Nussbaum, "Missiology as the Queen of Theology?," 64.

The Bible's story is of God's purposes being fulfilled as a "blessing for all nations."[121] The message of the gospel is not one of escapism for the one who is "saved," but the message is that God is at work and he will bring the world to its true end. This is the movement of God that is ongoing and the institution of the church must therefore submit itself to God's movement.

Mission, Therefore, Must Be Conducted as a Harbinger of the Kingdom of God (*missio Dei*)

Since we earlier discussed the development of the *missio Dei*, we can now place it in context with an understanding of mission, church, and kingdom. God has called out the church to conduct his mission in the world. He has elected his people to carry his message. This is his pattern in the Scriptures. Consider, for example, when Jonah carried the message to the people of Nineveh or Paul carried the message to the gentiles. These few were called for a purpose: to work for the sake of all. In the same manner, the church is called to carry the message to the world.[122] In the mid-twentieth century, the term *missio Dei* came to be used in missional theology to attempt to define mission and its relationship to the church and the Kingdom of God. Wickeri says that this idea has received widespread acceptance in mainline denominations and the ecumenical movement. He is correct to assert that the *missio Dei* emphasizes God's work in history and rejects the ideas of piety or good works in mission. This has thwarted both liberals and conservatives. Mission should not be seen as something initiated by the "deeply committed or well meaning."[123] It is not another area of the church to be run as a program. *Missio Dei* looks at all the aspects of the church, both as a movement and as an institution, and sees the need for the church to be centered around mission, not mission centered around the church.[124] So, then, how is this mission to be conducted? Mission is to serve as a harbinger of the Kingdom of God. Who inaugurated the Kingdom of God? I have shown above that Jesus announced that the Kingdom of God is come near. Thus, the church, as an agent of the *missio Dei,* must do the same.

Jesus often used parables to explain the Kingdom of God. The church should follow this precept. There were times in Jesus' ministry when he taught and people clearly heard the message. Others heard the same message and turned away. God's election is still at work: there are those who are

121. Newbigin, *Missionary Theologian,* 36.

122. Newbigin, *Missionary Theologian,* 36–37.

123. Wickeri, "Mission from the Margins," 187.

124. Wickeri, "Mission from the Margins," 187.

called to fulfill God's purposes for the benefit of the masses. Those who bear witness to God's work are not the ones who open peoples' eyes. The work of God remains a mystery unless it is revealed by him. Such a proclamation is made in weakness, not in human power.[125] So must the church, an agent of the *missio Dei,* proclaim the Kingdom of God in parables of acts of service to demonstrate the healing and wholeness Christ offers. The bearers of mission should proclaim the Kingdom of God in words and action alike. When John the Baptist sends his question to Jesus, "Are you the One who is to come or not?," Jesus does not respond with a lecture. Instead he points to the signs he has demonstrated. So must the church, as bearers of the mission, point to the signs done in the name of Jesus. The works of the *missio Dei* have the "same two-edged character the parables have. They can cause those who hear of them to stumble, or for some—and blessed are these—they can be the occasion of faith."[126]

THE MISSION LANDSCAPE

So far, we have taken a sweeping view of the landscape that includes the recent developments of a theology of mission. This provides a framework that will inform the discussion of STM that follows. The historical understanding of a mission that propagates faith, expands God's reign, offers conversion for the unbeliever, and establishes new churches is important when establishing the terrain of contemporary mission. I articulated some of the difficulties these presented when mixed with governmental interests of commerce and colonization. The leaders of the church, understanding that it had the right to dictate how and where mission should be conducted, contributed to these difficulties. It is not the church nor government that dictates mission. Rather it is the *missio Dei* that should dictate all activities of the church, especially those done in the name of mission. I again emphasize the triangular relationship: mission needs theology needs biblical engagement. This is a central theme to bring into the conversation with STM. Since STM is a significant contemporary practice, it is important to explore in what manner its practitioners are engaging these three important principles in relationship to one another. These were important principles that framed my discussions with STMers as we will see in later chapters.

The movement of Fresh Expressions and the ECM are significant outcroppings of the contemporary missiological landscape. Both should be commended for their efforts to engage in presenting the gospel message in

---

125. Newbigin, *Missionary Theologian*, 38, 137.
126. Newbigin, *Missionary Theologian*, 36–37.

new ways to new people. They should be affirmed for their efforts to involve the laity in ministry. However, they should be cautioned against a disregard for the ecclesiological and theological work that shapes their current thinking. Efforts to dismiss historical mission for a contemporary expression of church are short-sighted. The church is to be an agent of mission that has been at work for millennia and whose work continues. The leaders of Fresh Expressions and ECM would do well to affirm the way mission has used the church in history alongside their correct call for needed reforms.

We then examined the proper relationship of mission, the church that serves it, and the Kingdom of God it proclaims. As a harbinger of the kingdom, the church is to be an agent of God's mission in the world for the aforementioned propagation of faith, expansion of God's reign, offer of conversion to the unbeliever, and the establishment of new churches. In the latter half of the twentieth century this was articulated in the concept of the *missio Dei*. The working out of the formulation of the *missio Dei* and its implications in mission practice drives much mission thinking and activity today. This is done in the careful examination of mission as the source of theology. I want to explore the manner in which STM participants may see themselves as harbingers of the Kingdom of God as they serve in mission.

Having established the broader landscape, our attention now turns to the understanding and practice of one particular denominational movement: Wesleyan theology. Paying careful attention to this part of the terrain will be necessary to understand Methodist STM, of course. Begun in Britain in the 1700s, Wesleyan theology is now a global influence in missional and ecclesial practice.[127] Indeed, it is of importance to the teams that I will study as they all come from an explicit Wesleyan tradition. Wesleyan Methodism will be the main focus of further discussions of the theology and practice of mission.

127. Jenkins, *Next Christendom*, 67, 80.

3

A Wesleyan Theology of Mission

"[A] Methodist is one who has 'the love of God shed abroad in his heart by the Holy Ghost given to him'; one who 'loves the Lord his God with all his heart, and with all his soul, and with all his mind, and with all his strength'. . . . And while he thus always exercises his love to God. . .this commandment is written in his heart, that 'he who loveth God, loves his brother also'. . .His obedience is in proportion to his love, the source from whence it flows. And therefore, loving God with all his heart, he serves him with all his strength. . . . Lastly, as he has time, he 'does good unto all men'—unto neighbours, and strangers, friends, and enemies. And that in every possible kind; not only to their bodies, by 'feeding the hungry, clothing the naked, visiting those that are sick or in prison', but much more does he labour to do good to their souls, as of the ability which God giveth."

—JOHN WESLEY[1]

In the opening chapters, we saw several key ways in which missional service in the *missio Dei* has been expressed throughout the history of the church. Now our attention turns to one particularly strong movement, the Methodist Revival that began in Britain in the eighteenth century. The movement spread to the American Colonies and served as a dominant influence

---

1. Wesley, "Character of a Methodist," 35–41. NB: Wesley was a product of the time and did not use gender neutral language.

in the new nation. Though Methodism does not hold the same influence in North America that it once did, the Methodist influence is increasingly strong in the widespread Protestant movements in Africa, Asia, and Latin America.[2] I now turn to a discussion of the historical and contemporary understandings and expressions of such a missional thought. In this chapter, we will discuss Wesleyan theology as the missional theology that it is. We will examine some of the motivations for service that Wesley expressed through his theological pedagogy. Next, our attention will turn to the emphasis Wesleyan theology places upon the call for service among the clergy and laity alike. Then our attention will turn to a discussion of the *missio Dei* in Wesleyan theology. I close this chapter with a synthesis of our discussions so far by outlining five key principles of Wesleyan missional theology. These principles are foundational to the examination of Wesleyan STM practices that follows. For these discussions of North American Wesleyan theology, I will focus on the largest American Wesleyan denomination: United Methodism.

METHODIST FOUNDATIONS OF MISSION

The Methodist movement was among the most potent forces in religious life in the eighteenth century.[3] Led by John Wesley, the Methodists sought to reform the church and the nation, and spread scriptural holiness across the land.[4] John and his older brother, Charles, did not distinguish between evangelism and service to others, rather the two were inextricably linked. This movement served as a catalyst to the Evangelical Revival in England and the Second Great Awakening in America.[5] Among the strengths of the message was the emphasis on salvation of individual souls who would then influence personal and societal change.[6]

Wesleyan theology is a missional theology. Its teaching, preaching, and practical ministry stresses a call for service to others. Wesley sought to spread this call for service through the formation of people gathered for discipleship in the Methodist classes and societies, the publishing of pamphlets, sermons, manuals and other literature, and prolific letter writing.[7]

2. Bonino, "Wesley in Latin America," 171; Jenkins, *Next Christendom,* 80; González and González, *Christianity in Latin America,* 270–71.

3. Hogg, "Rise of Protestant Missionary Concern," 105.

4. Wesley, " 'Large' Minutes, A and B," 845.

5. Bevans and Schroeder, *Constants in Context,* 209–10.

6. Bosch, *Transforming Mission,* 285.

7. Snyder, "John Wesley's Theology," 62–63.

Such a theology was formed not in isolation from theoretical consideration but in Wesley's life and practice. Sometimes his efforts were met with bitter disappointment, for example his work in the Georgia Colony.[8] However, his emphasis on the theology of the love of God balanced with the love of neighbor shaped the eighteenth-century revival in Britain and the young America.[9] This practiced theology continues to echo through current Christian movements, particularly in what Philip Jenkins called the "Global South." Jenkins utilizes "Global South" as an overarching term for Africa, Asia, and Latin America to emphasize the unity of religious beliefs in those contexts. He correctly stresses that the Global South is the emerging center of Christianity.[10]

I discuss Wesleyan theology not to establish a John Wesley hagiography. Nor do I emphasize the influence Wesley had (or should have) upon other theological expressions. Instead, I seek to explore Wesley's unique framework for missional theology. Wesley was influenced by several schools of thought including Puritanism, Anglicanism, Lutheranism, Roman Catholicism, and Eastern Orthodoxy. One strength of Wesleyan theology is the ability to hold several of the tenets of these schools of thought together in theological and practical expression.[11] William Abraham is correct to admonish, "any attempt to reinstate Wesley's [theology] without attending to the intervening developments is simply a non-starter."[12] With such attitudes in mind, I will discuss a Wesleyan understanding of the Christian's role in God's kingdom and what that might mean for mission. I will then turn to some brief comments about the influences of this theology in current missional and ecclesial practice. This will be helpful in the study of STM since many United Methodists participate in such short-term service projects. Though not exclusive to Wesleyan denominations, STM trips are commonplace in many United Methodist congregations. I will elucidate both points below. It is beyond the scope of this project to examine STM from the myriad of theological backgrounds of its various practitioners. For purposes of delimitation, I have chosen United Methodism. I do so for several reasons, including: the missional nature of United Methodist theology, the widespread use of STM in The United Methodist Church, and the global nature of both STM and The United Methodist Church.

8. Hogg, "Rise of Protestant Missionary Concern," 209.

9. Bevans and Schroeder, *Constants in Context,* 210.

10. Jenkins, *Next Christendom,* 15.

11. Runyon, "New Creation," 6; Maddox, "Wesleyan Resources," 40.

12. Abraham, "Saving Souls," 15.

The Christian's Place in the Kingdom of God

Wesley understood that the Christian is initiated into the Kingdom of God by grace, through faith, in the pardon offered in Jesus Christ. "'He pardoneth and absolveth all that truly repent, and unfeignedly believe his holy gospel'. . .Believe this, and the Kingdom of God is thine."[13] Pardon and absolution is how Wesley understood justification, the forgiveness, that comes by the merits of Christ.[14] Upon justification, the Christian is "pardoned *in order to participate*" in God's divine nature.[15] Justification is not the end of the salvation process; it is the beginning. The Christian's participation in the loving relationship with God "brings about the renewal of the image of God. This change begins with the new birth, which inaugurates sanctification. Justification, says Wesley, 'restores us to the favour,' sanctification 'to the image of God.' The one takes away the guilt, the other the power of sin."[16]

Randy Maddox points out that, in Wesleyan theology, salvation "is focused on the renewal of persons" to bear God's image in the world.[17] In his sermon "On Original Sin," Wesley asserts "Ye know that the great end of religion is to renew our hearts in the image of God."[18] This renewal does not end at justification, but is to be experienced through the ongoing sanctification through a continued relationship with God's love by the power of the Holy Spirit.[19] Theodore Runyon affirms that Christians are "to *reflect* God's perfect love into the world, to share it with our fellow creatures—and to share it *perfectly*, that is, to share it in such a way that is can be received and appropriated by others as a love whose source is God."[20] The Christian is not saved merely to be removed from this world. Nor is the Christian saved in isolation.[21] The Christian is saved within the connection of God's movement of re-creation in his people and in the cosmos, his creation. Wesley found solid scriptural precedent for the expectation of God's restoration of God's creation.[22] In his thinking, since God created the world as good, he will redeem it. The Kingdom of God is at work on earth and will be fulfilled at

---

13. Wesley, "Way to the Kingdom," 230.

14. Maddox, *Responsible Grace*, 166–68.

15. Maddox, *Responsible Grace*, 168. Emphasis original.

16. Runyon, "New Creation," 11.

17. Runyon, "New Creation," 7.

18. Wesley, "Original Sin," 185.

19. Runyon, *New Creation*, 225.

20. Runyon, *New Creation*, 225. Emphasis original.

21. Marquardt, *John Wesley's Social Ethics*, 136–37.

22. Snyder, "John Wesley's Theology," 70.

the eschaton. Wesley affirmed that God could redeem the Creation, and he expected God to do so.[23] The redemption of Creation was to be brought about, in part, by the Christian's reflection of God's love to those in the household of faith and those who were "not only *our* enemies. . .but even those we deem to be 'the enemies of God.'"[24]

Wesley saw grace bringing the new creation in both cosmic dimensions and in the renewal of the individual, and "this *renewing of the image* is what Albert Outler calls 'the axial theme of Wesley's soteriology.'"[25] Wesley put forth that God will renew the earth and that renewal begins with the first fruits of that creation: humans. In linking the cosmos with human redemption, Wesley affirmed the teachings of the Eastern fathers whom he admired. Humans hold a unique place in this renewal, the special relationship with God through Jesus. This relationship is possible by the love of God received by humans. That love is then, in turn, reflected toward "all other creatures, but especially toward those likewise called to bear 'the image of the Creator.'"[26]

The binding of God's love to all creation, and the Christian's participation in that love, is a key theme in Methodist theology.[27] This participation is done correctly when the Christian reflects God's love to the rest of creation. Such a reflection cannot be done of one's own accord. A Christian's calling and destiny is illustrated in the analogy of a mirror: "a mirror does not possess the image it reflects—but [to act] as an agent who must constantly receive from God what it transmits further. It images its Maker in its words and deeds."[28] This is a key motive for mission in Wesleyan theology. Wesley taught that the Spirit was at work, to bring about the Kingdom of God, in those who were still far away from the gospel and those whom he saw as nominal Christians, both of whom were equally in danger of spiritual demise apart from the saving grace of Jesus Christ.[29]

Making REAL Christians

The nominal Christian was a strong focus of Wesley's preaching and teaching as he sought to awaken them from spiritual death. His observation

23. Tuttle, "God at Work," 112–13.

24. Runyon, *New Creation*, 227.

25. Runyon, "The New Creation," 7. Emphasis original.

26. Runyon, "The New Creation," 8.

27. Meistad, "The Missiology of Charles Wesley," 212–13.

28. Runyon, "New Creation," 8.

29. Tuttle, "God at Work," 114.

of the churches of his day "convinced Wesley that the major reason why churches were nurturing so few *real* Christians was the prevalence of an inadequate notion of the 'salvation' that Christianity proclaims."[30] Wesley was not satisfied with an anemic understanding of Christian life and admonished his hearers to "[l]ean no more on the staff of that broken reed"[31] of their baptism. He called nominal Christians out of their complacency and admonished them instead to participate in the means of grace God offered. While Wesley strongly emphasized salvation by faith alone,[32] he also emphasized that the marks of such salvation are evidenced by a life of love of God that seeks to draw closer to him.[33] Such a love would produce the fruit of love, "a love whereby we love every man as ourselves; as we love our own souls."[34] Wesley rejected any notion that the individual is saved for personal salvation alone.[35] Moving people from complacency in Christianity to participation in Christian ministry is a key theme in Wesley's preaching and teaching. "[H]olding together in tension inward and outward holiness, worship and mission in the world, grace given and grace lived, and preparatory waiting and prophetic act" was Wesley's solution to the problems inside and outside the church.[36]

The foundation of such a theology is Wesley's teaching on Christ's example for all. Christ is properly seen as the incarnation of God's love, redeemer from the guilt of sin, and, as Methodist scholar Manfred Marquadt puts it, "the One who filled the justified person with faith and love and made it possible for that person to have a new humanness according to the likeness of God."[37] Wesley expected Christians to see Christ as the perfect example. He saw this as normative for those who were seeking the sanctification that God offers through the power of the Holy Spirit. Wesley expected Christians to imitate Christ and to be controlled by Christ's love in all things. Just as Christ was filled with love for all, Christians were to be filled with love for their neighbor. Therefore, "following Jesus means having His mind, walking as He walked, and doing good."[38] Wesley stressed that when Christians are transformed by God's love they can then express

---

30. Maddox, "Wesley's Prescription," 17. Emphasis original.

31. Wesley, "Marks of the New Birth," 430.

32. Wesley, "Scripture Way of Salvation," 162.

33. Wesley, "Scripture Way of Salvation," 166.

34. Wesley, "Marks of the New Birth," 426.

35. Wesley, "Marks of the New Birth," 417-30.

36. Meeks, "Home for the Homeless," 2.

37. Marquardt, *John Wesley's Social Ethics*, 114.

38. Marquardt, *John Wesley's Social Ethics*, 114.

the love of God and others as the natural course of life. Wesley expected that acts of love would flow from a heart filled with God's love. This was foundational to his expectation that God's grace is greater than any sin and those transformed by that grace would demonstrate it through acts of personal piety and loving actions towards God and others. Such an expectation is what Wesley meant by his teachings on Christian perfection.[39] An expectation that all Christians could expect to go on towards perfection is foundational to Wesley's missional theology.[40]

Saved for a Purpose

Wesley also saw that deliverance from sin continued through a life that went on towards entire perfection in this life.[41] There is not space here to fully illustrate Wesley's teaching on Christian perfection. However, it is important to note that seeking perfection is understood as the participation in the true mark of Christianity: love. As influential Wesleyan theologian Albert Outler says, "Wesley's evangelistic message *combines* radical faith in God's reconciling love in Christ (the inward, personal dimension of salvation) *with* a moral social agenda implied in and by this love that energizes and guides the Christian life from new birth to maturation, always 'in Christ.'"[42]

For Wesley salvation was not to be merely expressed in personal holiness. It must also be lived in community with other Christians and expressed in acts of love. Wesley emphasizes "[t]he gospel of Christ knows of no religion, but social; no holiness, but social holiness."[43] Liberation theologies have sought to use this teaching as a call to rework political systems, economic structures, or social norms. These theologies have sought to uncover systematic "oppression and injustice," particularly among the poor in the Global South in recent years.[44] However, social gospel or liberation theologies misunderstand the "social holiness" aphorism when using it in isolation to justify political activism. Instead, Maddox points out:

> Wesley assumed that consistent and faithful social action must be grounded in such communal spiritual formation. The tendency to counterpoise concern for spiritual formation against

39. Macquiban, "Work on Earth," 187–88.
40. Marquardt, *John Wesley's Social Ethics*, 106–09.
41. Maddox, *Responsible Grace*, 180.
42. Outler, *Evangelism and Theology*, 108–09. Emphasis original.
43. Wesley, *Hymns and Sacred Poems*, viii.
44. Jennings, "Wesley and the Poor," 24, 30.

concern for social service and activism, which his twentieth-century heirs appropriated from their culture, has inclined [such theologies] to overlook this connection.[45]

Correctly understood, social holiness is to be expressed in the Christian community for an "ongoing growth in grace."[46] Stephen Rankin says that as one grows in love for God, so does the love for one's neighbor

> because God's own Spirit instills this love in the believer. Since neighbor love is a reflection of God's image in the believer, and since full restoration of the image of God is the goal of Christian perfection, love necessarily motivates one toward service, because it reflects God's own relational nature as well as God's determination to reclaim what has been lost.[47]

Any sort of expectation to change society must begin with a Christian's pursuit of holiness of heart and life.[48] This movement in Christian perfection is first the goal of the individual. This renewal of the image of God in the individual engenders a hope "that the future can surpass the present."[49] This leads to what Runyon describes as a

> holy dissatisfaction [that] is aroused with regard to any present state of affairs—a dissatisfaction that supplies the critical edge necessary to keep the process of individual transformation moving. Moreover, this holy dissatisfaction is readily transferable from the realm of the individual to that of society, where it provides a persistent motivation for reform in the light of 'a more perfect way' that transcends any status quo.[50]

Therefore, Methodist theology moves the question beyond "How can I be saved?" to "For what purpose am I saved?"[51]

Expressing Holiness

The strong conviction to teach others of God's offer of freedom from slavery, sin, and death moved Methodists to spiritual and physical action. From his

---

45. Maddox, "'Visit the Poor," 64.
46. Maddox, "'Celebrating the Whole Wesley,'" 81.
47. Rankin, "A Perfect Church," 89.
48. Maddox, "'Visit the Poor," 63–64.
49. Runyon, "The New Creation," 11.
50. Runyon, "The New Creation," 11–12.
51. Meistad, "The Missiology of Charles Wesley," 220.

days at Oxford (hence before his time in the American colony of Georgia and the "Aldersgate experience"), Wesley sought to minister among the poor, the outcasts, and the imprisoned. It was after the formative experiences in Georgia (and the subsequent influences of those he met through that encounter, not least of which were the Moravians) and at Aldersgate that Wesley sought to implement a scriptural holiness that demonstrated a love of God and neighbor in tandem. Wesley sought to serve the poor wherever he could find them, defining the poor as "those who lacked the necessities of life."[52] In his sermon "On Visiting the Sick" he says, "By the sick, I do not mean only those that keep their bed, or that are sick in the strictest sense. Rather I would include all such as are in a state of affliction, whether of mind or body; and that whether they are good or bad, whether they fear God or not."[53] Wesley clearly understood that those in need of demonstration of Christian love were not to be limited to physical symptoms or to those already inside the church. Additionally, he strongly instructed his hearers to be physically present with those in need as the only proper way to be in mission service.

> Many are so circumstanced that they cannot attend the sick in person; and where this is the real case it is undoubtedly sufficient for them to send help, being the only expedient they can use. But this is not properly visiting the sick; it is another thing. The word which we render visit, in its literal acceptation, means to look upon. And this, you well know, cannot be done unless you are present with them.[54]

Wesley saw those in need in London and as he traveled throughout England preaching in the open fields, city centers, and industrial areas. Moving out of the parish setting of his Anglican ministerial past meant that Wesley encountered populations to which he was unaccustomed, among them servants, miners, farmers, and other working class people. He was moved by the great need he witnessed first-hand.[55]

Wesley's belief that all people are redeemable by God's grace also held that redemption meant a relief from physical depravation as well. Wesley saw the poor as more than objects of mission and recipients of charity. He saw them as children whom God loved. Wesley sought to share this lesson, in word and deed, with the Methodists under his care. As Harrison Daniel puts it, "Wesley learned through mission that nominal Christians without

52. Heitzenrater, "People Called Methodists," 27.
53. Wesley, "On Visiting the Sick," 385.
54. Wesley, "On Visiting the Sick," 385–86.
55. Heitzenrater, "People Called Methodists," 28; Heitzenrater, *Wesley*, 127.

an experience of the new birth available in Christ were caught in their original sin to the same extent as non-Christians."[56] One of the most powerful ways to teach Christians to, instead, demonstrate a love for God was to put them near their neighbors in need. Being involved in God's mission is the key to understanding the Good News.[57] He encouraged the Methodists to do all within their power to meet the very real physical needs before them.[58] Wesley saw that one way to exercise such power was to leave little to happenstance in terms of the effort given to service. Rather, Wesley and his followers systemized their efforts to seek maximum effectiveness.

Organizing to Beat the Devil

As the title of Charles Ferguson's book, *Organizing to Beat the Devil: Methodists and the Making of America,* so aptly puts it, the later American Methodists learned this practice from Wesley's example.[59] "Wesley was a master of small details. . .[h]e did not just recommend that his people go about doing good, he set about organizing goodness."[60] Since Wesley understood holiness in a holistic manner, he organized the Methodists into structures that would facilitate personal and social holiness. The strength of the practical theological expression of the Methodist movement was the small groups in which the people were organized, known as classes and societies. They were to meet "having the Form, and seeking the Power of Goodness, united in order to pray together, to receive the Word of Exhortation, and to watch over one another in Love, that they may help each other to work out their Salvation."[61] These classes (groups of about 12 people) were to spur one another to good works and continue in showing the evidence of their salvation by following the general rules: "First, by doing no Harm. . .Secondly, By doing Good. . .Thirdly, By attending upon all the Ordinances of God."[62] Wesley organized and encouraged the classes and the larger societies to demonstrate the General Rules he articulated through a variety of practical demonstrations of the Love of God they professed. The Methodists distributed food and clothing and offered medical assistance to the poor. They pioneered free pharmacies and clinics. They sought to provide community

56. Daniel, "Young John Wesley," 455.

57. Daniel, 455.

58. Marquardt, *John Wesley's Social Ethics,* 27.

59. Ferguson, *Organizing to Beat the Devil.*

60. Miles, "Moral Life of John Wesley," 209.

61. Wesley, *General Rules,* 4.

62. Wesley, *General Rules,* 6–9.

health education about proper nourishment and hygiene and offered self-help treatment ideas for various illnesses. Interest-free loans were available to those who showed need and pledged to repay the loan in three months. Projects were arranged to employ those who were out of work.[63] Methodists opened (or took on existing) schools intending to form the spiritual, physical, and mental training of children whom society had shut out of quality schools. Educational programs were established for adults as well.[64] Such projects are commonplace in Methodist missions today.[65]

Granted, Wesley was not always successful in implementing these programs. However, his work set new theological premises for the missional service of the time. Assistance became an activity of the Christian community rather than one to be relegated to the structures of the parish church leadership. Methodists were expected to help others of the community of faith and those still outside of it. Wesley challenged the "us-and-them" dichotomy of class and Christian fellowship. He confronted unrealistic, stringent definitions of poverty that were popular in Britain in his time, and which kept many needy people from receiving help. Wesley emphasized the need for every Christian to participate in works of charity.[66] Such participation in Christian mission remains an important practice in United Methodism, as we shall see.

Serving with a Foundation

Wesley was firm in his belief that God raised up the Methodist movement to "reform the nation, particularly the church; and to spread scriptural holiness over the land."[67] This was to be accomplished by the Spirit of God working through the people of the church. Christians were to spread the message of God's gift of salvation through their scriptural witness. The joining of evangelism and mission service would be accomplished by, what Jeff Conklin-Miller calls "a People with the mind of Christ, living in the way of Christ, and serving others, engaging the world in the name of Christ."[68]

---

63. Marquardt, *John Wesley's Social Ethics,* 27–29.

64. Heitzenrater, "People Called Methodists," 34.

65. I plan to illustrate this further in my research on mission development and short-term mission.

66. Heitzenrater, "People Called Methodists," 35–36.

67. Wesley, "'Large' Minutes," 845.

68. Conklin-Miller, "Leaning Both Ways," 164.

These "servants" and "martyrs"[69] were, as Richard Heitzenrater says, to "imitate the life of Christ not improve the national economy."[70] This was to be done in a way that affirmed every person as a child of the God who loved them and to whom salvation was offered in the person of Jesus Christ. He worked "to remove the stigma of poverty" and most importantly to "affirm that we are all poor in some way or another."[71] The Methodists ministered among the poor, in part, because the poor were so often among Methodists.[72]

These acts of mercy were not good deeds as an end to themselves, nor were they mere philanthropic enterprises. Wesley did all this work in a solidly theological framework. They were deeply rooted in a theology of a holistic evangelism. As Theodore Jennings points out, "[T]he announcement of good news to the poor must at the same time be the enactment of good news to the poor. . . . If this does not occur there can be no talk of evangelism that has anything to do with the gospel of Jesus Christ."[73] Acts of love as a means of sharing the gospel are foundational for Wesleyan theology. By practicing the commands of Christ, others will not be susceptible to stumbling blocks that piety without solidarity with the poor presents.[74]

Wesley's Experience in Georgia and a Theology of Mission

We have thus far seen a Wesleyan missional theology that expresses a response to God's activity in the believer and is focused upon the Other. Yet, this legacy of mission and service represents a significant shift from Wesley's early understanding of mission. Wesley served as a missionary to the American Colony of Georgia in what was, at best, a contentious endeavor. His motives were misplaced in a self-seeking effort to earn God's favor through his good works. In his letter to John Burton, written just prior to Wesley's departure for the Georgia colony, Wesley admitted, "My chief motive, to which all the rest are subordinate, is the hope of saving my own soul."[75] Read in view of some of his other works, Wesley seemed to be seeking a way to move beyond a book knowledge of God and his love, but to learn of it in service to others. I have noted above that Wesley later rejected any notion of

69. Outler, *Evangelism and Theology,* 66. By "martyrs" Outler means those who bear the witness as instructed in Acts 1.

70. Heitzenrater, "People Called Methodists," 36.

71. Heitzenrater, "People Called Methodists," 36.

72. Marquardt, *John Wesley's Social Ethics,* 34.

73. Jennings, "Wesley and the Poor," 22.

74. Jennings, "Wesley and the Poor," 29.

75. Wesley, "To the Revd. John Burton," 439.

works to earn God's favor. However, in the rest of the Burton letter there are some interesting parallels among Wesley and some of the problems mentioned earlier with misunderstandings of mission. Wesley revealed some of his romanticized views of the "heathen" to whom he sought to minister. He saw the "other" as one who was not bound by the trappings of his own comfortable life. He believed that they were not bound by the temptations of food, drink, clothing, philosophy, or other distractions of the English society he was leaving behind. Instead, he saw the Indians as little children in the faith, humble and ready to learn all that Wesley would teach them and to do the will of God with joy. His encounters with the tribes in and around Fort Frederica did not fulfill his romanticized hopes.[76]

This does, however, present some interesting parallels to the practice of STM. The idea that the romanticized "other" will be receptive to the gospel because of their lack of material distractions is not a new phenomenon. Just as Wesley had an inappropriately naive view of the objects of mission, so do some who currently serve in mission. It could be said that the ones with a similar naive view, experience the same results. I will illuminate this in the following chapters.

THE LAITY AND A THEOLOGY OF MISSION

Now that we have seen the Wesleyan foundations for mission service, we will further examine how these were used to incorporate the laity in service efforts. The Methodist movement was a movement among the laity.[77] For Wesley, the empowering of the laity in ministry was the way "the Kingdom of God is made visible by believers in Christ joined in community to love God and neighbor and to fulfill God's whole law."[78] Such empowering, among other issues, caused tensions among Wesley and other leaders in the Anglican Church of his day. Despite the tension between the Methodist movement and established Anglicanism, Wesley did not seek to establish a new church. Instead he sought to revitalize the Anglican Church to which he held so firmly by re-energizing the laity in the Christian faith they seemed to profess, but failed to demonstrate. The Methodists demonstrated the lesson that the laity embodies the church, visible in the world. This was an important lesson for Wesley as it ran counter to his clerical training that centered ministry in the ordained.[79] However, a growing movement of laypeople

76. Wesley, "To the Revd. John Burton," 439-42.

77. Heitzenrater, "People Called Methodists," 118–19.

78. Rankin, "A Perfect Church," 95.

79. Outler, *Evangelism and Theology*, 24.

presented problems for Wesley. He had difficulty managing the theological training of those he had empowered for ministry. Only a small number of trained Anglicans joined John and Charles in their efforts. Therefore, they recruited and empowered lay preachers to spread the work of Methodism. These lay preachers were forbidden to administer the sacraments, a right reserved for the priests, but were encouraged to preach the Word of God on the circuits. Because of their traveling requirements, they did not participate in the regular class meetings. Those in pastoral leadership were, at times, without corrective leadership themselves. This vacuum led to problems of theological deviation among those entrusted with proclaiming the message. This was a problem American Methodists would inherit.[80]

Luis Wesley de Souza points out that English and North American Methodism emphasized the ministry of the laity in several ways, "It was a movement of the people and, as such, it trusted the Holy Spirit to inspire people as they exercised their ministry in the world."[81] He is correct to emphasize the need for lay ministry, under the guidance of the Holy Spirit, in the churches of the West and the Global South. However, de Souza goes too far when he said that Wesley's ecclesiology gave "unlimited room to the laity."[82] The Wesley brothers struggled with how to best manage the growing need for ministers and see that the ministers under their care were fit to serve. They carefully examined their ministers and expelled those who did not meet their doctrinal and ministerial standards. The traveling preachers who were not purged were asked to uphold a covenant of ministry under the careful supervision of John and Charles.[83]

THE *MISSIO DEI* AND A UNITED METHODIST THEOLOGY OF MISSION

Now that we have seen the role of the clergy and laity in mission, how then are they to serve the *missio Dei*? Some Wesleyan scholars have engaged the *missio Dei* as it relates to current expressions of Wesley's original missiology.[84] In local congregations, Methodists, both lay and clergy, continue to serve in mission. Hundreds of thousands of United Methodists participate in service projects at home and abroad each year. However, the minority do so under the purview of official United Methodist agencies. Whereas

80. Maddox, "Untapped Inheritance," 24–25, 36.

81. De Souza, "Challenges of John Wesley's Theology," 86–87.

82. De Souza, "Challenges of John Wesley's Theology,," 87.

83. Heitzenrater, "People Called Methodists," 182–87.

84. See Gaines, "Politics, Participation, and the Missio Dei."

Wesley sought to organize and oversee his followers in mission service, it would appear that utilizing denominational connectivity is not a priority for many American United Methodist churches today. In 2012, more than 500,000 United Methodists reported serving in mission at home or overseas. However, less than 11 percent of them did so through the guidance of agencies affiliated with The United Methodist Church, such as United Methodist Volunteers in Mission (hereafter UMVIM).[85]

The reasons for this are not entirely clear, and they raise several questions. Why are such large numbers of laypeople forgoing official United Methodist agencies? Do they do so under the guidance and example of their pastors? Are the laity serving in mission by engaging with the Wesleyan practices of accountability? Is this a new movement of the *missio Dei* that is designed to equip the laity for mission which should be embraced by church leadership and should the current systems be radically overhauled to embrace it? I address these in the discussion of STM below.

Current mission patterns in United Methodism seem to be indicative of the larger American mission movement. An increase in service by the laity, a move away from the power of centralized organizations to local congregations, and the increasing influence of a "market state" rather than nation state can all be seen in United Methodist mission. The increase in focus upon the decisions of the local congregation were discussed in the previous chapter. I will discuss the market state model in the next chapter. Additionally, there is a perceptible move away from a designated international missionary who is supported by local congregations and supervised by leaders with a missional hierarchy. Instead, international mission work is becoming increasingly centered in the local congregation. One indicator of such a movement to the local congregation is the evidence that more United Methodist congregations are not utilizing the denominational connections available to them (noted in the opening paragraph of this section). Studies by anthropologist Robert Priest and sociologist Robert Wuthnow indicate a similar trend in STM more broadly.[86] The laity, with various levels of training, preparation, and oversight are deploying themselves to bring their understanding of mission and ministry to nearly every continent. They encounter new patterns of Christian living that are sometimes difficult. Such is but one challenge of United Methodist mission.[87]

---

85. According to reports complied by the General Council for Finance and Administration. Whitney Washington, e-mail message to author, March 12, 2014.

86. See Priest, "Short-Term Missions." Wuthnow, *Boundless Faith*, 162–75.

87. Marquardt and Klaiber, *Living Grace*, 368–69.

Perhaps the ongoing Wesleyan movement can embrace the lessons of its origin to catch a glimpse of its participation in the *missio Dei* and to do so in the mutual accountability of clergy and laity. Key components of the work of the *missio Dei* in the current context will include a radical solidarity between the missionary and those served, an embracing of the world as the parish, and a recognition that all are poor in some way.[88] Maddox is correct to say that "[w]e face a dire need for reintegrating the practice of theological reflection and activity into the life of the community of believers if we are to foster authentically Christian responses to the urgent problems of our times, including the problems of poverty and economic injustice."[89] This is particularly true for the growing movement of United Methodist STM. Its leaders must assess their priorities in formation of the laity to "labour to do good. . .as of the ability which God giveth."[90]

FIVE PRINCIPLES OF A WESLEYAN MISSION THEOLOGY

To codify a Wesleyan mission theology, I suggest that there are five principles that should be considered. To synthesize what I have illustrated thus far, Wesleyan mission, correctly understood: 1) is rooted in Scripture, 2) embraces the role of the broader church, 3) affirms that evangelism is mission, 4) insists that mission is not merely evangelism, and 5) expects ongoing discipleship in the lives of practitioners and recipients.

1) *Rooted in Scripture.* Wesleyan motivation for participation in God's mission comes from an understanding of the mandates of Scripture to do so. This is the first principle of Wesleyan theology of mission: it is to be rooted in Scripture. As mentioned in chapter 1, a correct understanding of mission theology presupposes the primacy of Scripture for motivation, instruction, and example of how mission should be conducted. Wesleyan mission is no exception. It is in Scripture that the missioner also finds the source for service activity: the redeeming work of Jesus Christ.[91]

2) *Embraces the role of the broader church.* Wesleyan missiology embraces the gifts of the broader church for new contexts, settings, and expressions. By "broader" church I mean an embracing of the width of the church's current expressions and depth of its historical expressions. However, it is not bound to those historical traditions merely for tradition's sake. Those

---

88. Daniel, "Young John Wesley," 454–55.

89. Maddox, "Wesleyan Resources," 44.

90. Wesley, "The Character of a Methodist," ¶16.

91. Snyder, "Wesleyan Theology of Mission," 21.

traditions are weighed in consideration with the other principles. Maintaining such traditions can be seen in Wesley's use of standards in expectations for leaders, preachers, and teachers. The innovative work in new contexts, settings, and expressions can be seen in things like the use of field preaching. Laceye Warner points out that such a practice was, at the time, "highly irregular, especially among respectable Anglican clergy."[92] I have also shown that the laity's innovations in the areas of medicine, education, and economics among the poor and working class people were, in many ways, new practices. Concurrently, Wesley did not seek to dismantle nor deconvert from his church, nor did he ask his followers to do so. Rather, his aim was to serve with the foundation of the broader church while reforming his own church. Recall the assertion in chapter 1 that, even in midst of new expressions of church, leaders must remain "committed to an exacting orthodoxy and a committed theology."[93]

3) *Affirms that evangelism is mission.* Mission is a broader action of the work of the kingdom while evangelism is, as Kimberly Reisman illustrates, a "narrower concept; however, it is 'the *core*, *heart*, or *center* of mission.'"[94] The Spirit's movement to bring about the New Creation includes an invitation for all to participate in the New Creation and the redemption the Spirit is offering through it. Recall Wesley's message of invitation for any who would believe in the gospel's message: "'He pardoneth and absolveth all that truly repent, and unfeignedly believe his holy gospel.'. . .Believe this, and the Kingdom of God is thine."[95] The offering of the gospel's story is a key motivation for a Wesleyan mission theology.

4) *Insists that mission is not merely evangelism.* I have shown several ways in which Wesleyan missional theology is more than merely verbal proclamation of the gospel. Warner points out that such an approach finds its roots in a biblical theology of mission and evangelism:

> [B]iblical foundations such as Luke and Paul developed the term *evangelizo* to explain the mission *and* message of Jesus. Therefore, to focus too narrowly on evangelism as verbal proclamation rather than an all-inclusive description of Jesus' whole work of ministry is to neglect the biblical foundations for a faithful theology and practice of evangelism.[96]

92. Warner, "Spreading Scriptural Holiness," 119.
93. Ward, *Liquid Church,* 56.
94. Reisman, "Restorative Witness," 99, quoting Bosch. Emphasis original.
95. Wesley, "The Way to the Kingdom," II.9.
96. Warner, "Kingdom Witness," 453. Emphasis original.

This "whole work" includes meeting the physical, emotional, and social needs of others as an integral part of the message of the restoration of Creation. These efforts were often maintained at the "grassroots" level. Yes, Wesley did at times seek to influence national policy, but without local action such national action was considered less than effective. Recalling his urging to visit the sick, of body and mind, we see that Wesley was an advocate of a message of the Good News that joined words and deeds alike. As I pointed out in chapter 1, "Evangelization is mission, but mission is not merely evangelization."[97]

5) *Expects ongoing discipleship in the lives of practitioners and recipients.* Those who responded to these invitations of words and deeds were expected to grow by the grace they had been given through participation in the bands and societies established by those in the Methodist movement. It was in such groups that people were expected to grow in their Christian discipleship as they prayed together, studied together, and watched over one another. They were expected to grow in the love of God and of Neighbor: "First, By doing no Harm. . .Secondly, By doing Good. . .Thirdly, By attending upon all the Ordinances of God."[98] Those who serve in mission, and those who were receptive to the gospel message presented through that mission, are expected to grow together. The participation of the newly converted, and the mature Christian alike, in a small group of other believers for the purposes of mutual edification and personal discipleship is tantamount to a full expression of Wesleyan mission and discipleship. These five principles are not necessarily exclusive to Wesleyan missional theology. However, they are key to understanding mission practice in the United Methodist tradition.

In this chapter, we have narrowed our focus of the mission landscape to the theological motivations of the Wesleyan missional service. I have articulated the role of clergy and laity alike. Using the survey of the mission terrain from chapters 1 and 2, I illuminated five specific principles of Wesleyan mission theology. As I said in the introduction, the aim of this project is to investigate contemporary STM activities by United Methodists. My aim thus far has been to establish the terrain of prominent figures in mission studies in general and then move to a more specific understanding of the history and principles of Wesleyan mission. In the next chapter, we will discuss STM and its unique role in contemporary mission. We will then be prepared to hear from current United Methodist STM participants.

---

97. Moltmann, *Power of the Spirit*, 10.
98. Wesley, *General Rules*, 6–9.

4

Short-Term Mission and
a Theology of Mission

Having now established this specific view of the terrain as it relates to Wesleyan Mission theology, our focus now turns to the practice of STM. Robert Priest, one of the most widely published writers on the subject of STM says, "Probably no other dimension of American religious life is so extensive while being so little studied or understood by scholars."[1] Yet, the practice of STM is a vast and growing movement. It is a "grassroots and populist phenomenon [that is] almost completely divorced from scholarship, from missiology, and from seminary education."[2] Much of the work that has been done focuses on a debate on the efficacy of the practice from a success-of-the-missioner point of view, and seeks to explore the change brought in the missioners themselves. A large number of articles that do discuss STM relate anecdotes or personal accounts of the cultural or theological miscues of the American missioners, and closes with a bullet point list of ways to improve the practice of STM. Much of this work is offered by career missionaries or STM brokers.[3] The personal stories, while somewhat helpful, are not offered with academic rigor.[4] The number of researched-

1. Priest and Ver Beek, "Short-Term Missions."

2. Priest et al., "Short-Term Mission Movement," 434.

3. In using the term "broker" I am referring to for-profit or not-for-profit agents and/or agencies who facilitate STM teams. This could include church-based or para-church-based individuals and/or organizations.

4. Raines, "International Perspective," 24.

based works is sparse.[5] Little material is offered from theologians or from a theologically significant missiology. Much of the academic work that is available focuses on the effect STM has on the participants by seeking to measure a change in their giving to charities, participation in civic causes, increased church participation, or similar areas.[6] These exercises seem to indicate that there is little lasting change in the STMers as STM is currently practiced.

With such an assessment of the current material in mind, in this chapter, I offer a fuller treatment of the available resources. I begin with an account of the origins of STM. Next, I will engage the work around more recent practices. Here I will examine STMers in the Third Wave Mission movement and their under-realized global impact. Next, I will recount some criticisms and affirmations of STM before moving to a treatment of the sparse literature from STM hosts. I close the chapter with a discussion of the lack of robust theological work in the field and the resulting unrealized potential.

EMERGENCE OF SHORT-TERM MISSION

The STM movement is a relatively young one. Those at the 1910 Edinburgh Missionary Conference mentioned in chapter 1 would have expected missionary service to be a lifelong commitment. However, this attitude soon began to change. Churches and parachurch organizations began new programs of mission that were designed for shorter terms of service. One such program was started by the Methodist Board of Missions in 1949. This radical new program sent recent college graduates out to the mission field for a three-year commitment to nations like Japan and India. With 45 days of training, they served in practical venues like rural development projects, hospitals, and schools. Religious groups such as Operation Mobilization (1957) and Youth With a Mission (1960) and secular efforts like the U.S. Peace Corps (1961) began sending workers into the field for periods of time ranging from a few weeks to a few years. George Verwer, founder of Operation Mobilization, began sending young people on short-term evangelism trips to Mexico to work with existing long-term mission efforts in the 1950s. A key strategy of these trips was the distribution of evangelistic literature.

---

5. Howell, *Short-Term Mission*, 26.

6. Beers, "Faith Development"; Beyerlein, et. al., "Youth Civic Engagement"; Campbell et al., "Reduction in Burnout; Hopkins, "Effects of Short-Term Service; Norton, "Changing Our Prayer Behaviors." Such works were representative of several sources.

By the early 1960s Operation Mobilization was sending over 2,000 people annually.[7] The 1980s saw a proliferation of groups specializing in providing STM trips for youth.[8] Today, American congregations expect youth pastors to take their groups on domestic and transnational mission trips. Additionally, congregations are increasingly adding "mission pastors" to their staffs to implement and maintain mission trips for youth and adults alike.[9] In addition to the congregations that send teams, there are more than 3,700 organizations designed to support international STM.[10]

CURRENT SHORT-TERM MISSION PRACTICES

Between 1.8 million and two million Americans participate in STMs annually. Approximately 83 percent of these trips last two weeks or less. The average length of a STM trip is eight days. Therefore, I define a "short-term" mission trip as one that lasts two weeks or less. STM teams serve on nearly every continent in a variety of contexts. Typical projects include evangelism, outreach activities aimed at children, repairing existing buildings or constructing new ones, giving technical advice to business leaders, and providing medical and dental care. The United States sends the most STMers, though other countries are seeing an increase in the practice. Nine of the top fifteen STM destinations for American teams are in Latin America and the Caribbean.[11] Each participant pays, on average, $1,000 in expenses, excluding transportation. This translates to approximately $2 billion in cash expended on in-country expenses, project costs, hotels, and the like. Additionally, these teams contribute over 30,000 person-years of service which can be valued at over $1.1 billion of time and contribution in the field. Congregations support teams with prayers, financial contributions and logistical support. Parents and family members contribute to youth trips.[12] This multi-billion dollar venture involves millions of people in the United States and in their targeted countries of service whose true numbers are difficult to ascertain.

---

7. Andrew Scott, e-mail message to the author, September 29, 2014; Priest, "Short-Term Missions," 84–85.

8. Priest, "Short-Term Missions," 85.

9. Priest et al., "Short-Term Mission Movement," 433.

10. Offutt, "Short-Term Mission Teams," 798.

11. Priest and Priest, "'They See Everything,'" 53–63.

12. Wuthnow, *Boundless Faith*, 167, 71; Howell, *Short-Term Mission*, 27; Priest and Priest, "'They See Everything,'" 57–63.

A Third Wave Mission

Very recent scholarship has couched STM in what has been termed the "Third Wave Mission" movement. Robert Schreiter explains the three waves of mission and the accompanying dynamics of globalization. The first wave, he said, was approximately 1450–1750 when Christian missionaries accompanied European explorers and military personnel. The second was, more or less, from the start of the nineteenth century until World War I. During this time, advances in travel and communication accompanied the forming of foreign mission efforts in both Catholic and Protestant churches. The third wave, the present wave, began in the 1980s. Advances in air travel and the advent of digital technologies are featured prominently in this wave of mission.

As it is an ever-developing phenomenon, implications of globalization during the Third Wave are still being realized. Some impacts include the compression of the conceptions of time and space. Travel that used to take days can now be completed in hours. Communication that used to require weeks can now be completed in seconds. Such compressions of time and space can also distort boundaries. Images of the collapse of the Soviet Union in the 1990s and the Arab Spring of 2010 were transmitted around the world almost instantaneously. Travel that allows mass migration of peoples has led to an increase in pluralism of both ethnicity and religions in places where homogeneity had prevailed for generations.

The STM movement is, in many ways, riding this wave. Globalization makes possible an increased awareness of global needs as well as the means to try to do something about it. Images of the effects of natural disasters or the effects of poverty can be seen by millions of Americans on their tablets and phones. Faster and cheaper travel allows them the opportunity to go overseas to attempt to do something about it in a time frame that fits with their work and family schedules. Coinciding, but beyond the scope of our discussion here, is the "twinning" of congregations. Twinning seeks to foster meaningful cross-cultural exchanges between congregations who would otherwise remain unknown to one another. It is in this rapid wave of globalization that STM grew. The role that STMers play in such globalization should not be underestimated.[13]

---

13. Schreiter, "Third Wave Mission." See also Gable and Haasl, "Third Wave of Mission." Howell, "Short Term Mission." Schreiter, Gable, and Haasl place Third Wave Mission as a predominately Catholic movement. However, the characteristics of Third Wave Mission are demonstrated in several Protestant expressions as well.

The "Overlooked Globalizers"

Considering these factors, it is easy to see why the trend of STM continues to increase in number and scope. In a study by Robert Priest, Terry Dischinger, Steve Rasmussen, and C.M. Brown, nearly half of seminary students (n=2208) surveyed said they had participated in one or more short-term, transnational service experiences. Priest's research indicated that it is likely that a clear majority of future pastors will support and lead future STM trips and/or expect their staff members to do so.[14] If current trends hold, 20–25 percent of American church-goers will be involved in STM at some point in their lives.[15] It is likely that "American pastors and their congregations are among the 'overlooked globalizers' of our world."[16]

The leaders of the STM movement carry a great deal of responsibility and influence. The growth of STM has moved faster than theological research and subsequent education related to such a widespread practice. This is cause for concern. For example, though youth workers lead a large percentage of STM trips, most youth workers have not been formally trained in STM. Those that do have a seminary education probably had little, if any, training in STM. Even senior pastors, who may have been required to take mission courses in seminary, probably did not receive training on STM.[17]

It is beyond the scope of this project to engage with STM dynamics in every context in which they serve. Because of the predominance of Latin America and the Caribbean in STM interactions, much of my discussion will focus upon teams who serve there. I am sensitive that there are cultural differences throughout this delimited context. However, I will try to speak to their commonalities without minimizing unique contributions that each culture in the region makes.

Criticisms of Short-Term Missions

Though many affirm the practice of STM, it is not without its detractors. Marian Adeney summarizes well the criticisms lodged against many STM practices in "When the Elephant Dances, the Mouse May Die." She offers an analogy of two friends, the elephant and the mouse, dancing at a party.

14. Priest et al., "Short-Term Mission Movement," 434; Priest, *Effective Engagement*, iii.

15. Wuthnow, *Boundless Faith*, 171. Wuthnow defines "church-goer" as someone who attends worship at least once a month.

16. Priest et al., "Short-Term Mission Movement," 434.

17. Priest, *Effective Engagement*, v.

Though the elephant was having a great time, he was unaware that his good time was putting the fragile mouse in great peril. Such is the case when exuberant, well-meaning North American STMers neglect the considerations of their more fragile mission partners. Adeney emphasizes that the lack of contextualized methods in ministry and sensitivity to cultural needs can undermine well-intentioned mission efforts. Attitudes of superiority (either intentionally or unintentionally) can lead to problems of neo-colonialism when American STMers impose their ideas and material solutions on their mission hosts without appropriate understanding of the complexities of local ministry settings. Those who travel to exotic locales on STM trips may neglect the mission's purpose in favor of the attraction of perceived adventure to be had.[18] Adeney puts it well when she writes:

> When medicine is practiced poorly, when engineering is done badly, when cooking is unsanitary, people can get hurt. Despite well intentioned efforts, patients can die, bridges can collapse, and families can get sick. In the same way, STM efforts done poorly can cause damage, sometimes great damage.[19]

Millions of STMers serve cross-culturally every year. However, many have done so without appropriate knowledge of the larger issues surrounding their short time in contact with others in a foreign culture.[20] Therefore, it is no surprise that the anecdotal accounts, limited surveys, and sparse ethnographic/anthropologic research expressed appreciation for, and cautioned against, STM.

An international short-term service trip is often billed as a way to increase participation in mission in the home church, reduce ethnocentrism, and raise active awareness for the plights of others. However, some studies contradict such claims. In one such study, Kurt Ver Beek followed STMers who rebuilt homes in Honduras after Hurricane Mitch. Upon the teams' return to the United States, he looked for an increase in time spent in prayer, charitable giving, or time spent volunteering. No significant change was found.[21] Priest and others pointed out that there has been little or no change in ethnocentrism among STMers after their international encounters.[22] Considering such issues, STM was criticized by some as "Religious

18. See Adeney, "When the Elephant Dances."

19. Adeney, "When the Elephant Dances," 1.

20. This observation comes from Priest et al., "Short-Term Mission Movement," 434–35.

21. Ver Beek, "Impact," 492–93.

22. Blezien, "Impact of Short-Term Missions," 111. Priest et al., "Short-Term Mission Movement," 435–44.

Tourism."[23] Some studies reported that when changes were evident after a STM trip, the effects faded over time.[24] After more than fifty years of sending STM teams, Operation Mobilization, one of the first to send short-term teams, reported no lasting increase in the number of long-term missionaries or giving to missions despite the widespread growth of short-term teams. This was likely due to a rapid replication of the model without replication of the key principles.[25]

The negative impact on multi-cultural relationship development is a cause for concern.[26] Teams can overburden receiving communities, missionaries, and hosts and distract them from other important work.[27] Participants' lack of the local language can be a hindrance and a severe cultural barrier. Short-term medical teams sometimes put an inappropriate focus upon treating presenting symptoms as opposed to committing to a long-term preventive healthcare management plan, which was seen as more effective.[28] STM teams can displace local laborers who may be more skilled and have a better understanding of local building practice.[29] Short-term missioners can ignore local customs, reinforce imperialistic tendencies, and put pre-conceived projects (and their quick completion) above the actual needs of the people.[30]

Affirmations of Short-Term Missions

There are some studies that point to positive aspects of STM. International mission service can begin to shape a deeper understanding of God's work in the world, God's nature in caring for others, and God's presence in the participants' lives.[31] STM can be "a transformative experience insofar as it galvanizes American adolescents in terms of their religious beliefs and practices."[32] Participation in international service opportunities, in some cases, can increase engagement in political movements and charitable ac-

23. Root, "Youth Ministry," 315; Parades, "Short-Term Missions," 257.

24. See Friesen, "Improving"; Ver Beek, "Impact."

25. Andrew Scott, e-mail message to the author, September 29, 2014.

26. Zehner, "Short-Term Missions," 510. The following citations also have root in his synthesis.

27. Van Engen, "Cost of Short-Term Missions," 22.

28. Montgomery, "Short-Term Medical Missions," 335–36.

29. Van Engen, "Cost of Short-Term Missions," 21.

30. See Adeney, "When the Elephant Dances."

31. Trinitapoli and Vaisey, "Transformative Role," 141.

32. Trinitapoli and Vaisey, "Transformative Role," 139.

tion.[33] First-hand reports of personal change are common, such as "I received more than I gave," "I was changed," and "I learned that people are the same everywhere."[34] Multiple qualitative studies reported that STM impacted participants in significant ways. Such reports continue to drive the STM movement.[35] The research conducted by Professor Dennis Horton of Baylor University shows several benefits to participating in a STM trip. His qualitative and quantitative research among ministry students at Baylor reveals a positive correlation between serving on STM trips and reductions in ethnocentrism and materialism. He also points out that students who had been on STM were more likely to be involved in service activities at home and serve as long-term missionaries later in life. Yet, most reports of the "success" of a STM trip were centered upon the conceptions of the STMers themselves. One such concept was of personal growth and, in this regard, Horton's research is no exception. The clear majority of his participants scored "spiritual and/or personal growth" among the highest when considering the benefits of such an experience.[36] I will discuss such issues of STM at length in further chapters, including exploring if the impact on the STMer is the desired outcome of the STM trip. But first it is important to consider STM from the perspective of the hosts.

The Short-Term Mission Hosts

There is limited literature on the effect of, or feelings about, STM from those in the receiving communities.[37] In 2007, Priest edited a thematic edition of the *Journal of Latin American Theology* devoted to STM. Hearing from the voices of the "objects of mission" is valuable. The literature provided conflicting points of view. STM teams were criticized for the brevity of their visits.[38] Teams were denounced for not coordinating with their host churches and not listening to the opinions of their host communities and churches.[39] Some authors wondered if it would be more beneficial if the STM teams simply sent the money that they spent on their trips. Billions of dollars to Latin American churches would be a significant windfall.[40]

33. Offutt, "Short-Term Mission Teams," 798.

34. Howell, *Short-Term Mission*, 171.

35. Blezien, "Impact," 113.

36. Horton, "Effects."

37. Zehner, "Short-Term Missions," 510.

38. Linhart, "They Were So Alive!" 459.

39. Maslucán, "Short-Term Missions," 141.

40. Ver Beek, "Impact," 490.

STM leaders were criticized for, often naively, attempting to manipulate the people or buy their approval with money or resources.[41] Teams were noted for ignoring cultural sensitivities and thereby hindering ministry.[42] More than eight out of ten national leaders surveyed by Martin Eitzen lamented the fact that most STM teams did not demonstrate knowledge of even a few basic Spanish phrases. Such an absence hindered the mission efforts. STM teams are often housed away from the people they seek to serve. Instead they often look for, even sometimes demand, hotels with amenities to which they are accustomed thereby running up large bills and building walls of social separation.[43] National pastors reported feeling more like tour guides than ministry leaders.[44] Tensions of paternalism and financial dependency were also addressed. It is commonplace for STM to provide thousands of dollars of cash and in-kind donations. Lopsided material and monetary transactions sometimes led to unintended consequences. Some members of host communities saw STMers as a way of providing easy access to American financial and material resources. Some reported placating STM teams to continue to receive those resources.[45]

However, the reflections on STM by Latin American leaders were not always negative. Eitzen's survey of national pastors seems to be indicative of positive feelings about the practice. Nearly 70 percent of national pastors saw STMs as a benefit to their church and ministry. The same percentage wanted STMers to participate in preaching, education, and special events in the future. It is significant that the pastors were more interested in spending time with the team members than merely receiving money from them. Only 10 percent of respondents said they would not want to receive a STM team.[46] Some mission hosts expressed a desire to receive teams in order to develop deeper understandings of scriptural principles through multicultural exchanges in the name of mission. Ulrike Sallandt, a scholar and pastor in Peru, encouraged teams to visit other nations, including her own, to seek a deeper understanding of Scripture through multi-national discussions of the Bible and one another's theologies. Interactions with STM team

41. Parades, "Short-Term Missions," 257.

42. Alegre Villón, "Short-Term Missions," 137; Eitzen, "Short-Term Missions," 42. See also Adeney, "When the Elephant Dances."

43. Eitzen, "Short-Term Missions," 43.

44. Raines, "International Perspective," 25.

45. Eitzen, "Short-Term Missions," 39; Jeffrey, "Short-Term Mission," 6.

46. See Eitzen, "Short-Term Missions." While others expressed similar feelings, Eitzen seems to be summative.

members and their hosts were seen to be mutually beneficial for practical and spiritual development.[47]

A VACUUM OF A THEOLOGY OF MISSION

The STM movement grew from a handful of participants to a movement involving millions of people in just a few decades. Though the practice is pervasive, Priest and Howell point out that "STM did not have a significant presence in research literature until recently" and that populist literature dominated the landscape of STM writings, beginning in the 1990s and lasting more than a decade.[48] This coincides with the fact that, while STM movement is affecting millions of people and several continents, those leading the movement are largely untrained and inexperienced. Priest and Karla Ann Koll both note that missiological education is not predominant in American seminaries and Christian colleges. Those that do offer mission education seldom offer explicit teaching on STM.[49] In Priest's survey of American mega-churches, nearly all reported sending STM teams. Indeed, 73 percent had someone on staff identified as a "Missions Pastor." While two-thirds had some sort of mission education, only 22 percent had a degree with a mission focus.[50] Many participants in STM are youths.[51] Pastors to youth are generally not expected to have the same level of theological education as other members of the church staff. Additionally, smaller churches without the human resource capabilities of the megachurches cannot designate someone on their staff as a "Missions Pastor." Even the senior (or only) pastor in these smaller churches is not likely to have a great deal of mission education, let alone an education specifically in STM.[52]

Problems were not isolated to church staffing contexts. Some who seek to train others in STM practices discouraged would-be adherents from engaging in too much critical reflection before departing on their trips. In what Robert Wuthnow calls "the most comprehensive guide to these programs,"[53]

47. Sallandt, "Short-Term Mission," 204.

48. Priest and Howell, "Introduction," 125.

49. Priest and Priest, "They See Everything," 53; Koll, "Taking Wolves among Lambs," 93.

50. Priest, "U.S. Megachurches," 101.

51. For our purposes "Youth" is defined as middle school and high school students, who are typically 13–18 years old.

52. Priest, "U.S. Megachurches," 101. Priest et al., "Short-Term Mission Movement," 434.

53. Wuthnow, *Boundless Faith*, 168. More robust works than the one Wuthnow referenced have been published since. See the works by Robert Priest and Brian Howell below, among others.

the writers of *Maximum Impact Short-Term Mission: The God-Commanded, Repetitive Deployment of Swift, Temporary, Non-Professional Missionaries* discouraged their readers from spending time in "academic anarchy" and to instead whittle down the hours of preparation and training, lest any more should go "to hell without Jesus Christ."[54] Contrast this with some congregations that require a commitment of a year of preparation before the mission trip and six months of follow-up afterwards.[55] With such a wide range of the expectations for theological reflection before a trip, among the nearly 100,000 congregations who participate in STM, one might expect such a wide range of reports regarding the practice.[56] The STM movement, for good or for bad, has deployed millions of laypeople to participate, at least in name, in the mission of the church. Yet they do so with a wide variety of training. In the absence of theological leadership that leads to orthopraxy, STMers are left to impose their American cultural expectations on their "objects of mission."[57]

For example, there is a danger in becoming enamored with the "adventure" of a STM and risking losing sight of the significant role the team should play in the mission of God.[58] Writing in *Effective Engagement in Short-Term Missions,* Richard Slimbach blames American television media for portraying unrealistic expectations about "parts of the Third World [that] become commodites to be voyeuristically 'consumed' as part of the overall experience" of international travel.[59] Citing Ben Feinberg's observations with study-abroad students, Slimbach goes on to argue that the youth and young adult generation most active in STM was raised on television "reality" shows like *Survivor* and *Amazing Race.* Feinberg is right to criticize shows like these for their portrayals of exotic locations in which participants were sealed off from the inhabitants who conduct their lives under real conditions and real pressures. Given the cultural impact of such media offerings, it is possible that the quest for an adventure-experience, like the ones portrayed on such television offerings, may influence the way some frame their expectations of a STM offering. When participating in service activities, the participants seek to seal themselves off in a similar manner. Such misplaced motivations and unrealistic conceptions may replace appropriate

---

54. Peterson et al., *Maximum Impact*, 26–29.

55. Howell, *Short-Term Mission*, 121–45.

56. Wuthnow, *Boundless Faith*, 168.

57. Linhart, "Planting Seeds," 268.

58. Wuthnow, *Boundless Faith*, 182.

59. Slimbach, "Mindful Missioner," 163.

theological reflections on one's motivation for mission.[60] I will discuss this desire for these types of experiences at length below.

American cultural views of success may be at odds with how "success" is viewed in mission. Andrew Walls quotes Japanese theologian Kanzo Uchimura as he laments the Americans' participation in mission: "To win the greatest number of converts with the least expense is their constant endeavour [sic]. Statistics is their way of showing success or failure in their religion as in their commerce and politics. Numbers, numbers, numbers, oh, how they value numbers!"[61] Indeed, this sentiment about the STMers was also expressed by pastors in Latin American contexts. Edwin Zehner points out while many national hosts appreciated the work of American STM teams, others have grown to find them "terminally offensive" to the local culture. Attitudes of cultural and ethnic superiority from the American team members were understandably problematic. Misappropriation of scriptural interpretations by STMers who failed to consider the cultural limitations of those teachings strained relationships with national hosts. Either by design or by ignorance, American teams often stepped in to take control of a ministry project without fully consulting those already running the ministry. This led to feelings of resentment of the paternalism and accompanying humiliation. However, they related accounts of genuine ministry progress when the American teams focused on relationships over perceived objective goals. When team leaders and members focused upon affirming current work by national pastors, and offering partnerships to support that work, ministry progress was affirmed. When STM participants demonstrated cultural sensitivity to the contexts in which they served, ministry progress was celebrated. When STM workers positioned themselves as long-term learners who wanted to support national pastors in ways that such pastors requested, ministry progress was acknowledged. When STMers sought to learn from their hosts rather than accomplish a specific project in a short time at all costs, national pastors were encouraged by the time the American teams spent and wanted to continue ministry partnerships.[62] Overall, the literature indicated that STM is a huge phenomenon with vast potential. However, this potential is vastly under-realized.[63]

---

60. Slimbach, "Mindful Missioner," 163. Feinberg, "What Students Don't Learn," B20.

61. Walls, *Missionary Movement*, 221–22.

62. See Zehner, "Short-Term Missions."

63. Priest et al., "Short-Term Mission," 445.

AN UNREALIZED POTENTIAL

As we have seen, the transnational short-term service project is a wide-spread practice affecting millions of people. Evidence seems to suggest, however, that little theological reflection has been done about the practice and what motivates those who go on such trips and those who receive them. As I demonstrated in the previous chapters, anything done in the name of Christian mission should be examined in light of the biblical understanding of the mission, which the church is called on by the inauguration of the Kingdom of God.

By his actions, teachings, proclamation, death, and resurrection, Jesus inaugurated the Kingdom of God. Subsequent generations of Christian disciples have sought to carry on the mission of the Kingdom of God demonstrated by Jesus. The early church embraced the idea that the kingdom of which Jesus spoke was not yet fully realized and that it was incumbent upon the church to continue the mission that Jesus began. Each generation of Christians has sought to articulate the expression of that mission. In modern contexts, such an endeavor is demonstrated in several different forms, as demonstrated in chapter 1.

So then how should STMers see their role in the participation of the Kingdom of God? The church is poised to be used by the *missio Dei* in some new ways. For better or worse, the churches based in America have already reshaped how mission is conducted. These churches have a responsibility to make a careful reflection upon their motivations to seek an orthodoxy that reflects an orthopraxy. Such a reflection on a variety of factors is necessary for the church to realize its role in the opportunity now presented.

Participating in World Christianity

The contemporary church is faced with a world that is becoming increasingly transnational. This has contributed to continued growth of Christianity in the Global South.[64] Such growth occurs, in part, due to the influence of encounters with American preachers, teachers, and business leaders. The growth of Christianity around the globe owes a great deal to the ready access to media and the travel of Americans abroad as well as the influence of visitors to the United States. While America continues to export music, movies, products, and even theologies, labor and capital also flows from the Global South back to the United States. The impacts of these factors on

---

64. Jenkins, *Next Christendom*, 4–5.

transnational religious exchanges has yet to be fully researched.[65] The STM mission movement puts millions of laypeople in direct missional contact with other laypeople of a variety of ethnicities and expressions of Christianity. As transnational flow occurs in other areas, so it does in Christian expressions. Global Christianity, the duplication of European models of church, is a thing of the past. Instead, World Christianity is "the result of mission as translation—radical embodiments of the faith."[66] Scholars and ministry leaders must address these issues to help the church express its role as a harbinger of the Kingdom of God.

Americans are uniquely poised to participate in the *missio Dei* by the tools many use every day. William Carey, in 1792, proclaimed the mariner's compass an important breakthrough in the mission movement. Easy access to e-mail, the internet, and increasingly quick and inexpensive travel are the same such tools for this generation. The pace of these global connections is increasing rapidly.[67] These realities of a global interaction becoming the "norm" means that previously ethnocentric American Christians have the opportunity, and responsibility, to be a part of what God's Spirit is doing around the world. This means they should proclaim the gospel's message of reconciliation while coming to a fuller understanding of God by learning about his work through other cultures.[68]

Linking Social Capital

American churches who participate in STM have a unique opportunity to share social capital with communities in which they serve. Social capital is "the norms and networks that enable people to act collectively."[69] To understand the *linking* of social capital, it is helpful to first examine the important roles of *bonding* and of *bridging* social capital. The bonding of social capital is "inward looking and tend[s] to reinforce exclusive identities and homogeneous groups."[70] Gender-specific church activity groups, exclusive country clubs, or other such inward-looking groups based upon ethnicity or status are all examples of groups that seek to bond social capital. Bridging social capital is done by networks that are "inclusive. . .and outward looking and

---

65. Wuthnow and Offutt, "Transnational Religious Connections," 210–11.

66. Raines, "International Perspective," 103.

67. Wuthnow and Offutt, "Tansnational Religious Connections," 212.

68. Fenrick, "Missional Experiential Education," 15.

69. Woolcock and Narayan, "Social Capital," 225.

70. Putnam, *Bowling Alone*, 22.

encompass people across diverse social cleavages."[71] Bridging social capital occurs when ideas, resources, teaching and labor are mutually shared despite socio-political structures that would otherwise hinder them. Power structures are re-arranged for mutual benefit.[72]

When speaking of the role of social capital in STM, it is helpful to think of *linking* as the preferred use of social capital by STM participants. This includes the "vertical connections across marked differentials of wealth, status, and power."[73] The linking of social capital is essential for collaborative STM projects.[74] Linking social capital changes the question from "What is wrong with you and how can I fix it?" to "What is right with you and how can we work together to be a part of what God wants to do in your ministry?"[75]

STM must be done in a collaborative spirit. STM leaders and participants must put aside monochromatic images of their hosts as the universally materially poor and spiritually wealthy "Other." Instead, STM must be reworked into a movement in which worldwide Christians partner together for collaborative ministry. At times, the American church will lead. In most instances, however, the host church should lead the establishment of the projects, ministry boundaries, and methodologies.[76]

STM must be done within long-term expectations, goals, and plans of the host churches. STMers should be a small part of a much bigger picture. The work began before they arrived. The work will continue long after they are gone. The lifetime of mission work continues in both the STMers and the hosts. Each Christian is called be a part of the *missio Dei*. A week of STM may be a small part of the way one can learn about the Christian's role in the mission of God. However, it is just that: a small part. Any participation in mission must be done in the larger context of discipleship in each one's home church.[77] Marcos Arroyo Bahamonde emphasizes that "Short-term mission is an inappropriate adaptation of [David] Bosch's" understanding of the *missio Dei*. He went on to say that the struggles of the host churches cannot be addressed or understood by STM "since these issues require a

---

71. Putnam, *Bowling Alone*, 22.

72. Priest, "Peruvian Churches," 181.

73. Priest, "Peruvian Churches," 181. See also Woolcock and Narayan, "Social Capital." Wuthnow, "Religious Involvement."

74. See Priest, "Peruvian Churches."

75. Corbett and Fikkert, *When Helping Hurts*, 109–13.

76. See Rickett, "Short-Term Missions."; Parades, "Short-Term Missions."; Friesen, "Improving."

77. See Parades, "Short-Term Missions."

long-term effort and commitment."[78] For this reason STM teams must always serve a larger part of the mission of the local church and its leaders.

Engaging Mission Principles

We have seen some of the problems that STMs face, or cause, from the perspectives of both practitioners and scholars. Anthropologist Brian Howell points out that, "[s]een from the anthropological perspective, STM may seem to be the worst combination of religious fundamentalist zeal and touristic superficiality."[79] I have shown above that these problems are a result of the lack of robust theological work. One of my aims is to establish a mission theology that engages STM. I wish to address the issue of a large gap in research that is among missional theologians.[80] It is incumbent upon theologians to provide a rigorous study of the practice to be shared and taught among pastors and lay leaders. Are such principles being utilized by STM practitioners? Since STM is largely absent from theological education amongst pastors, staff members, and lay participants, it is unclear to what degree robust theologies motivate its practitioners. Thus, it seemed to me that the time was right for such a study. In the follow chapters, I will use my original ethnographic data to discuss these operative motivations. First, however, I will close this chapter with a brief summary of the research of STM movement and point out some of the gaps in research that my work seeks to fill.

Researching the Short-Term Mission Movement

The rise of STM has attracted the attention of some sociologists and anthropologists. They too have produced only limited literature on the subject. Many available studies from the fields of sociology and anthropology: a) focus on youth and young adults who participate in STM, and b) examine STM's effect on later civic involvement or charitable giving of those who participate in STM. Researchers admit that there is a lack of research in STM and call for more work to be done to examine the movement. Robert Priest and Joseph Paul Priest point out that this limited research has provided some helpful discussion. Speaking of the work of missiologists, they say:

---

78. Bahamonde, "Contextualization," 230.

79. Howell, *Short-Term Mission,* 27.

80. Howell, *Short-Term Mission,* 26. See footnote 9.

Missiologists, until recently, have ignored and sometimes disdained short-term mission. We have not systematically re-searched it, have not produced high quality missiological analy-ses of short-term mission structures and have not oriented our writing or teaching to the large numbers of our students whose connection to mission and the global church is through STM.[81]

Such "high quality" missiological research should consider the relationships of church, mission, and kingdom, as previously mentioned, in the contem-porary practice. Such is a key goal of my research. One aim of this project is to hear from those who are connected to the global church through STM and who represent a much broader age range than just youth.

Not only is the practice of STM common in America, it is becoming increasingly common for churches from Asia, Europe, Australia, and Africa to send transnational STM teams.[82] If STMers are to avoid the calamities Howell mentions a more theological examination of this practice in the name of mission is required. It will require long-term integration of educa-tion and experience.[83] The field of STM research is primed to examine areas such as corollaries between STM service and spiritual pilgrimage, what role "image" plays in how STMers conceptualize the "Other" as the object of their mission, the role of mission and hospitality (particularly for hosting churches), the role of liminality and communitas amongst STMers and their hosts,[84] and how STMers identify themselves as agents of the *missio Dei*. By examining such areas, scholars can help the practitioners develop an orthopraxy of STM rooted in appropriate theological reflection. The socio-logical and anthropological studies have provided some helpful description of the landscape of STM. However, a significant gap in the development of a theology of STM remains. I suggest that it is necessary to work towards a theology of STM that utilizes some of these previous studies and scholarly research in the areas of pilgrimage and tourism.

Missiology and practical theology are focused upon appropriate praxis of theological work. Praxis is the direct and active expression of theology. To put it another way, theological reflection begins in the praxis and is thereby expressed in faith-based action. Such an understanding properly puts, as Dave Hazle says, "mission at the centre of the theological enterprise."[85] By extension, then, mission practitioners who are engaging in robust theolo-

---

81. Priest and Priest, "They See Everything," 67.

82. Priest and Priest, "They See Everything," 167; Wuthnow, *Boundless Faith*, 185.

83. Park, "Researching Short-Tem Missions," 524.

84. See Howell and Dorr, "Evangelical Pilgrimage."

85. Hazle, "Practical Theology Today," 349.

gies, which I have attempted to illustrate thus far, will demonstrate, in their own words, the deeds done in the name of mission. Perhaps it could be summed up this way: theologies shape motivations and motivations shape actions. Therefore, another aim of this project is not to investigate changes in social or civic behavior after a STM trip. Rather, I want to hear the theologies that shape motivations and thus, actions. Our attention will turn there in the following chapters.

In this chapter, we have focused upon a particular outcropping of the theological landscape: short-term mission. We have seen its populist, grassroots origins and subsequent spread. We have seen some of the conditions that have allowed it to flourish, such as globalization. Other conditions that allowed STM to flourish will be addressed in subsequent chapters. We have heard some of the affirmations of fruitful work and criticisms like insensitivity to cultural considerations and power-sharing concerns. We heard from STM hosts and the desire by many to continue such work, but under certain considerations. However, the key issue is the theological vacuum in which the practice has grown. Leading scholars have called for a theology of STM to be developed that engages important principles like pilgrimage and tourism. I intend to contribute to this development. Considering this call by Howell and Priest to work towards a theology of STM, I wanted to hear the theologies of contemporary STMers. Hazle's model of practical theology is helpful for our discussion. If, as Hazle said, praxis is a reflection of theological enterprise, and the praxis of STMers was seen to many as less than ideal, I wanted to explore the implicit and explicit theologies of the STMers themselves. What theologies were motivating STMers and how was this shaping their work on transnational service projects? With this in mind, I set out to hear from the practitioners themselves. Now that we have established the essential elements of a Wesleyan Missiology and have established the landscape of STM we move to my unique field research to explore these principles in current STM practice among United Methodists.

SECTION II

The Practice of Short-Term Missions

5

Hearing from United Methodist Short-Term Missioners

Hearing the narratives of STM participants is important to gain a greater understanding of the theological motivations for their work in STM activities. Before moving into the narratives of the STMers, it will be helpful to briefly review what we have discussed about mission theology previously. As noted in the last chapter, there has been a severe disconnect between STM and the requisite theological reflection by pastors, leaders, and other practitioners. This is due, at least in part, to the absence of theological work in this area by leaders in seminaries, colleges, and universities. Since these service activities are done in the name of mission, it is important to explore the understanding of a theology of mission among those performing such activities. Theologies shape the development of theory and subsequent practice. Practitioners often demonstrate their motivation and justification from the tools they use to arrive at their theological conclusions. Richard Osmer identified these as "Scripture, reason, tradition, and experience." Such terms are familiar to many United Methodists as some Methodist scholars list these as the primary resources for a United Methodist theology.[1] Since two million Americans are putting their theologies to practical application each year by participating in transnational STM trips it is important to hear more from them in regards to just what theological constructs are shaping their motivation and justification. Additionally, it is important to see if these theologies align with the missional teachings of the tradition they may represent. Specifically, to what degree do United Methodist STM participants

1. Osmer, "Practical Theology," 3; United Methodist Church, ¶102

85

express a Wesleyan theology of mission? To what degree are other influences shaping their motivations and justifications? Hearing the answers to such was the goal of my conversations with STM team leaders and their respective team members.

This is a unique study of STM participants. In what follows, I present an ethnographic study that is different from others in the field of mission studies. Existing ethnographic work in STM has been and includes both quantitative and qualitative methodologies. Howell's *Short-Term Mission: An Ethnography of Christian Travel Narrative and Experience* provides some helpful insights with his participant observation study. However, his study was limited to one particular team of college-aged students.[2] Priest and his co-authors have contributed works that are mostly quantitative research that provide a map of the STM landscape in terms of size, scope, and depth of short-term and long-term engagement.[3] Ver Beek provides a mostly quantitative survey of STM participants following their work in Honduras after Hurricane Mitch.[4] Linhart's embedded study of high school students' STM trip focuses upon the narratives of one team's experience in a cross-cultural context.[5] There are very few studies that include a wide age range. Rather, many are focus on student-aged participants.

Though students-aged participants are often the face of STM in popular accounts and advertisements, the average STM participant is more likely to have school-aged children than to be a student.[6] Wuthnow's profile of the typical STM participant was a guide for hearing from the representative STM participant:

> Although people of all ages, locations, occupations, and church traditions go on mission trips, the typical participant is a white, married, college-educated male in his forties or fifties whose children are grown and who lives in a relatively homogeneous suburb in the South or Midwest. Religiously, he is affiliated with an evangelical church where he has been a member for at least three years, attends every Sunday, and holds a lay leadership position such as chairing a committee or teaching Sunday school. The short-term mission participant is thus similar to the person

2. Howell, *Short-Term Mission: An Ethnography.*

3. Priest et al. Priest, "U.S. Megachurches." Priest and Priest, "They See Everything."

4. Ver Beek, "Impact."

5. Linhart, "They Were So Alive!"

6. Wuthnow, *Boundless Faith*, 172.

who is simply a faithful churchgoer, period, with the exception that active churchgoers are more likely to be women.[7]

So it was with many of the participants in my field of research, though I did solicit from a range of churches and ministries to provide a richer dataset.

Since there is a need for a more reflexive practical theology that utilizes ethnographic tools to further understand the STM phenomenon, I wanted to hear from those who were among the "overlooked globalizers." They should be recognized for their role as an important force in the transcultural exchanges of theologies and their influences on the churches that send them.[8] The ethnographic research I present here is from individual and focus group interviews and online surveys. They came from seven different STM teams in four different states and four different annual conferences of The United Methodist Church.[9] Fifty-five people participated in the pretrip interviews, thirty of whom completed the post-trip online survey. Team members ranged in age from 18 to 81. The average age was 54 years old. A clear majority had participated in STM before. Nearly all (n=50) were active members of the sponsoring congregation and/or ministry.[10]

To maintain anonymity, I will utilize pseudonyms for participants and their churches. I have also removed identifying information. I am not aware of any research projects that directly match my own.

PARTICIPANTS

The participants in this study, in many ways, reflect Wuthnow's profile of the typical STM participant. Further, seven out of the top ten destinations for STM trips are in Latin America or the Caribbean.[11] Therefore, I chose to interview STM teams who were serving in this region of the world. By choosing teams and team members that fit such a profile, I wanted to provide a window into an important part of the of STM movement.

---

7. Wuthnow, *Boundless Faith*, 172.

8. Priest and Priest, "They See Everything."

9. An annual conference in The United Methodist Church refers to not only an annual meeting, but also a regional body and organizational unit. An annual conference may cover an entire state or span multiple states. In addition, each annual conference is under the leading of a bishop and professional conference staff. Therefore, each conference has its own missional identity and priorities. Utilizing representatives from multiple annual conferences provides a more diverse research body.

10. See Appendix.

11. Priest, "U.S. Megachurches," 98.

Recall that the work of STMers has been brought into question in limited literature. The solution for many writers was to offer a short, bulleted list of "best practices." However, these lists of "shoulds" and "should nots" fail to address the underlying issues. Merely responding to the visible symptoms, be they positive or negative, fails to examine the systemic issues that present those symptoms. This is what much of the literature did: neglect the important principle that theologies shape motivations and actions. This has left a great need to develop a theology of mission that takes into consideration the STM movement. As Robert Priest pointed out above, STM is a grassroots movement. To explore the theologies behind the movement, it is necessary to take exploration to the grassroots level.

This meant that my effort to find teams for the study was a bit of a journey itself. It showed me a glimpse of how the grassroots movement gathers individuals to form a group of people to give time, money, resources, and service in the name of mission. In this chapter, we will investigate the journey further. Our attention will first turn to the way STM members are recruited for a trip. Team members were recruited and formed months in advance. The time before their trip was often just as important to the team as other activities on the trip itself. After examining recruitment, we will hear how team leaders prepared their teams. Some teams dedicated months of pre-trip work for an overseas excursion that would last less than two weeks. The explanation of this work proved helpful in understanding the operant theologies of STM leaders. The ways team leaders select team members, and the things they emphasize in preparing that team for the trip, are a part of the overall STM narrative. The team leaders' explanations of their area of emphasis are analyzed. After an examination of such emphases, we will then hear the implicit and explicit motivations of mission from the STMers. We will pay particular attention to the narratives around scriptural and denominational understandings of mission. Then we will hear from STMers about the way they view the people they met and the places they visited, and the impact these had on those who sought to serve. The idealizations they expressed are helpful in our pursuit of identifying theological constructs. The explanations STMers gave to the importance of going on such a trip will follow. The STMers' preference for proximity to their host church and mission leaders is our next area of discussion. Lastly, we will hear from those who look for labels for the purpose of their work, be they evangelists, missionaries, a combination thereof, or something else entirely.

The account I present here is a result of conversations with STM teams prior to their trips. Most of the time, our conversations were held during one of their regular pre-trip meeting times. Our discussions were casual and relaxed. Usually these were held in spaces familiar to the group members, like a Sunday School room or Fellowship Hall. The concept of "team" is important in many STM trips, so we discussed their thoughts about their STM efforts in a group format that included the members of their team.

When I began this research, I planned to interview with each team some three to six months after they returned from their STM trip. The intention of the post-trip interview was to assess to what degree the goals and expectations expressed in the pre-trip interviews had been met. I explained this to the team leaders as we set up the meetings and mentioned it a few times during the arrangement of the pre-trip interviews. Most team leaders admitted that a post-trip meeting was important, but many confessed to having done a very poor job at follow-up with their previous teams. Prompted by my requests related to the research (and because they felt it was the right thing to do anyway), many told me they would attempt to hold a follow-up meeting. The team leader for Riverbend UMC was an exception. He told me that it was not his custom to hold a post-trip meeting. It was not clear why he would not hold follow-up conversation with his team members. Granted, some of his participants lived hundreds of miles away. Yet, he did not conduct such a meeting with the portion of the team that lived nearby. A month or so after a STM team's return I contacted the team leader about arranging a follow-up meeting. Most often, my calls and e-mails were not returned. The few who did respond expressed their regrets that they were unable to bring the team members together again. Only Ramen UMC held a post-trip event.

Such lack of post-trip de-briefing and mission education is often pointed out as a problem by those who study STM. Though team leaders may acknowledge its importance, few follow through with their good intentions. Because the post-trip focus-group interview did not develop, I utilized an alternative instrument for post-trip reflection. As an alternative to meeting together, I designed an online survey.

It is important to note that many team leaders expressed a desire to hold a post-trip meeting, but felt that it was impossible to hold such a meeting due to circumstances beyond their control. For example, some members of the Christian Campus Ministry team did not return to school the following term. Others no longer participated in the ministry's activities for one reason or another. Another team leader had a series of personal and family difficulties beyond his control.

Churches

Six churches participated in the study. All are United Methodist churches located in the southeastern part of the United States. One Methodist ministry for college students also participated. The size of the churches varied greatly. The smallest church had approximately 200 members. The largest had over 6,000. Teams ranged in size from six to eighteen people. Most of the churches have ongoing STM programs. For some teams, I was only able to talk with a few members of the teams.

Most teams were working on construction projects in their host nation. Some were working with ministries to children and their families. One was almost exclusively a medical team. Regardless of other ministry goals, one common component in the teams' mission efforts was working with children. Teams conducted Vacation Bible School (VBS) activities. VBS uses arts, crafts, games, and other activities to teach Bible stories and principles to children. Adult leaders often prepare crafts before leaving home and bring the appropriate supplies for the VBS with them to their hosts nations. Frequently, VBS utilizes contemporary thematic elements to teach Bible stories. Such activities are normative of many STM trips.[12]

The likelihood that a church will send a STM team is not affected by its location in an urban, suburban, or rural setting. However, larger congregations are more apt to send international teams. Churches with more staff members are more likely to have active STM programs that send teams overseas on a regular basis. With these factors in mind, I secured teams from churches in all three settings: rural, suburban, and urban. These included teams from large churches with paid staff members dedicated to coordinating mission efforts, as well as churches with no employees other than the pastor.

The STMers were undaunted by the language barriers that they were to encounter. Only two reported fluency or proficiency in the language of their destination country. Twenty-two reported having no knowledge of the language of their hosts. The remainder indicated various degrees of ability with the language, ranging from "very little" to "I know enough to get by." A few indicated that they were making efforts to learn the hosts' language. The fact that the language barrier was not a concern for many of the participants was likely due to the fact that teams hire translators in the host nation. The translators were connected to the church and/or agency that attended to the other aspects of the team's needs that included food, housing, transportation, and the securing of worksites.

12. Priest, "U.S. Megachurches," 99.

All the team leaders had experience in STM. Three team leaders had led STM teams at least twenty times each. The remaining leaders had been to the destination country a few times before. Only one team leader reported an advanced knowledge of Spanish, his hosts' language. One reported a job-specific knowledge of the language, a doctor who is experienced in medical Spanish for routine examinations.

Ideally, team interviews were held immediately before or after a regular meeting time. However, team business sometimes overlapped into the interview periods. As a result of the priority of team business over the interviews, some focus groups were as small as two people. The team leader at Riverbend UMC, Dr. Timothy Lyons, would not allow me to come to his pre-trip team meeting. He only held one pre-trip meeting with his team and the agenda was already filled with items of logistical considerations to cover with his participants. He felt that his team members would not have time to talk with me. I offered to modify my research by remaining a detached, silent observer. He rebuffed my suggested modification. Dr. Lyons insisted that his team had a great deal of logistical work to do. Some of his team members were traveling from long distances to attend the meeting. He seemed to feel that my presence would not allow him to cover his agenda of trip plans, flight schedules, packing considerations, and similar concerns.

RECRUITMENT

Many team leaders and pastors spent a great deal of energy to recruit and retain STM participants. In this section, I will illustrate how team members were recruited and organized. Next, I will illustrate how team leaders were recruited. Lastly, I will touch upon how sites for STM trips were selected.

Team Members

Several of the churches, even those with vibrant STM programs, actively sought out new participants for their mission trips. To do so, the larger churches held "Ministry Fairs" in which the missions committee took the opportunity to tell others about their upcoming trips. Posters were displayed with pictures of the previous mission trips. Veteran STMers were available to answer questions and encourage new participants. Churches made announcements during worship gatherings about trips. Notices were placed in church bulletins. Mass e-mails were sent to advertise upcoming trips. Social media was utilized to solicit participants for trips. STM leaders felt particularly proud when their pastor had participated in a trip and made references during the Sunday morning message encouraging others to go. This, they felt, brought an extra level of endorsement to their efforts.

The denomination's regional mission organization (covering several states) regularly advertised availability of upcoming trips through mass e-mail lists, their website, and social media outlets. This was often done on behalf of local church congregations, similar to the ones in this study. Potential new members did not have to be otherwise affiliated with the sponsoring church or even a member of the denomination. The available spots on a trip were advertised in a manner that encouraged anyone with interest to apply. It was rare that qualifications or prerequisites were listed in the advertisements. Indeed, there seemed to be few required prerequisites or proficiencies to join a STM team.

Team Design

Teams were often formed around common interests or life situations. While many churches send STM teams that include all ages and stations in life, some offer trips designed around varying mutualities. Some churches offered teams specific to teenagers, college students, women-only, men-only, single adults, retirees, and multi-generational families. Groups designed around such categories mirror what Wuthnow found in his study of American small-group ministry activities. Americans often make associations along classifications of age, gender, or marital status for participation in small-group church activities, though not exclusively.[13] Of the teams in this study, one was designated for college students and sponsored by a college ministry parachurch organization. Another was designed for "senior adults," though a few experienced STMers of younger ages also participated. The work on the senior adult trip was modified for the abilities of the participants. The team leader communicated with the host pastor in advance to assure that the team members could alter their participation as their health required it. Another team was made up of individuals from a particular Sunday School small group in a very large church. It was not necessary to look very far beyond their own small group to find enough people to form a team. Their group pre-existed as a study group made up of individuals and couples of similar life situations. The remainder of the teams in this study were of somewhat different ages and stations in life, but only nominally so. Additionally, many members of those teams had previous connections with one another.

13. Wuthnow, *Sharing the Journey*, 78–83.

As is typical of many STM teams, the teams in this study were often designed for the convenience and comfort of the participating team members. Some trips were scheduled around holidays and vacation times to maximize the potential participation of the STM team members. This may be convenient for the STM team, but this can become problematic for the mission hosts, as these times may or may not be most advantageous for the mission hosts or for the intended projects.[14] This can undermine the intended efforts and cause problems in the host nation, and the STMers may not be aware of the limitations their needs place upon the work overseas. One account provided a poignant example:

During the field work, I met Dean Becker, an American who has served as a missionary in Central America for more than twenty years. As a part of his work, he coordinates the hosting of STM teams. Dean recalled a time when a STM team was to work for an indigenous tribe by constructing a new building using bamboo walls. The team arrived and Dean directed them to cut the bamboo and build the walls. The elders of the tribe attempted to stop Dean and the team. Bamboo should only be cut, they said, on a waning moon. Dean reminded the elders that the waning moon was two weeks away. The team was here now. Dean dismissed their objections and admonishments to wait two more weeks. He told the team to cut the bamboo anyway. Not long after the team left, the bamboo was infested with insects and the walls were unusable. Dean asked the elders why the walls failed. The tribal leaders told him that the moon affects the amount of sugary nutrients in the bamboo. On the waxing moon, the sugar content of the bamboo is higher. Cutting the bamboo at that time traps those sugars in the bamboo and makes it more attractive to the insects. The sugar content of bamboo cut on the waning moon is not nearly as high in sugary nutrients. Insect-proofing the bamboo is as simple as waiting until the right time to harvest.[15] Such issues of national hosts acquiescing to the wishes and conveniences of the Americans, at times to the detriment of the community, was not isolated to this one.[16] I will say more below about the problems that mission that is centered on the missionaries can present.

Other considerations used to make the trip comfortable for the STM participants were things like group dynamics, age-appropriate work schedules, and the perceived safety of the trip. Anna Barrows and Tracy Pierson said that they were attracted to their mission trip because it was

14. See Priest et al, "Short-Term Mission."

15. For a discussion of such phenomena, see Zürcher, "Plants and the Moon-Traditions."

16. See chapter 3.

"non-threatening." They appreciated the ease of travel and looked forward to doing something enjoyable. They were traveling on mission to a place where they could avoid "the jungle" and not fear for their own safety due to criminal activity. This perceived safety, joined with a "little hard work" and assisting with a building with their own hands, was a reason why they chose the mission trip.

Team sizes were chosen mostly for practical considerations. One such factor was ground transportation in the host country. For example, if the vans used to transport the teams could hold six passengers, then teams were limited to twelve or eighteen people. Filling all available seats on the vans reduced the cost for the team members as much as possible. Team sizes were also chosen for their perceived ability to allow the team members to develop desired relationship outcomes. If too many people participated, then the team became disjointed. Rev. Keith Wallace described a team size of twelve as the "sweet spot." When I asked him to clarify, he said, "You have too many and you run into issues of travel; there's people [forming cliques]. A team of about twelve means that there is one cohesive group. . . . It is not that there are too few people where the experience is awkward. It's just the 'sweet spot.'"

Team Member Selection

The process for team member selection varied greatly. The selection of team members had much to do with the culture of the particular church and/ or organization. City Central United Methodist Church is a large member-ship church. They send several STM teams each year. The team leader was chosen by the missions pastor. The team leader had experience in the host country, but no formal team leader training. Nearly all the team members were retirees and most were former professional colleagues of the team leader. They were also connected through the church functions in which they participated. Such relationships were found in many teams through the dataset.

Ramen United Methodist Church also sponsors several STM trips a year. Teams may form as a part of an existing group, or team members may have just met one another in preparing for the trip. Ramen UMC requires an application as a part of a vetting process. The church's missions com-mittee developed guidelines which included this requirement. But this is not without its problems. The committee seemed to have been divided on whether or not everyone in the church had a right to participate in a STM trip. Team leader Richard Davis felt as though it was important to retain the right to reject certain applicants. Though it is rare that he will turn down a person for a STM team, he did admit that some people are turned away. Asked about what sort of things would prevent someone from participating, he said:

> [If] there's some things you see that led you to believe that they're not far enough along on their mission journey. They make some comments that lead you to believe that they would not be sensitive to the local people you're working with. . . . I think the main thing is, if they're not spiritually mature enough. If they're doing something that might be detrimental to the team or to the ministry you're serving with, then it's the team leader's prerogative to say that person can't go.

Husband and wife team leaders Larry and Carla Harris would agree that not everyone should participate in a STM trip. They recalled a trip to Cuba when they had to intervene when a team member was more interested in the rum and cigars than the work to be done. After that trip, they instituted an application process that included "three or four questions. . .so we can see where their heart is." When I asked what sort of criteria they used, they replied:

> You get a feeling in your spirit that this person is ready to go, especially to get them to start thinking about why they want to go. . . . Hopefully, [we can help] get them in a place where they can be in the right place to get what they need out of it, what God wants them to get out of it. And what God is calling them to see in their own lives.

Some teams seemed to have a wide-open selection process. Team leader Philip O'Connor was willing to take nearly anyone if they had the money and were ready to travel. Though he, and the team leaders mentioned above, seemed ready to have an "out" to refuse an interested party from traveling with the team. Team leaders reported that they were prepared to find a way to deny participation in the STM trip if they saw a problem that would be detrimental to the project or the experience of the team.

Team Leaders

Team leader selection varied among the ministries in the research study. Only one team leader was not a volunteer leader at the sponsoring entity. Rather, he was an ordained minister and a paid staff member. The remaining six team leaders had varying levels of experience leading trips to the respective destination countries. Three had each led teams on at least fifteen previous occasions. The volunteer team leaders were chosen by their respective ministerial leadership to guide this STM trip, though this had not always been the case. Many reported becoming team leaders through a process of convenience or by being selected by their peers to lead. Some were chosen for their particular expertise. For example, Dr. Timothy Lyons was chosen for his medical expertise. Philip was chosen, in part, for his Spanish language skills. A key trait for the team leader, at least in their own eyes, was the ability to handle the logistical considerations deemed important for international group travel. The team leader's ability to organize and coordinate the myriad of logistical considerations was of top priority in the many of the team leaders' narratives.

Training for STM trip team leaders is available through The United Methodist Church's mission agency which offers a one-day seminar. The training focuses on many of the practicalities of the STM travel needs, insurance guidelines, fundraising, and other such details. Team leader training participants are given a manual that points them to suggested resources. While some discussion of the biblical foundations for mission occurs, the training focuses more on best practices rather than the reasons for such practices. For example, in the list of "best practices" for preparing a United Methodist STM team, spiritual formation is listed last behind logistical and cultural awareness considerations. Spiritual formation resources were not provided in the team leaders' training manual. Rather, team leaders are directed to download it from the organization's website.[17] Four team leaders reported having participated in the training, though, for some, several years had passed since they participated. The other three had no specific training in STM leadership.

Site Selection

Selecting a site for a STM trip can be as easy as spending a few minutes online. A simple search for a "Short Term Mission Trip" will yield links to scores of organizations that offer to broker trips with the guarantee that they are "safe" and "affordable" while being "Christ-Centered." Akin to a travel agency portal, they offer trips customized by age group (for young people and adults) as well as offering a variety of locations according to regional preference.

17. See United Methodist Volunteers in Mission. I will discuss this in greater detail in chapter 8.

The ministries in my dataset did not indicate using such a service. Rather, they used pre-existing social connections to find a place to take their teams. Four churches had sent a STM team to the host site on previous occasions. Two ministries were sending teams from their church for the first time and did so because of pre-existing ministerial connections between their church leaders and the American missionary living in the host country. The team from Elmville UMC was traveling to Nicaragua because their pastor had traveled on a STM trip there with a church he had previously pastored. He enlisted the help of Philip O'Connor, a member of that previous congregation, to lead the trip since Philip had been on more than two dozen STM trips to Nicaragua.

PREPARATIONS

The preparations team leaders utilized for the STM varied widely. Some teams met for several months ahead of time. Elmville UMC and Riverbend UMC gathered only once before their scheduled departure date. Many members of the Riverbend team had not been introduced to one another prior to that meeting because some lived hundreds of miles apart. However, the remaining teams held multiple meetings prior to the overseas travel. My discussions revealed some common tasks amongst the teams as they prepared for their trip, including managing the logistical considerations and securing funds to pay for travel and project expenses.

Planning the Trip, Sorting the Details

The perceived need for a team leader with the ability to handle logistical concerns may be because there are, in fact, several important factors to consider. Team leaders recounted a considerable list of logistical considerations. There were several intricacies of international group travel: airline tickets, visas, ground transportation in the United States and overseas, meals, lodging, and others. Differences of language and varying access to reliable communication methods by mission hosts complicated planning further. Another layer of concern was related to the work the teams were to do. Teams who participated in VBS activities often brought hundreds of trinkets and toys for the children who came to the teaching times. Medical teams brought their equipment for examinations and hundreds of doses of several different medications. Construction teams worked hard to learn how to best pack safety equipment, hand tools, and power tools in suitcases. Team leaders often asked team members to designate one suitcase to the team's logistical packing needs. Close to departure, many teams held "packing parties" to determine ways to accommodate all the required goods. Team leaders spent a great deal of time mitigating such factors. Some team leaders sounded much like travel agents and quartermasters as they spoke of their team preparations.

When asked about spiritual preparations, team leaders were not as quick to answer. None of the teams reported a using an intentional Bible study or a designed spiritual preparation course. Most teams did have a team "devotional" at the beginning of a team logistical meeting. These devotionals often included a brief Scripture reading, a few minutes of reflection and/or instruction on the verse by a team member and perhaps a prayer. Carla and Larry Harris typified most teams' pattern, "We don't do any Bible studies. But we do ask each member, once a month, a different team member. . .to start our meetings out with a devotion." None of the teams reported using specific, cohesive, intentional strategy for the devotionals, nor did any report using a designed curriculum for spiritual preparation.

The length of time teams used to prepare varied. To meet all the needs of the team, some groups began preparations a year in advance. Contrast that to two teams who only had one meeting prior to their departure on the mission trip. This single meeting was designated for logistical concerns and to introduce team members to one another. In one case, some team members lived as many as 500 miles away from one another and therefore meeting together was not practical. In the other case, it was the team leader who lived a distance away from the team members. In the limited time they had together, they focused upon travel concerns in their group meeting time.

There was strong evidence in the narratives of the team leaders that the time team members had together before a trip was disproportionly spent on the logistical preparation for the travel before them rather than the addressing the biblical and theological issues around their efforts done in the name of mission. Biblical instruction or spiritual exercises were minimized. Additionally, there was such a heavy emphasis on the pre-departure work that some team leaders saw the work during the STM trip itself as secondary or relatively unnecessary. Team leader Will Manning, who was particularly adamant about the importance pre-trip logistical planning, typified the emphasis of work before the trip rather than during the trip. When I talked with him a few days before his team's departure, he told me, "Now it's all organized, so I don't have anything to do."

Raising the Funds, Building Community

Some team leaders sought to use the months leading up to the trip as time to prepare the team and to teach others in the church about the STM project. One common way to do so is by fundraising. Some teams used fundraisers as a way to allow congregants to participate in the mission. Teams held special church-wide meals where the proceeds were used to offset the cost of the trips. Some sold t-shirts or other goods. It was not unusual for a team to hold multiple fundraisers.

The use of those funds varied from group to group. Some groups allowed team members to solicit funds from church members and the community to pay for the expenses of their trip: travel, project costs, or other expenses. One large-membership church team I interviewed used church funds to pay for at least half of the costs of any STMer who wanted to go. These funds were assigned from the church budget, as received from tithes and offerings, or from special giving designated for the STM projects. If team members wanted to pay their own way entirely, the money was used for others to go. If a STMer was unable to pay, the church paid for the entire cost.

Some teams saw fundraising as more than just putting money in the travel accounts of the team members. Teams felt as though they were giving the entire church community a way to participate in the trip. When STM teams solicit money from the church, "It feels like more of a church involvement or sponsored thing, instead of just a few people going on it," Debbie Porter told me. Her teammate, Cecilia Snyder, affirmed this, "We are being representatives of the church, instead of us going as individuals." Contrast this to team leader Philip O'Connor. He is a member of a small, rural church which does not participate in fundraisers for travel costs of a STM trip. However, his community does hold a fundraiser to benefit the mission projects, but not the costs associated with an individual's travel to work on those projects. Talking to Philip feels somewhat like talking to a travel guide. When I asked him about the requirements for his mission team members, he answered, "First, you've gotta be able to pay your way. To me, it doesn't matter how you get the money. If you have it, and you're going to pay your own way, that's fine." Philip was reticent to involve the church ministry funds in the support of STM trips.

Other teams saw raising money as potentially difficult, but a way to build community. Rev. Keith Miller talked about raising money with college students, "There's a certain element of misery to it. When people are in misery together, it is a bonding experience. When they look back and say, 'We did this together. We raised the money together.'" Those "bonding experiences" were not always done in "misery." Some reported building team cohesion while raising money. Some teams made special mention of the fact that they wore matching t-shirts or aprons while serving meals to the church members and guests. Monies raised from these meals was used to offset the cost of the trip and involve the church. Perhaps just as significant was the way the team members were building community before their upcoming trip. Such "bonding experiences" seem to demonstrate the bonding of social capital Robert Putnam described among groups.[18] Indeed, the increasing homogenization of dress, of roles, and of misery was, for many, a way to strengthen a team before the upcoming trip.

MOTIVATIONS

Exploring the motivations of those participating in the STM movement is an important step in developing a robust theology of the practice. In our previous discussion of the way theology influences mission and practice, we saw that theologies shape motivations and motivations shape actions. Using the narratives of STMers I wanted to hear their implicit and explicit understandings of the sources of the motivations for their activities done in the name of mission. Did they feel called by God to do what they were about to do? How did the Bible inform their mission service? What role did a Wesleyan missional framework play in their actions? Or was there something else pushing, or pulling, them?

"We are going to obey the will of God"

Many STMers reported feeling that their participation in the trip was a result of a divine call of some sort. Of the thirty people who took the follow-up survey, twenty-four either strongly or somewhat agreed with the statement "I felt a call from God to participate in this particular mission trip." However, the expressed purpose of that call varied. Carla Harris grew emotional when discussing how she came to be involved in leading teams to the Caribbean. She recalled her participation in a short-term trip to Asia over ten years ago. She told me that while working with the children on that trip, she knew she was going to be called to go somewhere again for God, either back to Asia on a return trip or a STM somewhere else. She didn't know where she was going, but she had to go somewhere. This call, Carla went on

18. Putnam, *Bowling Alone*, 22–23. I touch upon this in relation to transnational mission in chapter 3.

to say, came when family members asked her to go with them on STM trips to Latin America and the Caribbean. When talking about her four trips that included three different countries, she described them as "a wonderful time." Such trips became a priority for her, and, in turn, for her husband. Carla later passed up mission trips so that her husband, Larry, could "have the opportunity to go." Carla seemed to be looking for something that was difficult to see whilst at home. When talking about her interest in STM, she told me about a quote she had found, "'Going on international mission trips is a little taste of heaven.'" She continued, "Because you'll see different faces, different colors, and once we're all in heaven we'll all be together again." This "little taste of heaven" seemed to be a sensation she wanted to experience again.

Many STMers reported that they felt a call to participate on this STM trip for some sort of personal growth and/or edification. But this was not so for all team members. When I asked teams why they wanted to participate in this mission, many spoke of a compulsion to respond to a perceived need. The location of that perceived need varied among the participants. For first-time STMers, it was often seen as meeting a need in someone else, in a far-off place.

Oliver Moore was a first-time participant in a STM trip. He spoke of his desire to be obedient to God by serving on this trip. His motivations seemed self-abasing and focused upon the others that he and his team members would encounter on the upcoming trip. He spoke of healing and restoration for those that they would serve. He spoke of practical projects that would be completed for spiritual reasons. Oliver was not focused upon what he would receive from participating in the trip. He said, "[I]f we get some pleasure and enjoyment out of it, that's a side benefit. But that's not the purpose of going. That's not the reason any of us are going. We are going to serve, and we are going to obey the will of God." He was focused upon the larger spiritual dimensions at work in his participation in the trip.

This was somewhat unusual. Many STMers spoke of God leading them, but their desire to experience something for themselves interacted with altruism differently. I will return to this idea in detail in the following chapters. It is, however, necessary to touch upon the reflection of some of the more experienced STMers. The idea of a personal satisfaction or personal growth was predominant in many of the narratives. Mack and Lena Anderson were preparing for their second mission trip together. They chose that trip, in part, because of the accommodations made for their physical limitations, e.g., not too much walking over difficult terrain for long periods of time. Additionally, Lena says, they felt like they heard a "small voice that says, 'This is something that you should think harder about doing.' And then you finally answer it and say, 'All right. I'll go.'" When asked why someone should participate in a STM trip, Mack introspectively offered, "It's going to mean a lot to you. In more ways than you can imagine. You're not going to experience it any other way than going and doing. You have to go and do. . . . I probably got more out of it than people I was trying to help."

The account from veteran STMers Mack and Lena was common to the dataset in many ways: people reported a sense that they were to do something and that it would be self-beneficial. This was, at least at first, different from Oliver's account. There are two important aspects to the sense of purpose in Oliver's narrative: it was somewhat unusual and it did not last. Remember that Oliver was a first-time participant. As such, he was in the minority on his mission team. Those who spoke in terms of a larger mission of God were usually first time participants. I had the opportunity to speak with Oliver after he returned from his trip. He spoke of the way the trip had affected him personally and spoke little of the motivations of a biblical mandate to serve the Other that he mentioned before the trip. Instead, Oliver compared his trip to a "retreat" in which one goes away for personal spiritual growth. He told me that the reason to participate in a STM trip is for the spiritual growth of the one going. When I tried to gently steer the conversation back towards those biblical motivations he mentioned earlier, he did not recall having spoken with such emphasis on benefitting the other first.

Team members often spoke of divine guidance in preparing for their trip or affirming their work. Though many team leaders mentioned personal references as an effective way to enlist team members, some team leaders and members alike spoke of contemplation and prayer as a guiding mechanism in deciding to participate. Charles Franklin spoke of his discernment process:

> I've just been praying a lot. At the beginning, it was more that I was trying to figure out if I needed to go on this. Was I being led to this? It was also trying to figure out how I was going to pay for this trip. As it got closer, everything started getting clearer. I realized that this path has opened for me. I need to take it. I have a job, so therefore I can pay for this trip. But for me, it has just been praying about it, trying to figure out if I need to go on the trip at all.

Team leader Sally Manning was not willing to let prayer stand alone in preparing for her team.

> We can't just sit and pray and, you know, we've got to do our part. You pray all along. You pray first, you pray middle, you

pray last but you still have to spend time to organize and get things done. I just feel like the more organization and the more preparation, the better the trip is.

Sally went on to emphasize the importance of the experience of the missioner to the success of the trip. She insisted that to maximize the STMers' experience, the leader must join organization with prayer.

Sally and her husband and co-leader Will looked for divine interventions during their service trips as an affirmation to their efforts. They recalled an event when a team member misplaced a passport in a crowded airport. According to Sally and Will, an angel in the form of a young girl intervened and returned the passport to them soon after it was discovered to be missing. They attributed this incident to an affirmation of God's call upon their work.

Laura Denson spoke of a personal conviction from God to return to the same STM destination country nine times. God was telling her, she said, to "go back and let people see the same face over and over again." The relationships with the people in the host country were important for Laura. Equally important (or perhaps causally) she traveled to the same country because "every time it's a different experience. . . . I always feel like God's stretching me a little bit. . .every time that I go down there."

Team members felt called to participate in STM. This call came through prayer or other signs attributed to God's direction for the individual. These messages were seen as ways to confirm to the STM participants that they were to experience a message from God while journeying in the name of mission service.

"I Am Not Driven, Personally, by Verses from the Bible to Go Do Missions"

Theological motivations are often developed out of an understanding of the teachings of Scripture. Therefore, I wanted to explore biblical motivations for mission among my participants. I asked each team leader and team focus group about their mission service. I phrased the question in the form of a hypothetical situation. I framed a situation where the team leaders were invited to speak to the congregation, during a regular worship service, about STM service. For team members, I framed a similar situation where they were asked to speak to a small group Bible Study or Sunday School class about their mission work.[19] I then asked what Scripture passage they might

19. I did so due to the fact that many teams spoke of the support of the whole

use to talk about the work. I did not ask participants to name a specific book, chapter and verse, necessarily. Rather, recalling a biblical story or account was sufficient.

There was often hesitation on the part of participants and apologies for not being more familiar with the Bible when trying to recall a verse. Answers to this line of questioning varied, and were among the most difficult to elicit during our discussions. Rev. Keith Wallace recalled John 21:15–19 when Jesus commands Peter to "feed my sheep." Patrick Stone pointed to the teaching in 1 Corinthians of the various gifts the body have to the benefit of the body overall. Others recalled the commands to put works to faith (James 2) or Paul's missionary travels or the question posed to Isaiah as to who would go for the Lord (Isa 6) or Jesus washing the feet of the disciples (John 13). College student Christina Potts was quick to answer when she recited John 15:15, "I no longer call you servants, I call you friends. Because the servant has no idea what the master is doing. Yet everything I have let you know has been known through me by the Father."[20]

Some team members and leaders referenced Scripture principles that pointed to aid and comfort for the STM participants themselves. Wayne Kennedy shared, "This trip has caused me some anxiety since I have never traveled on a plane, and I have never traveled this far before." He mentioned that he had a "kind of personal verse. . .'The Lord has not given us a spirit of fear, but of power and of love and of sound mind.' And I feel like that has really helped me get through this."[21] Other participants pointed to verses that describe God leading those who were seeking direction in their own lives or ways in which they could overcome personal difficulties.

However, generally speaking, scriptural references in regard to service in the name of mission were slow to come from the accounts. After I posed the scenario about scriptural references, there were often long pauses or nervous laughs. I found this to be the case among team leaders and team members alike. When I asked Dr. Timothy Lyons (a fifteen-year veteran team leader) for a scriptural allusion, he indicated that I should speak to the team member who was running the children's outreach activities as he was unsure of any such references, with the exception perhaps of the command to go into all the world, saying that the Bible was a weakness in his personal faith life.[22]

---

church, a particular small group Bible Study, or Sunday School class as supportive of their efforts in service.

20. I have included the scriptural reference as she recounted it.

21. This is a likely reference to 2 Tim 1:7.

22. Though he did not specify, this is likely a reference to Matt 28:19–20.

Will and Sally Manning regularly lead teams of their peers to the Caribbean. In conversation, they seem to place a priority of biblical teaching in the life and teaching of the church. They told me that bringing a Bible to church worship services was a priority for people at City Central UMC. Doing this meant that their church "isn't your typical [United] Methodist Church." They spoke of their leadership in children's ministries at City Central UMC and the importance of biblical instruction in these ministries. Bible reading at Church and Christian education were important for them. However, if these highly valued principles translated into mission education is unclear. While they spoke of the importance of Bible reading for the members of the church, they had difficulty expressing biblical principles underpinning their mission activities.

I asked Sally and an experienced team member, Nancy Denson, about the Bible verses that shape STM at Central City. Nancy referenced Acts 1:8 when Jesus says to the disciples, "'But you will receive power when the Holy Spirit has come upon you; and you will be my witnesses in Jerusalem, in all Judea and Samaria, and to the ends of the earth.'" Sally, however, was much less clear or confident. She told me, "Probably, 'Go into all the world. . .and preach the gospel too.' That's at the very end of Acts. And um, I don't know. There are lots of different ones." Her voice trailed off as though she were unsure what to say next. Her answer may be a conflation of Nancy's reference to Jesus' command at the beginning of Acts and the command at the end of Matthew's Gospel, "'Go therefore and make disciples of all nations, baptizing them in the name of the Father and of the Son and of the Holy Spirit. . .'" (Matt 28:19) Will and Sally later told me that, when thinking about mission, a motivating principle is the adage, "The more you give, the more you get." Sally offered, "Well, the Bible basically says that." She did not offer references to any passages or teachings that illustrate such a principle.

Richard Davis is a life-long Methodist. He is a team leader with over twenty years' experience and often leads multiple trips a year. When I asked him for his thoughts on biblical motivations for mission by requesting a Scripture reference for his mission sermon, he told me that he was caught off guard by the question. After long pauses for reflection, he finally answered, "I am not driven, personally, by verses from the Bible to go do missions. I guess, you know, the message, Jesus' message of go, serve, love. . . . I guess the whole thing about doing unto your neighbor. . .that whole message is what I go by. Not specific verses." To give him another opportunity to expand the concept by asking for a biblical image or command, he followed up with "Loving and serving others. That's the thing I think that drives me."

Loving and serving others is certainly a Christian priority. I probed Richard's thoughts about how, then, Christian mission is different from secular groups who want to love and serve on humanitarian mission around the world. Again, the question seemed to give him great pause. The main difference, he told me, was to build relationships and in doing so one would show the love of Christ. When we discussed the fact that non-Christians could build relationships with others, Richard pointed to the motivation of the one who is seeking to serve as a key difference. I pushed a little further looking for the motivation that he sees as making Christian mission distinctive. He affirmed that mission is what "Jesus told us to go do." However, he had quite a bit of difficulty in pointing to distinctions between his Christian mission and secular compassion projects. Looking for how this might be exhibited in the motivations of his team members, I asked what he thought motivated those who signed up for this trip. Service was mentioned, but curiosity was a prime reason for new people. Such curiosity was about a mission trip that, for previous STM participants, was "a great experience. . .how it changed their lives."

When asked about scriptural references to mission, Larry and Carla Harris instead pointed out that they often embrace a "team song." The team song was one that was popular in Contemporary Christian Worship Music during the particular year that they traveled. The song included allusions to Scripture or used Scripture as a part of the lyrics. The lyrics they mentioned alluded to Isa 40:29–31:

> He gives power to the faint,
> and strengthens the powerless.
>
> Even youths will faint and be weary,
> and the young will fall exhausted;
>
> but those who wait for the Lord shall renew their strength,
> they shall mount up with wings like eagles,
> they shall run and not be weary,
> they shall walk and not faint.

When they did offer a particular scriptural reference, it was one of personal growth and development rather than upon service to another.

The scriptural references that were offered in the dataset often reflected the issues that the STMers faced in the journey of ahead of them. They recalled passages that provided them a sense of comfort through the uncertainty ahead, a comfort that Jesus considers them a friend, or that they will receive something for themselves through what they are about to do. Granted, some did report a feeling that they were being instructed to "Go," but there was not always the requisite reflection as to why they were going there. As mentioned in chapter 3, a Wesleyan understanding of mission is firmly rooted in scriptural mandates of service to another with recognition that the one serving is but an agent of the gospel's transforming message. The mandates the STMers seemed to be heeding were those that offered personal comfort and growth rather than the proclamation of the liberating message of Jesus as demonstrated in, say, Luke 4. I discuss these motivations of experience and life-change, mentioned above, over biblical constructs in the exchange of mission at length below.

A Role in Wesleyan Mission

Since all the groups for this study were sponsored by United Methodist churches and/or parachurch ministries, I wanted to explore the participants' understanding of Wesleyan mission in their current mission activities. As discussed in chapter 3, Wesleyan theology has a strong history of embracing service as a means of grace. The people called Methodists have used biblical mandates of service to the poor and disenfranchised as a key trait of the movement. I expected to find some articulation of this in the conversations I had with the STM participants and their leaders.

The most common answer I received when I asked, "What makes Methodist mission distinctive?" was, "I don't know. I have only done Methodist mission." This was particularly common among team members. It may seem that the question may not have been fair to laypeople with little or no mission experience. How could laypeople know how to practice mission for themselves, let alone know how it is distinguished among other ways of service? However, the answer to the question, or lack of an answer, is telling. If participants cannot give an answer for how Methodist mission is exercised, then they are likely not being taught a theology of mission in a historical Methodist understanding. It is possible that their mission team leaders, pastors, and others are not placing an emphasis on the rich history of service among the Methodist movement.[23] Though some members of the interview groups did list advantages to participating in Methodist mission projects. The advantage to Methodist mission was seen in three areas: connectionalism, organization, and approach to faith-sharing.

---

23. Of the focus groups, the college students expressed the most familiarity with the Wesleyan history of mission service. It is not clear if this was an emphasis of the team leader's teaching or some other source.

"The connection. Plain and simple."

Rev. Keith Wallace valued the ability to reach out to other United Methodists directly and arrange international work trips because of the experiences
they had in seminary together. Richard Davis appreciated the other resources he had in finding new personnel to lead future teams. Philip O'Connor
was firm in his answer about the distinction of Wesleyan mission:

> The connection. Plain and simple. . . . You're in a little rural
> Methodist Church that sits out there by itself. But we belong to
> a district of Methodist churches in the south part of our state.
> Then the. . .Annual Conference. We are all connected there.
> And then the General Conference. With the UMVIM office that
> we can go to register our trips that provides some options for
> places to go and serve. Some resources are consolidated there
> that you will need to give focus to your team. Then, even when
> you go to that foreign country, there's the church with the same
> emblem. The same UM hymnal, maybe in a different language.
> They have a district and a conference, just like we have. So, that
> connection and organization has been the biggest benefit that I
> see in doing mission with the Methodist Church.

Other team leaders also expressed their appreciation for the connectional nature of The United Methodist Church to provide resources for
selecting mission sites, offering tools for organizing groups, or supplying
teams with forms to use for logistical considerations. Many team leaders
saw these as not only helpful, but a key component in what made a team
successful. It should be noted that such ideals embrace the notion that mission should accept its role in the broader church, a key principle in Wesleyan mission theology. Recognizing that it is but a small part of the church
universally, such connectional partnerships do affirm the interconnectivity
of the work of mission.

Organization

For Will Manning, organization is a key component in a successful mission
trip. When I asked, "What makes United Methodist mission distinctive?"
he compared the trips he organizes with the trips from a church in another
denomination. He was previously a member of that denomination and expressed a confidence in being able to distinguish organization that led to a
sense of purpose for the team members between the two:

When we go, we have a goal, we have a purpose. Not all of us are speakers. Not all of us work well with children. . . . But we can all hug and we can all smile and we can all care. And I think, building the relationships, like I have said over and over, and having a focus to get every person involved in the mission that does go is critical. I think we all feel better after going. The people I talked to at First [Church], when they go . . . 'Well, they went.' And that's not good enough.

"Well, they went" referred to an account he gave of friends who participated in a mission trip and were disappointed by a lack of a sense of personal accomplishment after they returned home. Will seemed to insist that his role was to organize the trip for the purposes of accomplishing the mission the team set forth. Such accomplishments included the work projects the team set out to do, "build relationships," and provide a sense of satisfaction for team members.

Dr. Timothy Lyons would agree with Will. Dr. Lyons often spoke of his role as organizer and trip planner and taking on roles that may have been the job of a travel agent or guide. These included the purchasing of tickets, organizing room and board for the team, and transportation logistics. He worked hard on the organizational tasks to accomplish his stated goal of providing a certain satisfaction for the team members and to fulfill their sense of success and accomplishment. He did say that he would thank God for that success. He did so while asserting that if the team members did not find it rewarding, they would not be going. He did not make a direct connection to the principle of organization as being distinctly United Methodist, but such a notion paralleled what other team members found as a strong principle for United Methodist missions. He admitted that he does not take advantage of the opportunities The United Methodist Church offers for organizing trips and instead completes those tasks himself.

"Oh, by the way, we're doing evangelism"

When describing United Methodist mission, many team members found it easiest to describe the distinctive approach that United Methodism holds when combining service done in the name of Christian mission and the verbal proclamation of faith sharing. The accounts given often described United Methodist faith-sharing as something grounded not in words but in actions. To illustrate this, STM participants contrasted their efforts with the STM teams from other denominations. The points of contrast were difficult to articulate directly, so anecdotes were used. One team leader's story seemed to sum up such accounts. He recalls a conversation with another STM team leader:

> He's very big in mission in a sister denomination, as we say. And they go over and do things. And he talked to me one day about the mission trip. He said, 'Yeah, we got this big tent and they have to listen to our message and then they get a ticket, once they do that, to go see the doctor.' And I cringed. And I didn't [argue] with him. But my whole concept of Methodist mission and the way, I think, I teach mission, and the way we teach missions here in this church is. . .they were. . .to me. . .they were pushing Christianity down these people's throats. Requiring them to listen to their spiel first. Before they were served. My whole concept is let's serve, let's love, let's open our hearts, open our minds, open our arms. . .that opens the door. You are evangelizing when you do that. That opens the door. If the opportunity arises, you share your faith. To me, I guess the evangelism was number one. But almost a forced evangelism. . . . The Bible thumping is first. Not the relationship building. Not the Christian love. . . . What I see more in the Methodist church is we're doing, and we're working and we're serving. And, 'Oh, by the way, we're doing evangelism.'

While all of the groups were being sent in the name of Methodist mission, they seemed to have only a vague understanding of what that would mean. While groups were ready to engage Methodist mission for its mechanics, they seemed unaware of its purpose. The issues of evangelism, service, and some of the struggles their intermingling can bring are discussed at great length later in this chapter. Certainly, such a sentiment demonstrates that "mission is not merely evangelism," the fourth principle I listed in Wesleyan missiology. The holistic message of a verbal proclamation joined with meeting very real, immediate, physical needs is a key to practicing mission.

A Way to Feel Better

A strong and ubiquitous theme among the STM participants was the expectation that those engaging in service to another would be different after the experience. While STM trips engage in some sort of project or service component for another, there was a strong underlying expectation that those serving would receive as much or more than those whom they sought to serve. Frequently, this was by design. Team leaders structured their trips in such a way to provide maximum benefit not just for those they sought to serve, but also for the STMers themselves. Rev. Keith Wallace described his work with his college students in both local and international service. Local service is important,

> [b]ut there is something very transformative, often, with mission trips. So we, about every other year or so, try to go to a place that will completely put the students out of their comfort zone. To help them try to understand and experience something that they have never experienced before. A lot of times, those conditions do a lot of good in students' lives.

Leaving the "comfort zone" was a way to describe the separation from normal conditions through the experience of international travel. Team leaders saw the separation from familiar foods, customs, and environments and immersion in an unfamiliar language as a valuable contribution to the STM trip for the ones engaging in service. Just as Rev. Wallace expected such a separation to be a transformative experience for his students, Richard Davis designed his trips as a part of an "experiential learning" opportunity. For Richard, experiential learning was among his highest priorities, placing it alongside "building relationships" and "doing the work" of the construction projects his teams undertook. These three he placed above faith sharing. Because, he said, "You're sharing your faith with the first three." For him, "experiential learning means that you're experiencing, you got your hands dirty, you're feeling, you're smelling, you're hearing, you're tasting the things in that culture."

"Raise your hand if you're an adventurer!"

The STMers seemed drawn to the short, intense nature of the separation from the familiar that their trip would bring. This, they felt, would be beneficial for them. Those who had served on STM previously often expressed a desire for such an experience again. Those who had not served previously often recalled hearing the accounts of family and friends who had served. These accounts seemed to motivate them to participate in the upcoming trip. Tracey Pierson was going on her second trip and felt drawn to do so by the experience she had on a previous trip to South America:

> One thing that drew me to it was the sense of adventure. Not ever having been. . .outside the US, this was kind of exciting, adventurous. . .if you will. . . . Just meeting a different culture of people, the surroundings, the environment. . . . But of course, it was so fulfilling seeing what a difference we made in the church

building we worked on. . . . I mean, basically, four days. . .actually work days. What a difference a team can make in a project.

Richard gave a similar account of the people who served on STM under his leadership: they want to return to recapture something they experienced the first time. He described how people often viewed their everyday world in new ways, how they viewed their routine differently, how some behaviors changed after returning from overseas service. Connie Hughes would agree:

> Well, the first mission trip I went on, I thought I was just going to bring this wonderful Christian experience to people who had none. And I was so mistaken. The people I encountered had such great faith, it was unreal. And I think the sharing of the Christian faith, not only did a lot to renew mine that I got as much or more seeing how much faith they have under the circumstances that they're dealing with. It was just awesome. . . . I did the conduit, spread the electrical, and all that stuff. I did the physical stuff that they needed help with, but I think I came back more blessed, spiritually, than I could have ever done for them. So, it was an amazing experience.

In one team interview, Amanda told us, "I think I thrive on doing new things." In reply, her teammate Sharon wanted to describe the group to me by saying, "We have a lot of adventurous spirits in here. . . . Raise your hand if you're an adventurer!" Nearly every hand in the room went up. These ideas of adventures seemed to be mixed with ideas of personal growth, as well as service. One team member said she wanted to participate in this STM trip because, "I want to go on an adventure where I am not the central focus or beneficiary. I want to focus all my energy on the people and showing God's love." Another replied, "To explore new places and to become closer to God and to just help people." This sense of adventure was linked to a larger goal for college student Wayne Kennedy:

> I've wanted to get out of the country, and I've wanted to fly on a plane. . . . I want to live a more adventurous lifestyle, is a good way to put it. [It will be] adventurous in that I am going to experience a culture and a type of geography that I haven't been exposed to before.

Wayne's teammates seemed to agree. They expressed a sense of being focused upon someone else when thinking about their trip. They talked about their travel being a "godly experience." For Gregory Booth, who had been on several STM trips before, this was more:

I am going because every mission trip that I have ever been on has been life changing and it's been an amazing experience. And as soon as I heard that we were going on one, I knew immediately that I had to go. From experience, I know that all the work that goes into going is always worth the trip that you go on. And I knew that this wouldn't be any different. It's almost like an addiction. Since the first time I went on my first mission trip. . .I was like, 'I need to keep going on these.' I feel like I am at a point in my life where I need to go on one. Obviously for the people of Costa Rica, but I need one for myself personally.

A Contagious Feeling

After three dozen STM trips, Richard Davis was able to vividly recall what first interested him in the practice. He gave an account in which he went to the airport to pick up a STM team upon their return to the United States. Expecting them to be exhausted from their work and long journey, he instead found that they were "just joyous." This joy intrigued him and he signed up for a subsequent trip looking for the source of such joy. Now his church uses this person-to-person experience sharing as one of the primary tools to subscribe new participants. "75 percent of our new people are one-on-one invitations." These new people are "curious," he says, because "they've heard people come back from mission trips and talk about what a great experience it was, and how it changed their lives." One college student summed up such a notion when talking about her friends who had been on a STM trip before, "I saw how my friends had fun and they got a lot out of it. So, when the opportunity came this time around, I said, 'Huh. I want to do this. I definitely want to do this.'"

"I go on mission and help others because it makes me feel better"

For Paula Davis traveling and the immersion of oneself in a new environment was significant for personal growth.

[Y]ou hear it over and over again. . .that you benefit more than you ever would imagine. So from a personal standpoint, it is that opportunity to get beyond what we are here. When you go someplace and you smell and you see, it opens up your eyes in such a way. And you just leave part of yourself wherever you go. There's no way that you can come back and not have been impacted by it.

Her husband, Richard would agree, "You think you're going to help people, and change peoples' lives. And you do. But you come back changed."

Many team leaders spoke of the service projects in which they would participate as secondary to other goals for the STM participants.[24] Larry Harris said that his projects were not the reason they go. Instead, he asks his team members to "focus on their spiritual growth, getting closer to God and on trying to hear His voice. . . . The priority is the relationship with one another, and then trying to figure out what God has for them during the two weeks." Through connecting with those in the host community, he expected his team members to learn more about what God wants them to do. He went on to describe his trips as a way that people can learn where God wants to them go and serve in the future. Using the imagery from the Book of Isaiah, chapter 5, he likens the STMer to the prophet standing before God. The STMer is to be willing to go when God asks for someone to go. That principle, he says, is something that people should seek God to teach them during, and after, a STM trip.

Walter and Jaqueline Williams were participating in the STM trip with their home church, City Central UMC. They are veterans of STM trips and were asked to participate in this trip because of their experience in leading other trips and the unique projects those trips undertook. Walter and Jaqueline were involved in ministry to couples that focused on teaching of biblical principles in order to strengthen marriages. They teach courses in the United States and have also taught them in South America. After teaching one such course at City Central UMC, they were asked join the team to the Caribbean to teach parenting on the upcoming trip. An experienced leader and teacher, Walter spoke with enthusiasm about not only teaching the curriculum, but also the expectations he had that the trip itself would be a growth opportunity. "[W]e are always looking for international missions to take couples on. So that they can experience it together and further strengthen their family team, husband and wife, going on a mission team together." Jaqueline expressed strong expectations for those on her STM team,

> I firmly feel like short-term mission trips are very beneficial to whoever goes. . . . We certainly hope to grow in our relationship with the Lord and let the Lord work in us, however he wants to on this trip. [Y]ou get away from your usual responsibilities. . .you can have time for the Lord to speak to you. Although

---

24. Later in this chapter I will show that many participants would later contradict themselves on this point. However, for clarity I want to focus on the subservient place the projects had in terms of personal growth.

we do stay very busy, and we're very exhausted at the end of each day. But, it's definitely a time of spiritual growth.

Among the most experienced team leaders and the newest team members, STM was described as a challenge to oneself with a specific reward in mind. That reward was often seen as some sort of personal fulfillment. Will and Sally Manning, a husband and wife team, have led several mission trips. It is important, they told me, to have a sense of purpose and accomplishment when participating in a STM trip. Will told of a news report he heard in which studies found that serving another person increased chemicals in the brain that lead to good feelings. "I think that is a great way to think about why we go on mission. . . . I go on mission and help others because it makes me feel better."

The idea of growing in personal faith seemed to influence some who participated in STM trips. It was necessary, some said, to travel overseas to encounter something outside of the normal routine to experience such growth. Naomi Shaw took time away from work and arranged to have normal family responsibilities covered by others while she was away, as is common for many STM participants. When asked why she would be willing to do so, she was quick to answer that she was doing so to seek "spiritual fulfillment. [T]hey always say it makes you feel better to do for others than for someone to do for you. Well, that does work for me. It helps you kind of forget what's going on in your life."

What was required for personal spiritual growth was expressed in different ways. Issues of enduring personal hardship and encountering others to see the poverty experienced in the host countries are discussed below. Those were, at times, seen as a means to the goal of personal growth. Issues of spiritual growth influenced the conversations when goals and values surrounding STM were discussed. When asked what makes a trip successful, obedience to God, openness to cultures, and completed projects were mentioned. However, the team members' expressed goals for the trip included a desire to be different than when they departed with expressions like:

- "to grow together spiritually and maybe discover something new about ourselves"
- "come back closer to God and closer to each other than when we left"
- "We all grew in Christ and with each other"
- "The major impact is on the people that go"
- "I think it will change our point of view when we see things and not take things for granted that we have"

- "It will encourage us to get out more and serve others more. A kind of humbling experience"
- "To experience a new way to grow my Christian relationship"

The idea of personal growth was not only characterized directly by phrases such as these, but it was also underlying in many conversations. Quantifying its influence would be difficult to do. However, it should be noted that it was prevalent in conversations with research participants. Yet, personal growth does not stand alone in the expressed goal of the trip. In a pre-interview survey, STM participants were asked, "Why do you want to be a part of this particular mission journey?" To this question, answers like "service" and "help" and "love" were used throughout. The terms used seemed to be focused upon another: God and others. A follow-up question was asked later in the survey: "What are your expectations regarding this journey?" To this question, many participants gave answers that could indicate a focus upon self:

- "To grow spiritually"
- "Spiritual fulfillment"
- "I think it will make me stronger"
- "To grow personally"
- "To experience a type of humbling freedom from the spiritual experience and the nature and culture"
- "To grow in my relationship with God and fellowship with the Costa Ricans while doing the best to help out"
- "Come back with a changed heart and mind"

This is not to say that the two categories of responses, focus upon Self and focus upon the Other, were mutually exclusive. There was overlap, confluence, and mixing. This seemed to indicate that, concerning these issues, focus upon the Other and focus upon Self were not clearly distinguishable in the narratives of the participants. It would seem that one precipitates the other. I discuss this at length in the following chapters.

"It's my gift to myself"

Such personal growth was understood by some to come at a price. Not only was there a monetary price to be paid, but there was an intangible price to be paid by some team members. While in the host countries, STM teams often stayed in hotels or guest houses designed for housing such teams. In appointments and comfort, these hotels and guest houses were somewhere between what team members were accustomed to at home and what their hosts lived with each day. Team members expressed a willingness to do without certain everyday comforts. Such regular comforts included use of their mobile phones, easy access to the internet, or foods they normally ate. Some expected to have to walk further than normal, while carrying their own luggage. Some were prepared for the disadvantages that a lack of a working knowledge of the language would bring. Some were ready to room with a fellow team member, who may be a friend or a heretofore stranger, for a week or two and thereby sacrifice some privacy normally experienced.

These were seen as a means to a greater end. Rev. Keith Wallace, who above discussed putting his college students out of their comfort zone for their own benefit, described it as "a mission trip, but it is a retreat too: where you work your butt off." He went on to explain that the mission trip is a spiritual growth retreat in the sense that:

> We have so many things that make life convenient, like our phones, but they also tie us down. Netflix. . .a lot of things that make life fun and convenient, but people can become slaves to those things sometimes. It is a time to intentionally put everything down and only pick up the things that are going to draw *us* closer to Christ and others to well-being and to Christ.[25]

One team member and pastor offered that he did not feel that everyone in the church could participate in a STM trip because they may not be comfortable with the difficulties of the language barriers or lack of creature comforts. He would encourage his congregants to support the team with prayer, money, or logistical report, but he understood that some people could not or would not want to do without the familiarity of, say, a hot shower. These were seen as ways that different people could use their spiritual gifts to support the STM team sent overseas, who could endure these perceived hardships. Kate Powell was an experienced STM participant. She recalled how others asked her how she could go to a place where the weather was so hot and how she could go without a hot shower. "I hate it. I do. It's the only thing I really hate. But it's my gift to myself. Now that's something I can give up. I hate cold showers." Her gift to herself, she went on, "Is to say that I can do this, that I can give up something. I can give up having ice [in my soft drink]."

These perceived hardships were not merely an end to themselves. STM participants embraced the idea of leaving the mundane by making sacrifices

---

25. Emphasis original.

like not having the use of their mobile phones, going without ice in their soft drinks, or enduring hot weather. These sacrifices were seen as sacrifices with rewards. As one woman put it, by doing so, "I'd like to think that I am going to grow in my love for fellow man and for Christ. I want my faith to be stronger and grow."

So far in this chapter, we have discussed the recruitment and training of STMers and the motivations of STMers for enlisting in at STM trip. Several of the issues raised so far relate to the issues of pilgrimage and tourism I mentioned in chapter 4. I will elucidate these further in the chapters 6 and 7, but it is important to emphasize the prominence of participation for personal growth at this point in our discussion. The idealized things that STMers expected to encounter that would help facilitate such growth is the focus of the next portion of our discussion. Again, I will further engage these issues in relation to the principles around pilgrimage and tourism later.

IDEALIZATIONS

The casting off of the comfortable during a STM to gain something that cannot be found at home could be seen as an attempt to emulate what participants expected to witness in their mission hosts and one another while on their trip. Several STM participants seemed to endow their mission hosts with characteristics they wished to experience for themselves. Characteristics such as joy, happiness, Christian character, family values, and the like were attributed to those they encountered previously. Veteran STMers expected to see these qualities again. First time participants expected to see these qualities because of the accounts of the veterans. The idealization of these encounters mainly occurred in three areas: family relationships, issues of poverty, and relationship building. Some STM members expressed an affinity for the strong family ties seen among their mission hosts. A strong theme of the idealization of the people in poverty ran through many of our conversations. However, one of the most influential themes in the discussions was the idea of building relationships. It was important to build relationships among the team members as well as those whom they would be serving. The design of the teams' preparations and time in the host country provided for a space for idealizations to flourish.[26] Our discussion of idealizations will focus on three areas: issues of marriage and family, issues of wealth and poverty, and the desire for relationships with team members and mission hosts, both separately and commonly.

26. See Occhipinti, "Religious Idealism."

Marriage and Family

For some participants, issues of family were of key importance. While many STM participants admired the family dynamics they expected to encounter, they were also willing to be an agent of change in familial relationships. The relationship between these was, at times, complicated but it was unclear if the STMers were engaging with those complexities. Walter and Jaqueline Williams, the couple charged with the specific task of teaching parenting skills and marriage enrichment courses, were distressed that the divorce rate in their host nation was around 70 percent. The ruling communist government was to blame, in many ways, according to Walter and Jacqueline, because the government was taking away the role of the husband as provider or primary bread winner. Their solution was to offer classes that provided instruction using biblical references for marital and parental education. This curriculum was written in the United States for American families and thus provided challenges of cultural adaptation that seemed to excite Walter and Jaqueline. For example, the curriculum offered solutions for working through difficulties of adjusting to new teenage drivers in the home or coping with the changes that accompany a child moving off to attend college or university. These were situations their hosts (now students) would not have to face. The cultural differences between Walter and Jaqueline and their future students were significant. However, they planned on figuring out new examples of these sort of challenges upon arrival through a few hours of discussion. They were sure that they could help provide answers to the challenges their hosts/students would face.

Dennis and Vicky Oden were participating in the same trip as the Williamses. They said they are "excited about" the fact that the Walter and Jacqueline were "doing the parenting thing." While there seems to be a need for family and parental education, there is also great admiration for the families the Odens expected to see again on this their third trip. Dennis talked about the deep bonding that he saw amongst family members because of the perceived lifestyle difficulties that families face. "Everything is rationed. . . . It's amazing how the families will bond because they have no cars. . . . They walk together; they're so close. And if the kids are married and need a bedroom they build a second story on their house." Such differences seemed to lead the Odens to see their hosts as having much stronger family units than many families in their own country. However, it was difficult to ascertain if this stood in contrast to their teammates' efforts to provide marital and parental education based on an adapted American curriculum.

They were not the only ones who felt who felt as though their hosts would exhibit qualities of family life that the STMers did not have. Anna

Barrows was taking her first STM trip, sponsored by Clear River UMC. In Central America, her team would be working on a construction project under the direction of an American missionary in that country. The team went through some cultural sensitivity training material immediately before our focus group interview. One point mentioned in the material was that a stereotype of Americans is that they are all rich. However, Anna expected to see things in her hosts that were lacking in the United States. "They may be rich in things we're not." When I asked her for an example, she replied, "Maybe a closer family, because they have to depend upon each other more, [for example, the rely on their] extended family. I expect to see great things. Like I said, you learn about yourself. But I have no idea what I will learn. But I expect to learn a lot."

Paula Davis, from Ramen UMC, noted how children in families and in the larger community seemed to get along well together. "They had the best time with nothing," Paula said. "Those kids were out there playing in the afternoons. The little ones and the big ones were all playing together. I didn't see one mean word, the big ones were helping. . .they were playing some kind of tag game, going back and forth." She contrasted this with American children who have "too much stuff" but complain of boredom. At times, the expressed understanding seemed to be that those the STMers encountered in their travels had richer interpersonal relationships, and richer spiritual lives, because of their lack of material goods and/or basic needs.

Poor and Smiling

The notion that the STMers expected to learn from their hosts how to be more spiritual with fewer material possessions was prevalent in several narratives. The STMers often seemed to feel that they had many material goods, but did not feel as spiritual. This juxtaposition was often expressed in terms of wealth and spirituality. Such a juxtaposition could be summed up with a statement typical STMers might make about the people they would encounter on their travels: "They are so spiritually wealthy, but materially impoverished. I am so materially wealthy, but spiritually impoverished." Team leader Larry Harris expressed his admiration for Christian worship among those whom he saw as materially poor. He recalled his experience in a worship service:

> They're so uninhibited. They freely worship because the only thing they really have to offer is themselves to God. That's what makes them free. 'Cause they really don't have much. And even when they give an offering of the small amount they give, we

actually had a Conga line around the church, you know, dancing, around the church. . .after the offering. Which is truly amazing to me. For them to have that kind of joy to give what they have.

Team Leader Will Manning would agree. "Those people have little, but they tithe on what they have," he said. He marveled at the way that church leadership holds people accountable to the practicing of giving 10 percent of their income, and its effectiveness: "80 percent of the people tithe. And as you walk in the door, the main entrance of the church, there's this big bulletin board there with every church member's name on it. . .and their giving. Can you imagine if you did that in your church. . .or in our church? [Laughs]." He admired those who tithed on the little money that they had. He also lamented the idea that though members of his church had much more money, they did not give with the same generous spirit. This, he said, was due to these factors of poverty, material goods, and spirituality. His church has a multi-million dollar annual operating budget, and he affirmed that people do give.[27] Yet, he felt his own church lacked the spiritual power he perceived in the host church, and wished his church was more like the one they would see on the STM trip.

His teammate Laura Denson explained this a bit more when she talked about the joy she perceived in the churches she has seen:

> I wish we could show you the video of them jumping up and down and dancing and singing and they are so happy. They have literally nothing. They have nothing. And you come back and you see people with a lot of stuff here and they're not nearly as happy as those people that are down there. So many people [here at our church], you look at them, they go to church and they don't really have joy. They don't really seem to connect with the Scripture. So those are the people that you want to see have some joy. You want them to have that light. That burning faith. It gives you that burning faith. It lights you up.

I asked her what she thought her hosts would say if they could worship at her church where thousands worship each week. "I think that they would probably say our worship services are weak." This is because the hosts' church services are "spirit-filled." The superiority of the hosts' service over the American service, she said, could be seen in the length of the service. "When you go to a church service down there, it's not an hour; it's not a thirty-minute sermon. If someone gets up and talks for less than forty-five minutes, that's a short sermon. So, a church service there is two hours." By

27. This would be in addition to what would be spent for debt servicing and capital-related expenses.

contrast, most services in her church last approximately one hour. Such a dichotomy seemed to indicate to her that her Cuban host churches had something that hers desperately lacked: a spirituality whose source was the poverty in which the worshippers found themselves. This was despite the fact that Laura and Will's church is, by their own description, not a "typical Methodist Church" and is among the largest United Methodist churches in the United States.

The STM participants in the data set seemed to expect that their encounter with the poor but happy would have some sort of positive effect on them. Rev. Wallace spoke of the way he designs trips for his college students: "The bigger picture is to help students be disciples of Christ." His ministry seeks to invite students to participate in the "abundant life of Jesus Christ." This "abundant life" is for students to find for themselves and to share with others:

> Mission trips help us do both. It helps them to grow in that abundant life and experience that helps process what that is and what they could be and should be for their lives on down the road. But also share that abundant life with people that are often very poor and destitute. And it is eye-opening to see that a lot of those people already have an abundant life. And it has nothing to do with the technology or the conveniences that we have here. It is completely divorced of that. Students wrestle on mission trips. If it is done right, students wrestle. . . . I hope students wrestle and start to get uncomfortable with the way they've been doing things and hopefully. . .reorient their lives a little bit more towards the way that it is meant to be lived.

Earlier in this chapter Rev. Wallace spoke of the way he designs his trips to put students "out of their comfort zones." Such encounters with the poor are part of the movement outside of that comfort zone for the benefit of the students' personal growth. "I feel like that is part of what makes the conditions for that optimal. It's out of the ordinary." He went on to describe how the students' encounters with people who go to landfills in search of food or items, or seeing half-naked children, would lead them to wrestle with larger questions about the world, themselves, and the nature of God. This would lead them to take pause, he told me, and to give them an appreciation for their own lives. "There's a thankfulness for what you have for one thing. But there's also a desire to make it better. . . . [A] desire that says, 'What can I do to help these people?'"

The Benefit of Having Less?

Others mentioned the benefit of the absence of the distractions of technology as well. Without these hindrances, it seemed, those encountered on a STM trip had an advantage over the STM participants. Jeanette Adams, a veteran STM participant offered,

> [S]ometimes I think the more stuff you have and the busier you are the easier it is to get distracted and look at things unfavorably. [giggles] I mean the poor-pitiful-me kind of scenario that so many of us seem to fall into. The jealousy of, 'I don't have [the latest iPhone].' Well really? 'I don't have any food to eat.' I mean how is that even comparable? It's a perspective thing.

Others would agree with her. Pastor Mark Hughes described his encounters with his own children and the children he saw on a previous STM trip: "Our children think to be joyful you have to have a [new video game system] or a smart phone. All this greatest technology that we have." He went on to describe what he saw in Latin America:

> [I watched] the local children just laugh and kick a flattened soccer ball. Didn't have any air in it. Wouldn't hold air. But they didn't care. Just the sheer joy. We think, 'Oh, this is just devastating circumstances and these poor, poor people.' They have something that we don't, at times.

That "something" that they have, he would say, is joy. Pastor Mark went on, "What I generally get out of it is. . .it reinforces my faith. It certainly does that. Just to see joy. . . . And I think just connecting with that joy at that level of faith."

Arthur McFarland, of Ramen UMC, also recalled his previous experiences on a STM to lament the state of the American culture. He described a time when he saw children, young and old, playing a game of tag. "And they had the best time with nothing. Then you've got our kids in America that are just bored out of their mind because they've got too much stuff." The "stuff" that the STM participants described was not just technological. Naomi Shaw, of Elmville UMC, recalled her first STM trip in which she stayed in an orphanage in Latin America. She offered to show the slideshow of pictures of the mold and mildew in the rooms that she took while there. Though they have no hot water in the orphanage, Naomi told us, the teenagers shared a room with joy. Their beds were made and the small boxes that held their belongings were tidy. Upon her return from that trip, Naomi recalled, she pointed this out to her own children while lamenting the fact that they each have their own bedrooms and they have "a whole closet full" of clothes. Such an encounter, she said, should change the way Americans live.

A strong influence in the narratives was that the encounter with those in poverty would lead one to a deeper reverence for those who have little money. Those with little money seemed to have a much deeper connection to God than those who have their needs met. "Because without so many material possessions, they have a stronger relationship with God. Because they depend on him for their daily bread. And they're not hampered by all this stuff that, you know, we have," said Jaqueline Williams, of City Central UMC. For this reason, she told me, "I firmly feel like short-term mission trips are very beneficial to whoever goes."

The Burden of Having More?

These benefits came not only through what was perceived as a spiritual depth amongst the poor. Jaqueline went on to say that one of the ways these benefits occur is "because you're exposed to a world totally different from your own. It makes you so thankful for what God has given us in this country." Her team leader Sally Manning expressed a similar sentiment,

> [Going on a short-term mission trip has] been a marvelous experience for me. I told somebody today, somebody was complaining about America and I said, [adopts a sing-song voice] 'You need to go to Cuba and see the people there.' [Laughs] I mean I think it's. . .just such an eye-opener and it makes you appreciate what we have here in America.

Philip O'Connor seemed to think that this sentiment would go beyond just his mission team, but also into the whole church. When discussing the involvement of the whole church in fundraising to support mission projects, he spoke of what he perceived to be the impact on all of the congregation:

> Because members [of the church] that have gone and have had that experience have come back with a great appreciation of what God has blessed us with. And what's expected of us due to the fact that we have received those blessings. The church is the people. So, the people that have gone, it has had a positive effect on them.

Similarly, Peter Browning expressed that his previous STM trips were beneficial to his outlook on things: "[I]t really makes me appreciate more what I got. We take so much for granted 'til you go somewhere else and figure out, you actually got it made." In the same sentiment, Audrey Nevins was preparing for her first STM trip when she talked about the personal impacts she expected from the trip: "I think it will change our point of view when we see things and not take things for granted that we have. Not give up things because we have too much or we are just tired of looking at it. I think we will really appreciate what we have."

What Is to Be Done about It?

Some team leaders felt as though there was a larger purpose in such feelings. They seemed to try to use such encounters as a prompt to "wrestle with" ideas to "help these people." The fact that the STM participants were engaged in mission-related activities would suppose that, at least at some level, they were indeed seeking to help those they encountered. Paula Davis expressed such an idea, "My prayer is that every day we can be a blessing and a positive impact." However, the encounter with those perceived to be in poverty was likely to have a variety of impacts on people. Team leader Richard Davis talked about how his teams reacted to the difficulties they were likely to face: "Things are tough. We see things that are hard. I've had people come back, the night we get back here, they're just bawling their eyes out. . .at what they've seen. And that's okay. That's compassion." However, his team member Arthur McFarland might react differently to such difficult sights. Arthur recalled to the small group his own feelings about their host country and a family member's previous experience there.

> It's like you time travel, because you leave [Central America] and two-and-a-half hours later you're in [the United States]. It's like you've left the early 1900s in some respects. My daughter went to [Central America] on a [short-term mission] trip. She said when they got back to the Miami airport, they went, 'God Bless America! God Bless America! God Bless America!' [laughs] I thought that was great. Pretty funny.

Such expressed ideas provided an interesting tension among the narratives. On the one hand, there seemed to be a strongly expressed idea that the STMers wanted to be more like those whom they encountered on their trips. They seemed to want something that the mission hosts had and they did not: a deeper spirituality that came from their financial situations. The STMers lamented their own lack of faith and their own physical wealth. On the other hand, there seemed to be a strong sense that when one encounters the hardships of others on a STM trip, gratitude to God for one's place of birth and current place in the world is a valid response. While no one made a direct statement like, "I thank God that I am not like them," it seems appropriate to ask if that is the next step for such gratitude. The mix of gratitude for current blessings and a movement towards compassion was not clearly distinguishable. They seem to mix together and flow back and forth. In many regards, the STM participants in the dataset did not clearly engage with the larger issues around these ideas. Even when I asked directly, these principles of spirituality in poverty did not seem to transfer to those who are impoverished in the United States or in the local communities of the STM team members. This may be due to a lack of engagement with the poor in their home communities. Among those with whom I spoke about their overseas STM work and their mission work at home, there seemed to be a sense that some were called to work overseas and some were called to work at home. Many times, those two areas of service did not mix. To be fair, many STMers did say that they worked in local mission projects and many participated in domestic STM mission trips. However, there was also a clear distinction between the local and the foreign work in many discussions.

It is intriguing that the interview participants spoke little about what they had done with the feelings and/or information they had after returning from a STM trip. Though many spoke of the almost sacred encounters they seemed to have with the poor, their spirituality, and their desire to be more like that, there was an absence of narratives that expressed the steps people took to be more like the poor through, say, shunning worldly possessions. Many of those who lamented technology's interruption on their lives still used smartphones and computers. Naomi Shaw, who expressed appreciation for the teenagers in the orphanage and lamented her children's abundance of clothes, did not say that she sold those clothes to be more like those she saw on her previous trips. Jaqueline Williams felt hampered with all of her "stuff" but did not talk about how she unburdened herself of some of that "stuff."[28] She summed up well what many people expressed, "I firmly feel like short-term mission trips are very beneficial to whoever goes." But what those benefits are exactly, why they come about, and how they are used, is a picture still coming into focus. I will offer some lenses that should make this somewhat clearer in the discussion that follows.

For now, it is important to note that no one in the research group expressed a desire to make the significant changes in money or status to be more like those they seemed to idealize. While they appreciated seeing the poor and their wealth of spirituality, many also seemed to want to say what Arthur's daughter exclaimed upon arriving back to the United States, "God

---

28. Of course, it is possible that some participants did, in fact, take such steps. However, there was no evidence of such in the data.

Bless America!" Whether those encountered on STM trips were actually as poor as they were perceived to be, or as spiritual as they appeared, is difficult to ascertain. One limitation of this ethnographic study is that the STM participants were interviewed before their trip in an isolated context: their sponsoring church and/or organization. I had no contact with those whom the interviewees described. However, other research proves helpful in a discussion of the accounts above.

Are Things Really the Way They Seem?

Terrence Linhart's ethnographic grounded theory study of high school students on a STM trip to Ecuador provides some interesting parallels to my own field research. Linhart described how his research participants marveled at the perceived lack of material needs in the people of Ecuador, and at the great joy that they seemed to have in spite of this. His students saw their home culture greatly lacking in spiritual commitment for God, yet they saw their hosts as living with a spiritual depth they desired for themselves. The high school students saw themselves as "blessed" for where they were born and the opportunities afforded them by their upbringing. However, this also brought a perceived burden for the students: these material "blessings" were seen as distractions from an authentic faith as described in the New Testament. They found themselves in passionless churches, surrounded by material goods.[29] As a result, ministry leaders designed "short-term cross-cultural service trips [to] offer a brief moment for students to experience faith with a new passion and purpose that counters a consumeristic culture's influences."[30]

One difficulty with such brief cross-cultural encounters is the tendency for a short-term trip to "resemble an interactive museum"[31] where the visitors play with children, work alongside manual laborers on construction projects, or "perform religious dramas or programs, while waving or smiling across the chasm of [the] language barrier."[32] Interpreters are limited and communication can be stilted. Smiles and gestures and reduced phrases become an essential means of communication. Such encounters can lead STM participants to generalizations that gestures, smiles and lack of significant communication somehow hold profound meaning. "[T]hey reduce

---

29. Linhart, "They Were So Alive!," 451–53.
30. Linhart, "They Were So Alive!," 453.
31. Linhart, "They Were So Alive!," 455.
32. Linhart, "They Were So Alive!," 455.

their knowledge of the 'Other' to that particular encounter."[33] Linhart described a student who was a veteran of STM trips who later returned to live with her hosts from her trips. She was confronted with the reality that though her hosts were committed and loving Christians, they did not exude the same joy and happiness she had generalized them to have during her previous mission trips. Her unrealistic, over-simplistic conceptions of her hosts could not be applied to the workaday world in which they truly lived.[34]

Linhart gave a high school student's account of an encounter with a child in Ecuador. "Lauren" was moved to tears when a young Ecuadorean boy shared a bag of fruit with her STM team. She understood that

> he lived with five brothers and his mother in a hammock that was right beyond where we were sitting. I looked at the little hammock with all the little kids, I was completely broken. Uh, tears ran down my cheeks. I just thought of how much we have and [how] much we take it for granted. . .and these kids have nothing. No food. No house. They live in a hammock and that's it. And yet this little boy gave us this fruit. We didn't need it at all, but he wanted us to have it. . . . It's gonna be a hard week for me as I see these kids and just how little they do have. I'm so excited just to love 'em and just to be a friend to them. And, it was just an awesome, awesome experience.[35]

In reality, Linart reported, the young boy did not live in the hammock, but hung his hammock outside his family's store and lived in the apartment above the store. Lauren and her team later learned that the boy's family ran the store and he spent his days in the hammock when the store was open. Though she later learned the truth of the situation, her narrative of the encounter remained entrenched in the misinterpretation of what she first observed. Such inaccurate, and unrevised, conclusions were normative for Linhart's study:

> It is not fair to say that the students were constructing a meaning that was not present in the encounters. There was a sense of joy and excitement on the faces and in the lives of those they met. The problem was that the students generalized that observation to the entire existence of the lives of their hosts and to the culture as a whole. The short-term trip, by its very design and purpose, seemed to force participants to stereotype.[36]

33. Linhart, "They Were So Alive!," 455.
34. Linhart, "They Were So Alive!," 455–56.
35. Linhart, "They Were So Alive!," 457.
36. Linhart, "They Were So Alive!," 458.

My conversations with team members uncovered similar accounts of those whom the STM participants encountered. Does the church where Larry Harris worshipped have a conga line each Sunday after the offering? In Rev. Wallace's efforts to put students "outside their comfort zones," was he leading them to make false projections about the conditions they observed? Were they encouraged to stereotype their own little boy in a hammock to be typical of all of the people of their host country? Were the hosts truly holders of the "abundant life," as he proposed? Was there joy in playing with a flattened soccer ball, as Pastor Hughes purported? Did their lack of technology bring them inner peace that seemed so elusive to his STM team members? If families with fewer resources are happier because they must walk everywhere and therefore spend more time together, as Dennis and Vicky Oden recalled, why were their teammates offering marriage and parenting classes? This tension seemed lost on them. Did the orphans Naomi Shaw observed during her trip later encounter conflicts and struggles (as would be expected amongst any group of teens) when the STM team guests were absent? Again, the scope of this study does not permit a full answer to these questions. However, research suggests that the narratives of the STMers in the dataset are consistent with a larger body of work.[37] It is possible that, like Linhart's research group, my STM research participants "generalized [their] observation to the entire existence of the lives of their hosts and to the culture as a whole."[38] Vicky Oden told us, "[Our mission hosts], they're poor, but they're smiling." But for how long? Did those smiles continue after Vicky was out of sight? These are issues that a robust theology of mission should address and thus influence the shaping of motivations and subsequent practices. I will discuss this further in the following chapters.

Building Relationships among Team Members

Be they stereotypes or not, the STMers desired more than mere observation or small interactions with their national hosts. A predominant theme in our discussions was one of relationships. For many in the dataset, the building of relationships seemed a key component to a successful trip done in the name of mission. STM team leaders and members alike described their desire to form relationships with one another and with those whom they would encounter on their trip. For some team leaders, the relationship building among the team members was a prerequisite for effectiveness in the service work and an end goal of their efforts.

37. See chapter 4.
38. Linhart, "They Were So Alive!," 458.

As noted earlier in this chapter, teams were often formed according to the commonalities they have outside of the work they may do on their trip.[39] Who was participating in the trip was a determining factor for some when deciding whether to go with the team or not. Husband and wife Mack and Lena Anderson discussed their last mission trip, who participated, and the role they played in influencing their participation in this one.

> LENA: We became very close [last time]. As a group. [Mack affirms.] Because this is the second time that we are going with a number of the people on the team. And the friendships have remained when we returned.

> MACK: Yeah, I met a lot of people that were going back. Made me want to go.

> LENA: Because we really debated on whether we were going back or not this year. And then everybody else was going and we were feeling bad that we weren't going.

Their "feeling bad" to be left out may seem quite natural considering the way teams are described and designed. Team leader Richard Davis described the way he designed his teams to think of themselves as a family:

> When I train a team, I talk to them about . . . 'You're becoming a part of a family. You'll always be a part of this family. You'll see people five to ten years down the road and you'll stay a part of that family of that mission team that you went on.' It is always about building relationships among the team. . . . We'll have a chance to get to know each other. Because a lot of people [who] come on these teams. . .are people that I've been with several times. . . . [W]e get new people every year that have never been on a mission trip. So we get them incorporated in our idea how to do missions. . . . . You become very close. That doesn't always mean that you're going to agree. You'll have spats. Every family does. And that's fine. We'll work through it. But I think that's very important before you go. [During the trip it is important to have] time for devotions and not just working, but to really have time there to know each other. And share their experiences. I always have devotion in the morning, and in the evening have a

---

39. A notable exception to this was the medical team from Riverbend UMC. Many, but not all, of the team members from Riverbend were selected for their medical expertise. The team was also comprised of non-medical workers who were chosen for the commonalities over skills and/or experience.

short devotion and have time to share things that went on during the day.

In describing devotions, Richard and other team leaders often referred to a time of contemplation of God and/or Scripture reading and reflection upon the Scriptures. Team leaders reported that devotions before trips were typically held at the beginning of a team meeting to discuss ideas that team members may face on their upcoming trip. Reported devotions during the trip were typically to discuss a Scripture and/or ways in which the team sensed God was at work that day. Notice that Richard's discussion of devotions was couched in terms of the building of relationships among the team members. The devotional times were there to have time "to know each other" and to "share experiences." Note that earlier in this chapter, when asked, Richard did not describe his motivations for mission in any particular Scripture. Additionally, he wrestled with the distinctions of Christian mission and secular efforts at relief and development. The possibility that Scripture is used primarily for the building of relationships among team members rather than the training of those who seek to engage in mission service is potentially problematic. We will discuss this further in chapter 8.

Richard's language of family and mission going hand-in-hand occurred in other narratives as well. Larry and Carla Harris emphasized their role as leaders of the "team" and "family:"

> It's more about relationship [early on]. Trying to build a relationship so that we can have a connection with one another while we are there for two weeks. . . . [W]hat you need to do is look at each other, help each other, support each other, because these two weeks we're going to have together will never be the same as when these two weeks are over. So you need to find how you're supposed to connect with one another and with the people God puts in your path. And that's the relationship building we are trying to do for the whole year [of preparation for the trip]. Saying, 'Ok. Here we are for one another. We're trying to help each other, raise funds, work together, have fun, and just build those relationships.' And that's the main thing is building those relationships with one another. . . . I think it's very important to have a united team. If you don't the mission is just going to go downhill from there.

When I asked Larry and Carla to prioritize their goals for a STM trip, their response came easily:

> It's team building. I'd say the priority is building relationship with one another, feeling like we are family. . . . The higher

priorities [are to] let the Spirit use you while you're there to accomplish the mission we think they have been called to go do.
[O]ur team is to go work. But that's not the reason we go. We
have them focus on their spiritual growth, getting closer to God
and on trying to hear his voice. To be able to get in tune with
that to be able to say, 'God is calling me to talk to this person.
God is drawing this person to me. Why? Why am I here? Is it
to talk to this person? To be a friend with this person for these
two weeks?'. . . . The priority is the relationship with one another,
and then trying to figure out what God has for them during the
two weeks.

The team from Elmville UMC was also looking forward to the relationships with team members. Team member Peter Browning was looking
forward to getting away from it all. Speaking of his experience from his
previous trips: "The biggest thing you're going to learn when we go, is you
are going to forget about everything else. Because down there. . .we didn't
have TVs. . .we just kick back. We sat around. We talked. We joked. We play
around. Don't worry about nothing. Time is. . .irrelevant." When I asked
the team from Elmville how they would, months after the trip, measure the
success of their mission efforts, Naomi Shaw offered,

It's already a success. It's already brought us together. . . . [W]e
might have seen each other around town. I might have run into
him, but I didn't [know him]. . . . We've already built a relationship. And we know that we have that common goal [this trip].
We know that that's something that we are interested in.

The participants at Christian Campus Ministry with whom I spoke
seemed keen on building relationships with their team members. It seemed
to motivate Christina Potts in her decision to go on the team: "This is my
third year at [Christian Campus Ministry]. I have seen [people at the minis-
try] go on a mission trip before. And I saw how my friends had fun and they
got a lot out of it. So, when the opportunity came this time around, I said, 'I
want to do this. I definitely want to do this.'" When I asked what her friends
had told her about it, Christina replied that it seemed to "really impact"
them and such an impact was how God told her to be a part of it. They
spoke of the camaraderie they felt as they prepared for their trip. Getting to
know others who were going with them appeared to have opened new social
venues for them and this provided an extra level of what they described as
excitement.

Many team members and leaders alike said that preparing for a STM
trip was a labor-intensive and time-consuming process. As mentioned

earlier in this chapter, raising funds to pay for the trip was one way in which teams spent their time and gave their labor in preparation. Fundraising efforts included church-wide or community-wide cooking events in which the proceeds were given to the team's efforts. The Campus Ministry team seemed to participate in even more fundraising efforts than most teams, likely due to their current situations as college students. Their food sales, t-shirt sales, letter-writing campaigns, manual labor jobs, and other efforts provided more than just a chance to make some money to pay for their expenses. Recall Rev. Keith Wallace's reasoning: "There's a certain element of misery to it. When people are in misery together, it is a bonding experience."

The seeking of such bonding experiences was a common thread throughout many of the focus-group interviews. The STMers expected to bond with one another and grow closer to God on their short-term trip. Charles Franklin seemed to sum up the narratives well,

> I can say that I am friends with everybody in here. . . . But growing spiritually with them is such an awesome experience that I am so excited to do and have experiences together that we can talk about that we have all grown in Christ. We have all done something amazing. And we can talk about this later. And growing spiritually with them is what makes me excited about it.

When I probed the idea of removing the element of the team interaction as the goal of mission, the notion was not completely dismissed. However, there was a feeling that something important would be missing. "Part of the experience is sharing the trip with other people and you bonding with other people," said Gregory Booth. "If you're by yourself, you don't have that. It is all contained in you and there's no one to share it with. It is less enjoyable."

Accounts such as these, that affirm the importance of building relationships among the team members, suggest that one goal of the STM trip is for the benefit of those who go, rather than those in the host nations. That a venture would be made in the name of "mission" but have as its goal a sort of personal transformation runs counter to the theology of mission we have previously discussed. While we do not have time to fully engage this problem here, I will discuss this further in the subsequent chapters.

Building Relationships with Mission Hosts

The building of relationships with team members was but one facet of the relationship paradigm for the participants. Building relationships with the people whom they sought to serve was equally or more important. The short, but intense, time with their mission hosts seemed to provide the environment to grow what were perceived as deep bonding experiences for many.

Richard Davis' account again provides a helpful summary about STM and the desire on the part of the American service participants to build relationships with their hosts.

> It's good for me. . . . The people [we meet overseas invigorate me]. It's nice for me. I tell [my team members], you know the old thing about them: the first thing we do is build relationships, I really talk about that: among the team, among the church and the team, and among the people we're serving with down there. . . . I think. . .the relationships with the people you serve [are] as important or more important than building relationships with the team.

Richard provides many opportunities in his mission trips for team members to spend time with the mission hosts in an effort to build such relationships. These opportunities were on the worksite, during the children's ministry activities, or at special events for the people from the host church. Mack Anderson, who was in his seventies and had health problems that sometimes limited his participation, described the work he did, and the relationships he said he built, on his last trip.

> I was on a construction crew. I enjoyed seeing the people and watching them. And being around working with them. They're great people. They appreciated it, no more than I could do. I was there trying to help. And if things were too heavy on a particular job, I'd hand them nails. Anything to keep it moving. They were great. You could see them smile. They smiled a lot.

He went on to describe how this was the way that he built relationships with his hosts and contributed to the "good experience" that his mission trip was last time. This positive experience seemed to be a strong motivator for his return on this trip. The smiles were enough to lead him to believe that they had a growing relationship.

In several different ways team leaders and team members alike suggested that the essence of their work was to "build relationships" with the people they would see on their STM trip. James Fellows of Ramen UMC seemed certain that his simple proximity to his hosts would lead to positive outcomes for all involved. Team members from City Central UMC seemed to agree. Jaqueline Williams felt that the nurturing of relationships was primary among the goals for the service trip. The building of relationships, she said, was the way "to show them the love of Christ. To let them know that there are people, right across the Caribbean, that love them and care, care very deeply about what happens to them. And we want to support their church. And them individually. So, I'm very much into the relationship part of it." When asked about their motivations and expectations for participating in the STM trip, participants offered answers like:

- "We will [connect] with another community"
- "Getting to know the Nicaraguan people"
- "To learn more about the community and to continue our service to them"
- "To continue the work started last year and resume relationships"
- "Relationships with Cuban people"
- "Further bonding with Cuban friends"
- "To grow in my relationship with God and fellowship with the Costa Ricans"

Minimizing the Differences

The differences between the parties in these relationships did not seem to present a problem for many STMers. One such barrier, and perhaps the most obvious, is the language.[40] Recall that of the fifty-five focus group participants, thirty (56 percent) reported having no experience or training in the language of their hosts. Twenty-four reported varying levels of proficiency.[41] The remaining one reported fluency in the hosts' language. However, the STM participants were undaunted by the challenges this could bring. Gregory Booth was particularly confident, "Language barriers are issues, but it is surprising how much you can communicate without speaking the language." Additionally, all teams employed nationals secured by their host churches and/or missionaries to serve as translators. Not only did this serve to employ members of the local community and church, it also pro-

40. During a STM, it is unlikely that team members will be called upon to read and/or write in the host language to a great degree. Oral communication with mission hosts and leaders is the primary form of communication.

41. Language proficiency is difficult to measure in such focus group settings. Considering the combined data found in written biographical information and oral interviews, there is likely a wide variance of understanding when they reported having "some" proficiency of the language. It is likely that participants both over and under reported their abilities.

vided means for the team members to function on the worksites, participate in church activities, and move about in the host country.

The STM focus group participants may have felt that the language was no problem, but their mission hosts may have felt otherwise. As noted in chapter 4, Martin Hartwig Eitzen considered STM from a Latin American perspective. In his study of Latin American hosts of American STM teams, 81 percent of survey respondents considered the STMers' lack of a working knowledge of the language a hindrance to their mission work.[42] While many of the focus groups did offer some language training, it was often in the form of a handout of key phrases. Some team leaders offered further language training in team meetings. Some team members enrolled in courses outside of team efforts. However, there did not seem to be an emphasis on language skills. Rather, those differences were minimized or team members allowed the burden to rest upon the hired translators.

The relationships between Mack Anderson and his smiling co-workers may not have been as deep as they seemed. Again, Linhart's study is helpful in investigating these interactions. He pointed out, "Because of a limited amount of translators and a language barrier blocking their ability to communicate, [STM participants] will often smile and make gestures to their hosts, hoping they communicate the intended message of warmth and kindness."[43] As a result, STMers reduced nonverbal communication to simplistic understandings. When STM participants "essentialize and generalize the observed gestures of others to hold significant meaning, they reduce their knowledge of the 'Other' to that particular encounter."[44]

Those serving on STM teams in my focus groups also attempted to minimize discrepancies of wealth. One gave an account from a previous trip of the immaculate condition he observed at a home near where they were working. Though the home was small, and on a tiny piece of land, he noted that it "was just perfectly clean." This was admirable, he told his teammates, considering the difficult conditions near the home's location. Reflecting on it, he said, "I really have learned to appreciate her, talk to her, that widow. And I did communicate with her some. It was just real interesting observing her and trying communicate with her." Such encounters seemed to typify the entire culture for many STM participants.

The level at which participants expected to bond with their mission hosts was just as deep, or perhaps deeper, than the depth of relationships they expected to encounter with their fellow team members. As mentioned

---

42. Eitzen, "Short-Term Missions," 42.

43. Linhart, "They Were So Alive!," 455.

44. Linhart, "They Were So Alive!," 455.

above, STM members idealized their perceptions of the hosts' relationships with their families and their perceptions of the joy they saw in the midst of poverty. The relationships between team members and hosts were similarly idealized. They seemed to expect an outcome that was beyond the sum of its parts. A trip of two weeks or less, in a foreign culture, while working on projects outside their normal expertise, "while waving or smiling across the chasm of [the] language barrier"[45] can provide many difficulties when trying to build meaningful relationships. However, many felt undaunted. The solution for the members of Ramen UMC was to celebrate in some unique ways, as I illustrate next.

Partying through the Differences

When I spoke to Kate Powell, a long-time member of Ramen UMC, she was looking forward to her ninth STM trip. Several of these trips had been to this same location. She recalled her previous trips in which one of her mission hosts had asked, through an interpreter, about a work apron she had brought for her personal use. She reported that she felt a special bond with this "certain older lady" who asked about her apron. Rather than merely give one item to one person, Kate decided to return with an apron for everyone. Between trips she collected from the ladies of her home church enough aprons, many homemade, to share with the ladies in the host church. On her next mission trip, she presented the aprons to the ladies of the church at a party. For the presentation party, Kate brought several bottles of nail polish. The ladies of the STM team painted the fingernails and toenails of the mission hosts. Believing that the ladies of the host community wanted makeup and lipstick next time, Kate set the ladies of her home church to work again. Before her next trip, she again requested help in gathering items to take back. "The ladies in [our] church went really crazy helping me. We got makeup bags donated. Beautiful ones. And we filled those bags with stuff for those ladies and it was really special," Kate said. Kate presented these at a makeup party for the ladies of the host church on her following trip. Having exhausted those avenues, this time the team was planning on a "Holy Spirit on fire" dance party. The party portion of the trip seemed to become a normal expectation for the hosts and guests alike.

Kate's teammate, Jeanette Adams, spoke of such parties as ways to show the mission hosts that they are "valued" by the STMers. She described a time at the nail painting party when she was filing the fingernails and toenails of a leader in the community. She knew of the woman from her

---

45. Linhart, "They Were So Alive!," 455.

work there, but said that she was "just the one that I wound up sitting with." The woman was moved to tears by the attention she was receiving from the STM team members. Through an interpreter she asked Jeanette why she was doing this. "I said, 'God brought us together. And we're going to bond in this moment. And we are going to be friends forever. I'm going to think about you. You're going to think about me. I am going to pray for you and your community.' And as soon as we stepped off the bus, [on the next trip]. . .she came [running towards us]."

Experiences such as these were ways in which the STMers reported feeling a deep connection with their hosts. Many reported that they hoped to feel a deep connection with members of their host communities in the upcoming trips as well. The great distance, length of time between visits, limited communication between visits, language and cultural barriers, and other differences were minimized in order to seek a deeper something beyond themselves. Not only did STMers idealize the people and places, but they seem to idealize the time spent as well. The "connection" between host and guest was a prevalent topic in interviews with focus group participants. STM participants seemed to realize that their time was short and they should make the most of it. Though their differences were great, many STMers seemed to feel they were making significant connections with their hosts. STM team members asserted that their personal presence was important in order to serve appropriately. Whether this is for the benefit of the guests, the hosts, the mission, or some combination thereof is difficult to ascertain. Like the idealization of poverty, and the issues around it, the idealization of relationships was a dominant theme in the research data.

In the follow-up survey, participants were asked if they had been in contact with their mission host leader and volunteers and/or those they served in the host country. About half (n=16) of the respondents reported that they intended to see them on another STM trip. Nearly the same number (n=17) reported connecting with them through social media. Almost one-third (n=9) said that they have seen them in person.[46] This data, however, is somewhat difficult to interpret. Because respondents were allowed to select more than one answer it is difficult to discern in what ways these overlap. It is interesting that nine people reported seeing their hosts since their last trip. It is possible that some had made another trip to the host country before taking the survey. Or perhaps someone, or a group of people, from the host country made a visit to the United States. In the pre-trip interviews, I learned that some mission hosts do travel to the United States on occasion to visit churches with whom they have worked previously. The

---

46. Respondents were allowed to select more than one answer.

follow-up questionnaire did not ask participants to distinguish themselves as either a team leader or a team member. It is possible that some of these contacts were team leaders preparing for another trip. Due to the limitations of the survey question and the lack of the follow-up interviews, it is difficult to ascertain the nature of an ongoing relationship between STMers and their mission hosts.

As I pointed out in chapter 4, the practice of STM was criticized in some of the academic literature as doing little to make a long-term difference in the lives of either the STMers or their mission hosts. Ver Beek's study of STM teams indicated that the vast majority (76.4 percent) of participants do not remain in contact with their hosts after they return to the United States, despite feeling as though they had established a meaningful relationship during their trip.[47] However, more recent studies are beginning to show longer term partnerships between those in the Global North and the Global South. Hunter Farrell's case study in Peru showed a leveraging of "significant social capital, including media coverage, professional and political contacts and expertise, scientific information and services, as well as prestige, legitimacy, and political power in ways they could not have accessed without the relationship with STM groups from the U.S.A."[48] However, it is impossible to move towards a more comprehensive understanding of such relationships without hearing more from those who host STM teams. The 2007 issue of the *Journal of Latin American Theology*, which was dedicated to works on STM, provided some perspective from STM hosts. Though some compared STM to "a person shaking fruit off a fruit tree only to leave it on the ground to rot in front of you,"[49] there was a message that at least some mission hosts desired longer-term, more meaningful relationships of ministry partnership and development.[50] Since this issue was published, millions of travelers and hosts have been affected by STM trips, yet it is difficult to tell if these meaningful relationships are now being developed. This is one area that needs careful further study. This is complicated, however, by the lack of follow-up expectations placed upon team members, which is demonstrated (to some extent) in the difficulty I had in securing the agreed-upon post-trip interviews. Whether STM trips, which are characterized by their brief, but intense, periods of interaction, can truly bring lasting, meaningful relationships is difficult to ascertain. Many STMers in my study seemed to re-aggregate into their normal patterns soon after returning home. Only

---

47. Ver Beek, "Impact," 487.

48. Farrell, "Global Discipleship," 175.

49. Cook and Hoogen, "Missiologically and Morally Responsible," 49.

50. See Maslucán, "Short-Term Missions."

six strongly or somewhat disagreed with the statement, "I built strong rela-tionships with the people on my team during the trip, but now that I have returned my relationship priorities are with my work, my family and my home life."

One case of a team leader making meaningful long-term relationships may be the case of Philip O'Connor. Philip has served on STM trips for over two decades. He says that he has a strong command of the language, though he will not say that he is fluent. He regularly returns to the same places when he leads STM trips. He travels to these places even when he is not leading teams. Between trips, he reported that he communicated with his international connections by e-mail, telephone, and handwritten letters. Other team leaders reported ongoing relationships with mission hosts that revolved around project and trip planning. Philip's case was the only one that transcended to such a personal level.

In this section, we have heard the narratives of STMers and the ideal-izations they formed around their activities. These idealizations were made around the perceived family relations of their hosts. STMers expressed ad-miration for the perceived spirituality in spite of, or because of, the poverty observed. We also examined the pervasive idealization of the relationships between team members themselves and with their mission hosts. The is-sue of relationships, both with the team members and the mission hosts, flowed in and out of several aspects of the focus group interviews, team leader interviews, and written biographical information. It was particularly strong when I posed the question of if the STM teams should just stay home and send solely monetary support instead. The matter of relationships and proximities is important to the next part of our discussion.

PROXIMITIES

The idea that the team members must be present in the lives of those they sought to serve was strong throughout the conversations. This was particu-larly evident when I posed a hypothetical situation to the groups that voices a common criticism of the practice of sending teams out on short-term service trips.

Why Not Just Send the Money?

As mentioned above, research shows that those who participate in such service trips spend an average of $1,000 per person, in addition to expenses incurred for transportation to and from the international destinations.[51] The focus group teams in this research project were no exception, spending upwards of $30,000 to send a STM team. Therefore, I offered them the chance to respond to some of the criticisms of the efficacy of these trips for the finances expended. The situation I posed went as follows: Let us pretend we were having this discussion in a nearby café. A stranger at the next table happened to overhear us. The stranger politely interjected into the conversation with an affirmation of the efforts the group members were about to undertake. She then offered to make a financial donation equal to the amount that all the team members were about to spend on the trip, including transportation. The only requirement was that the team members must remain at home. Instead, all the funds would be sent directly to the mission and/or church they would serve. In other words I was asking them, "Why not just send the money?" The answers were a strong, and unanimous, "NO!" Their reasons for saying so generally fell along four different lines: 1) relationships, 2) showing love, 3) preventing corruption, and 4) the experience. I discuss each of these below.

Relationships

Some team members said that they posed the same question to their mission leaders before enlisting in their upcoming trip. In reply, one team leader offered, "we could [just send the money]. We could make an impact by sending money. But you miss that ministry of presence. You miss that opportunity to get to know people. You miss that opportunity to build those relationships with the people that you're working with." The idea of relationships was a dominant theme in the responses. Merely giving money was seen as an impersonal response to the issues their hosts faced. "I think it is an interpersonal relationship that makes a difference, for them and for us," replied Vicky Oden.

    Philip O'Connor gave a thoughtful response, as though he had previously been asked, "Why not just send the money?"

> Economically, efficiently, that's a valid criticism. But it's flawed. Where does the relationship come with that?. . . So, when you send the check, that's very efficient. But, where's the relationship? Where's the opportunity for the people in Nicaragua to see a gringo and say, 'You know, he left the comforts of his home to come work shoulder-to-shoulder with me.' How does that happen?

51. Priest and Priest, "They See Everything," 57.

Rev. Keith Wallace used a story from a previous trip to illustrate his assertion of the importance of participating in a trip rather than sending money alone. He recalled a time when he was helping lead a trip to Africa with a different ministry. While working on a construction site one day, he met a construction worker from a local company. The worker approached him with a big smile. When Keith asked why the big smile, his African host told him that he was glad that Keith was in his town. Keith's presence, he said, indicated Keith's love for him. Keith continued:

> You can't send money for that. People get aid. People find aid in places. But there's something about being there and making eye contact with [construction workers]. And that he's just giddy that you're there. That you care. That's the only reason that you cared, that you loved them. I know that doesn't happen all the time. . . . What judges success? That was a success moment for me.

Show the Love of Christ

Similar to Keith's story of showing love for the people whom he served, STM participants also wanted to show the Love of Christ to their hosts. As Arthur McFarland put it, by sending money alone:

> It wouldn't affect them the same way. They could get a check and get more done by hiring a contractor. But they wouldn't see the Love of Christ in the same way. . . . We are investing in them through our time and money. The time speaks more to them that we are there than if we just gave a check.

Christina Potts and some of her teammates would have agreed with Arthur. The investment of her time was a worthy venture. It was more important to "show God" to the people of their host country. It wasn't about the money, they said. It was about God. As Christina put it:

> Christ counted up the costs and said that we were worth it. Just like Christ counted the costs and said that the people of Costa Rica were worth it. We have a financial cost trying to get us there. But the real cost is the cost of our spirit that we are having to spend down there. You can throw millions of dollars down there. That could help them build tall buildings, but is it really going to help their spiritual life? Our lives may be the only Bible that some people may read.

Christina's affirmation that she may be "the only Bible that some people may read" may speak about the unknowns before her team. Despite being just a few months away from their trip, her team was not sure the location or the nature of the work they would have to do. However, it also belies the fact that her team was working through a local Christian missionary who had lived in Costa Rica for several years. Her hosts lived among some of the fastest growing Christian movements in the world.[52] Yet, she expects to encounter others who have little or no exposure to the Christian message. During our discussions, her enthusiasm was strong as she tried to bring her teammates to her way of thinking about the reason for their service.

Pastor Mark Hughes affirmed that money is important for STM trips, but it must be conjoined with a personal presence. He explained:

> It goes back to. . .being the hands and feet of Christ. And, money's important. You have to have money to make things happen. To pay for things. But you can't put a price tag on having Vacation Bible School. Even sitting and coloring with a child. You might not understand them; they might not understand you. They understand love. And they understand that you have taken your time to come down there and spend it with them. Whether that's painting a wall or coloring a picture. Or decorating a craft. They understand that and they understand you can't buy that. You can't just send money and communicate love. Yeah, money's important. And we need some to make things happen. We'll have to buy supplies. We'll have to pay folks to help us work. But the human connection can't be paid for.

Corruption Prevention

For some participants, being present along with the monies that were sent was as much for preventing the negative as it was for instilling the positive. It is common for teams to bring thousands of dollars in cash for construction projects they will work on during their week. They may also make a cash donation to the church and/or mission where they work to help with expenses throughout the year. Teams hire translators, cooks, drivers, and other workers during their time in the host country. If Americans are present with their cash donations they can help prevent its misuse. Philip O'Connor explains:

> [Y]ou're talking about an area of the world. . .part of that culture, and a part I don't appreciate is, there's corruption. There's

52. Jenkins, *Next Christendom*, 3.

corruption in the government. There's corruption at all levels. And they don't look at that corruption the same way we do. It's part of who they are. How are you going to ensure that the $14,000 is going to be used for the very way that you intend?

Philip's answer was to be present to ensure the money's proper use. Some of his team members would agree. Peter Browning wanted to know where every dollar of his donation was going. There was a feeling, as teammate Ed Grossman told us, that "Everybody wants a piece of America. . . . I mean, everybody would like to have your money."

Experience

Building relationships, offering Christian love, and preventing corruption were offered as reasons to not "just send the money." However, the reason that had the most influence on the data was something different. If the money were sent without the STM participants, then they would be missing out on something important: the experience. The assurance of the experience for the STMer was among the most significant reasons given for the international service travel. These reasons were also evident when it was suggested that the trip may be just as effective without the team members' participation.

Participants who were returning to communities where they previously served described in vivid detail the sights, smells, and sounds they expected to encounter. Another spoke of the richness of her own experience and how she expected to share that with another by hiring someone from the church to work at her home. Her goal was to allow the worker to earn extra money to pay for his immediate family to participate in an upcoming STM, thereby they could both provide an enriching experience for his family. Why is it so important to go? As one team leader illustrated:

> You miss the opportunity to experience first-hand what they're experiencing. And come back and share it with the people here in this church. That's what you miss when you don't go. . . . Missions is not just sending money. Missions is going and working side by side with other people in other countries and understanding their world from their viewpoint and you can't do that by sending money. . . . You have to go experience it. [He repeats for emphasis] You have to go experience it. And when you go experience it, again you come back a changed person. You can make a greater influence, a greater impact once you've experienced that than if you just sent money.

One's presence is required to experience an expected change, participants said. This was a recurring theme in the focus group data. When someone on her team mentioned the rewards for participating in a STM trip, Kate Powell had trouble describing such rewards. "I like to touch, see, and feel. And [our hosts] do too. . . . It's hard to put it into words. It really is. It is not like I want to feel extra special. But I do. It's not like I want to, it's just what happens. It's just like God putting that love in you. . . . You can't explain it." Her teammate Maureen Whitehall came a little closer to putting it into words,

> I felt like I was just on a mountain top. And I was so excited to get back to tell. . .what we did. The people we met. How wonderfully they would greet us. The children love on you. It was amazing to me. That's why I want to go back to that. I mean it's just an excitement that you can't explain.

Dr. Lyons, who has led more than a dozen STM trips, was clear that just sending money would be detrimental to his own teams and the people of South America. He told me that he did not feel the doctors in his host country could do the job as well as his team members could. Perhaps even more important to him was that without traveling on such a trip, his team members would be deprived of their value, satisfaction, and good feelings from the work they had done. Kenneth Frye, from the Christian Campus Ministry team, would agree with Dr. Lyons, "I also feel that we put a lot of work in trying to get there too. And then it would be like, 'Well, just send the money, and we won't go.' I feel like that would not be getting everything back for us. Like they said, it is a spiritual strength for us." Thomas Barber of Clear River UMC spoke of something similar, "We want the experience of it. We want the personal interaction. Through our actions, we want to express our love of God, and Christ. And we want them to experience that as well. You can't do that by writing a check."

Being present in the lives of the people was important for the team at City Central UMC. Team members wanted their mission hosts to know that they are not alone in a country where Christians are a minority. At the same time, there were expectations on the part of the team members for something to happen for themselves. Nancy Denson is a veteran STMer. Recall her desire to have an experience that will grow her in some way: "This will be my ninth time to go to Cuba. . . . [E]very time it's a different experience. . . . I always feel like God's stretching me a little bit, every time that I go down there." This stretching was described as a way of personal growth. Earlier in this chapter, Nancy's team leader Will Manning described some of his motivations for serving, "I go on mission and help others because it makes me feel better."

The expectation to experience something for themselves was an influential idea in the dataset. When it was suggested that the teams could "just send the money" the idea was unanimously rejected. Though there were various reasons, the experience was likely the most pervasive. STM leaders and/or members from each focus group team mentioned the expectation of a personal growth experience during their international travels. There were no team members who refuted such a suggestion or expectation. A discussion of the experience and its implications follows in the next chapters.

Gifts and Donations

The STMers' presentation of gifts and donations was also important for relationships and for the experience. Though they may not send the money alone, STM teams brought several in-kind donations as well as cash for their mission hosts. Teams provided work for the host churches and missions with the hiring of logistical support personnel during the trip, including translators, cooks, drivers, construction helpers, and others. There seemed to be an overall feeling that teams would bring whatever materials or goods the hosts requested including tools, Bibles, or personal items.

Personal gifts from team members to hosts were discouraged on Jaqueline Williams' team. That did not stop her from bringing things to some people whom she had met on a previous trip to the community. Making sure not to be heard by too many, she told me, "They tell us not to bring gifts on these trips, but I've got twenty-one gifts. Little gifts, earrings, things like that for twenty-one of my special friends. [laughs] So, I'm not going to tell [the team leader]. [Laughs] But, it's about relationships. And it's about showing the love of Christ." Jaqueline went on to tell of a time when a member of the host community asked for the shoes off her feet. She gave them to her and returned to her hotel barefooted. The next time, she brought the same woman "a new pair of sandals that I had bought for her. I mean, nice ones, really cushioned and pretty. And I found her and gave her those, and she was just so thankful."

Teams reported bringing in Bibles in numbers that were far beyond what could normally be obtained in a year. Others reported that they expected to distribute food to community members near their worksites. This food was to be provided by the local mission leaders. One team provided spectacles for those who requested them. Laypeople were trained to give an eye exam and did so as their area of specialization in the service work.

The medical team from Riverbend UMC provided members of the host community who attended their clinic not only with an exam, but also the medications they required and referrals to any necessary follow-up care. The children who attended the activities offered by Ramen UMC's team would receive items related to their construction-themed activities that included hard hats, nail aprons, and safety goggles. As mentioned in the section on "idealizations" above, the team brought community members several items in the past including aprons, makeup, and other such items. These were given in a special presentation to show the ladies of the community that they are of value.

Participants in the dataset seemed to want to use the exchange of money and gifts as a furthering of the ever-important relationships previously mentioned. However, only a few seemed to begin to struggle with the power dynamics that such gifts might begin to change. Vicky Oden briefly alluded to it. Like many of the others above, relationships in the trip were important to her and her teammates at Central City UMC. Vicky has been on a few STM trips before and has quite a bit of experience abroad. She said that she values the relationships of those that she meets overseas above all. However, she wondered if there were other motivations for the warm reception that she got from her hosts. Her trip of a week or two was not going to have a lasting effect, she told me. But she was ready to experience the relationships again.

> I think it's relationships more than anything. You know, I don't think in a week you're changing anybody's life. Let's be honest. The church we change. Because until this trip, we've taken quite a bit of money, to use for church construction. Which we aren't this time. So, it will be interesting. They may not love us as much. [She repeats] They may not love us so much.

As she said this, she finished with a chuckle. Vicky would later back away from that statement a little, saying that someone's life could change in a moment and that she felt like she was "planting seeds" that may grow later. Perhaps this snapshot of Vicky's feelings was indicative of many of the issues going on with others in the dataset. While Vicky was alone in stating that she didn't expect to change anyone's life in just a week, others fully expected their own lives to be changed.

As with the discussion of the impact of relationships, it is important to consider the voices of those who receive STM teams in the discussion of the exchange of money and gifts. Ver Beek's research is again helpful. In his study of community members in Honduras who received STM teams to rebuild homes after Hurricane Mitch, respondents had a difficult time deciding which was better: to receive the teams or receive more money. He reported that several in the community did, in fact, value the relationships and connections made with the North Americans. Several of the Hondurans conveyed a desire for the Americans to come and "build relationships" and "experience a change of heart or outlook."[53] However, when such experiences were considered against the additional homes that could be constructed and Hondurans employed with the funds spent upon travel there was a clear preference for the for Americans to remain at home and send the money instead.[54]

In this section, we discussed the power of proximity the STMers expected to experience in their host nation. The development of some sort of relationship and the engagement in an experience were key influences in the narratives of the STMers. Such notions deserve further discussion in relationship to a proper understanding of mission that I have illustrated previously. We will engage in such a discussion in the following chapters.

PURPOSES

First, however, it is important to discuss the way STMers expressed their understood purposes. We have shown above that participants wanted to be different when they came home than when they left. They wanted to see something that would move them deeply. They wanted to engage their senses in an immersive experience. They wanted to sacrifice and serve. They wanted to see the way the Other lived. All of these seemed to mix together into a conglomeration that made it hard to discern what was most important for many in the research groups. Such a lack of clarity was most evident in the discussion of the purposes of their trips.

"We are Not Evangelists"

To what extent the STM participant was to engage in faith-sharing varied among teams and among their individual team members. However, one tendency in the narratives seemed to be that those who spoke of plans for overt faith sharing opportunities during their trip were usually first time participants. Recall that Oliver Moore was one such first-timer and when asked about his goals before the trip, Oliver described his upcoming faith sharing efforts in a direct manner: "[I]t is really the great commission.

53. Ver Beek, "Impact," 483.
54. Ver Beek, "Impact," 484.

Spread the Word [of God. My wife and I] feel like we need to go and share in deed and word." He spoke about the focus of the trip being outside the individual person, and instead on the larger mission of a proclamation of the gospel, "[I]f we get some pleasure and enjoyment out of it, that's a side benefit. But that's not the purpose of going. . . . We are going to serve. . ."

However, his team leader, Richard Davis, a leader for over twenty years, confidently placed faith-sharing behind other priorities for his mission trips. "Sharing your faith, to me, is about fourth in line [of priorities]," he said. He went on to explain the priorities of the mission trip:

> "I'd say build relationships. Experiential Learning. Doing the work. And then sharing your faith. You're sharing your faith with the first three. So many people when they talk about a mission trip, they think you're out evangelizing and beating people over the head with a Bible. And my outlook of the mission is not that. You're sharing your faith by all that you're doing. . . . When you get the opportunity, yes, you share your faith verbally. Non-verbally, with a hug, with a smile."

He preferred to work, to serve, then be prepared to say, in his words, "And, oh, by the way, we're doing evangelism."

Richard seemed to heed the call by Stephen Chapman and Laceye Warner of embracing a style of evangelism that includes "a wide variety of practices, habits, dispositions, and non-verbal signs, in addition to spoken utterances."[55] Earlier in this chapter, I pointed out that such a notion does affirm a holistic approach to ministry: joining verbal proclamations with meeting very real needs. In the follow-up survey, the clear majority affirmed that faith-sharing must be done in both words and deeds. However, there seemed to be a strong priority on the deeds over the words in the narratives. Such a prioritization may be for other reasons as well. Richard's teams, like all the teams in the dataset, work with national churches and ministry leaders from the host nations. These churches, and the individual members among them, were seen by many as superior to the sending churches. As Richard went on to say,

> So often we go to these places and find their faith is stronger than ours. They're living in difficult conditions. Their whole view of the Bible is different from ours. . . . We aren't going to convert people. . . . We're going to work with brothers and sisters, to assist in however that local ministry wants us to assist.

---

55. Chapman and Warner, "Rethinking Evangelism," 64.

Assisting host churches in ongoing efforts led other teams to move away from even serendipitous opportunities for faith sharing. Central City UMC team leader Will Manning and his team worked in a "Christian church" and therefore, as he said, "Everyone's already a Christian." Yet, the church is in a country with a government-imposed restriction on religion and a limit on the number of Bibles printed by his host church's denomination. On this trip, his team brought two-and-a-half times the number of Bibles that were permitted to be printed annually. These Bibles were given to local national pastors for distribution rather than members of the STM team passing them out on the streets or in the churches during their construction activities. Rather than verbal faith-sharing, the leaving of a relatively large number of Bibles was their way of faith-sharing.

Much as Richard did, Will recalled his prior experiences with churches in his host country, he marveled at the spiritual depth he perceived at the host church. Such a depth far surpassed that of his own mega-church, he asserted. He was amazed at the way their faith seemed to be so very strong when they seemed, to him, to be so very poor. Therefore, Will determined the efficacy of the trip was not in their efforts of faith sharing. Rather, the efficacy of the mission could be measured by the experience the team members had while on their trip. Their measures of success often included things like personal spiritual growth, growing closer to team members, making new friends in their host countries, and experiencing other cultures and peoples. Recall Will's assertion: "I think that is a great way to think about why we go on mission. . . . I go on mission and help others because it makes me feel better."

Other team leaders and team members alike struggled with the words to describe their work. At Clear River UMC, Cecilia Chandler had experience working on short-term trips after stateside disasters, such as Hurricane Katrina. Preparing for her first international project, Cecilia insisted, "We are not evangelists." Rather, she offered, "'The Church Work Trip' would be better if you're trying to label it." Her team leader, Patrick Stone, was afraid to speak of their trips as evangelistic efforts for fear of being mistaken for other groups. "I used to not want to call them 'mission trips,' because I thought of the Book of Mormon kind of missionary. . . . But it's not like that at all." Patrick went on to say that their departure from prioritizing faith-sharing was a result of the denominational training he received: "I think Volunteers in Mission [UMVIM], in fact, discourages you from engaging in religious discussions with the people that you're helping. . . .We were told, this is not about us going down there and trying to save their souls. This is about us going down there to show God's love in action."

Some have tried to delineate mission and evangelism with definitions like: "Evangelism is the spreading of the good news by proclamation, whereas mission is the outflow of the love of God in and through our life, word and deed."[56] Many times these flow one into another. The balance of "proclamation," "deed," and "word" was not always clear cut in the narratives. Veteran team leader Philip O'Connor from the Elmville UMC team attempted to navigate the difficult terrain:

> How we carry ourselves in the community is evangelistic, but I don't feel the need to evangelize in a community that is churched. . . .Now, if the opportunity presents itself,. . . I will witness. But the main purpose of my mission trips is not to evangelize. What I see as my purpose, my calling, is to better equip those that are already there to be. . .the Methodist Church in that community.

The narratives here from both Philip and Richard earlier implied that there is a "right time" and "right way" to share one's faith with those whom the team members would encounter. Some participants wanted to make sure that they did not "beat anyone over the head with the Bible." There was a strong emphasis on "faith and work" going hand-in-hand. In the online survey, no one disagreed with the statement: "Sharing my faith means that I must do so with both words and actions." Wesleyan mission theology holds that evangelism is at the core of mission. Offering the gospel's story should be a key motivation for anyone involved in Methodist mission. However, neither of these team leaders, nor any of the other team leaders in the dataset, provided explicit pre-trip training for their teams in knowing when and how to engage in faith-sharing. There is certainly a biblical precedent for joining words and actions in mission and evangelism. However, many from the focus groups seemed to be much more comfortable in the area of actions rather than words. It was unclear if STMers were ready to share their faith with both their paintbrushes and their mouths.

All the team leaders expressed a desire to submit to the ongoing mission of the host church, which knew the special needs and concerns of their immediate constituency. They should be commended for doing so. As William Abraham rightly pointed out, such careful consideration of the needs and concerns of the hearers of the message is vital in evangelistic efforts.[57] However, because these international service trips, done in the name of mission, were working in established church communities, the dataset seemed to suggest that some STM team members saw themselves as now free from

56. Geevarghese Mar Osthathios, "Worship, Mission, Unity," 39.

57. Abraham, *The Logic of Evangelism*, 172.

the directive to engage in faith-sharing endeavors. In fact, many perceived a greater faith in their hosts than they themselves possessed. The literature has shown that, in general and for those in my dataset, STM trips are to places that are already among the new centers of World Christianity.[58] Perhaps there was a departure from faith sharing, because, as Will said, "Everyone [there is] already a Christian" and, in many ways, believed to be more devoted Christians than the STMers.

"Developing My Personal Faith"

This perception of Christian devotion in the mission hosts surpassing that of the STM was significant. For many in the dataset, there was an expectation that the devotion in others would lead to a deeper devotion in themselves. They expected to grow in their own faith while on the trip in part by what they observed in their mission hosts. While those interviewed expected to "share God's love" by their service efforts, they had other priorities for their time overseas. In the follow-up survey, participants were asked to rank the priorities of mission trips in general. "Preaching the Word of God" and "Serving the Poor" ranked among the least important. Rather, STMers ranked the development of relationships with team members and hosts alike among their highest priorities. These relationships were to serve a variety of purposes. There was a strong sense that these relationships, though short and intense, would lead to lasting ministry partnerships. However, both implicitly and explicitly, many saw the development of these relationships as a means to grow their own faith in new ways. Participants strongly emphasized "Developing my personal faith" as a top priority in both the pre-trip focus group interviews and the post-trip survey. They expected to be different upon their return because of the experiences they had while away.

THE NARRATIVES AND A THEOLOGY OF MISSION

At this point, it is helpful to recall what we said earlier about mission theology and the practical expression thereof in light of the accounts of the STMers in the dataset. Some key points from this chapter to recount:

- STMers often reported a sense of a divine call to participate in the trip and that call was for their personal growth.

---

58. Priest, "Short-Term Missions," 90; Jenkins, *Next Christendom*, 3–6.

- STMers traveled among a group of similars.

- STMers had difficulty explicitly articulating a biblical framework for their activities.

- Many STMers saw the experience as a gift to themselves and to improve themselves.

- STMers used idealized notions of friendships and family structures that were often shaped around issues of poverty.

- STMers affirmed the importance of proximity to others in order to develop relationships, show love, prevent corruption, and participate in the experience. The notion of experience was key.

- STMers largely rejected the idea that their service activities were for explicit faith sharing.

- Rather, STMers saw their activities as a way to strengthen their own faith, in many cases.

- STMers affirmed the need to work in group efforts, through existing ministries, to meet physical needs.

In previous chapters, I have affirmed David Bosch's definition of mission to include the propagation of the faith message, the conversion of unbelievers, the expansion of kingdom work, and the establishment of new church communities. Such a definition focuses the attention of the efforts of mission away from the center of the church and looks out towards others who are, as of yet, outside the Church. It places the focus of mission on the benefit of the other before the benefit of the self.

In chapter 3, I enumerated the five principles of a Wesleyan mission theology: 1) rooted in Scripture, 2) embraces the role of the broader church, 3) affirms that evangelism is mission, 4) insists that mission is not merely evangelism, and 5) expects ongoing discipleship in the lives of practitioners and recipients. Each of these bears consideration in conversation with the narratives of the STMers and as illustrated in the points above.

1) Rooted in Scripture. The absence of an intentional use of Scripture by team leaders to train their team members seemed to indicate that working towards a solidly biblical framework of mission was not the first priority for mission leaders. When asked to recall verses that applied to mission, many participants referenced passages that brought them personal comfort through the challenges they expected to face. There was little evidence in the dataset of engagement with the passages of scriptural mission teaching that I illustrated in the opening chapters.

2) Embraces the role of the broader church. The teams with whom I spoke did, at least in part, embrace their role in the work of the broader church. All of the teams were sponsored by church ministries and worked where ongoing church ministries took place. They connected with national pastors and missionaries to guide their service efforts. However, few of them utilized the resources of The United Methodist Church for training, or further connectional ministries beyond simple logistics, such as purchasing travel insurance.

3) Affirms that evangelism is mission. The reticence to engage in faith-sharing is a departure from historical mission activities. It is outside biblical and Wesleyan missional theological instruction that team leaders would minimize faith-sharing as a part of Christian service. STM teams participated in biblical instruction for children through VBS, delivered Bibles to Christian churches to further evangelism efforts, and openly participated in public Christian worship services. Yet, some were adamant that they were not serving as evangelists. This complexity needs to be explored further. For example, what can North Americans, though they describe themselves as being on a "mission trip," offer in the way of evangelism to a foreign context where Christian communities are already seen as vibrant, perhaps even more so than their home contexts?

4) Insists that mission is not merely evangelism. There was significant data in the narratives to affirm this principle. The United Methodist STMers in these narratives embraced their role of sharing in mission activities like construction projects, health clinics, and community development.

5) Expects ongoing discipleship in the lives of practitioners and recipients. While ongoing discipleship is expected, Wesley did not understand that doing things for another should be a means to one's own faith development. Rather, service for another should be done in the selfless act of the love God instills in the believer. Rankin is again helpful here:

> Since neighbor love is a reflection of God's image in the believer, and since full restoration of the image of God is the goal of Christian perfection, love necessarily motivates one toward service, because it reflects God's own relational nature as well as God's determination to reclaim what has been lost.[59]

Such love cannot help but put the needs of the other before self. Yet, if this were the case for the STMers, it was not clearly evident in the narratives or survey. The idea of mission service for the purposes of personal faith development needs to be explored further. In the next two chapters I

---

59. Rankin, "Perfect Church," 89.

will go into greater detail about the issues of traveling afar to perform acts of service with a group of peers for the expectation of personal growth. We have touched upon the issues of pilgrimage and tourism a few times already. I will examine these in greater detail and in light of both secular and sacred influences.

SECTION III

Short-Term Mission, Tourism, and Pilgrimage

6

Influences on the Practice
of Short-Term Mission

The implicit and explicit motivations that STMers expressed failed to align with the mission theologies I have outlined. Recall that the STMers often made, or affirmed, statements like, "You gain so much more than you give on a mission trip." This gain was frequently seen as their primary motivator. That U.S. Americans would seek an experience with a STM trip may be very natural considering the environment in which STM grew. Earlier in this work, I pointed to the fact that the development of the STM practice does not demonstrate a clearly defined theological and/or missional strategy. Much the same could be said of my qualitative data that revealed that team leaders were not utilizing training material provided by the denomination or other biblical training resources, for the most part. If such resources were not the primary influences to shape STM teams, the influences that could have shaped the implicit motivations and/or theologies of the members of the dataset should be analyzed. Therefore, an examination of the broader culture that influenced the practice is in order. The purpose of such an examination is to see how such cultural constructs may have shaped the practice where mission theology has not. In this chapter, we will discuss the changing nature of relationships in American culture, the role of small groups in faith development programs, and the way experiences drive the American economy. At first, these may not seem directly related to the Church. However, these conjoin to provide an environment in which STM flourishes.

A CULTURE'S CHANGING RELATIONSHIPS

As seen in the previous chapter, the STM participants spoke often of building relationships. Team members felt that it was important to build relationships, the data indicated, between the team members themselves and with those whom they intended to serve while abroad. These relationships were a critical component of the STM experience for many. The relationship component influenced people to enlist in the STM trip, was a vehicle for personal growth, and was an expressed goal of the overall experience. As such it was a key component for team leaders to consider when designing the trip. By the nature of such a trip, the intensity of these relationships could be very high. Team leaders reported that veteran team members often maintained a level of connection with fellow team members from previous trips, though the depth of these connections varied.

STMers reported a strong desire to build meaningful relationships with their mission hosts, but this is more problematic as there were several barriers to doing so. Such barriers include the short, but intense, nature of the STM trip, language barriers, cultural differences, and practical considerations. Recall that the average length of a STM trip is eight days.[1] The trips of the teams in the dataset were of a similar length. Many in the dataset reported participating in a STM no more than once a year. Such short periods of face-to-face contact, spread so far apart, do not seem conducive to building meaningful relationships. Most members of the dataset report no training or experience in the language of their hosts. Significant cultural differences exist between many STM participants, only some of which can be overcome in the short contact period of the actual STM trip. Though some members of the dataset did report efforts to maintain contact with their hosts after the trip, they admit that it is often difficult for their hosts to connect to the internet to communicate by e-mail and/or social media. However, the STMers seemed undaunted by such obstacles, if they acknowledged them.

While there was a desire to build a relationship with people thousands of miles away, many Americans do not seek to build the same such relationships with those within arms' reach. This emphasis on relationships, and the dismissal of the obstacles to such relationships, is particularly interesting considering the cultural period in which STM trips grew: the latter half of the twentieth century. At the same time these trips were increasing in popularity and scope, the dynamics of relationship building in the United States were changing significantly. Sociologist Robert Putnam, in *Bowling Alone*, points out several changes in social connections during this same

---

1. Priest, "Short-Term Missions," 85.

period. Americans entertained at home less, visited others less frequently, got together for social activities less often, and engaged with their immediate neighbors in waning numbers.[2] By the last decade of the twentieth century, "the average American came to spend nearly 15 percent more time on child or pet care. . . . By contrast, the largest changes of all involve time spent at worship and visiting friends, both of which fell by more than 20 percent."[3] A decreasing number of Americans participated in activities that involved others while an increasing number participated in more insular activities.[4]

Putnam further points out that several areas of generosity declined during the latter half of the twentieth century, while others increased. There was a decline in work on community projects. Reported charitable giving was down in several areas including overall philanthropic giving, donations to the United Way, and among Protestant and Catholic churches alike. However, volunteering increased over the same period. This is important to the discussion of relationships because participation in a social network is one of the strongest predictors of the participation in volunteer efforts or philanthropic endeavors, an even stronger predictor than altruistic attitudes.[5] Social connections are often an engine to one's determination to give time and money to a project or a cause. One-on-one requests to support an activity or philanthropic endeavor are among the most effective ways to enlist others to participate. People who were already connected with an organization, particularly a religious organization, were more likely to volunteer their time. "In round numbers, *joiners are nearly ten times more generous with their time and money than nonjoiners.* Social capital is a more powerful predictor of philanthropy than is financial capital."[6]

In addition to Putnam, Robert Bellah and his co-authors Richard Madsen, William Sullivan, Ann Swidler, and Steven Tipton point out that American individualism and the desire to connect to community are not at odds, but instead exist in an important relationship. "[P]eople evince an individualism that is not empty but is full of content drawn from an active identification with communities and traditions."[7] Their research indicated that participants felt that both are needed for each one to grow. The individual needs the community and the community needs the individual. These communities can be found in a variety of places including town

2. Putnam, *Bowling Alone*, 92–107.

3. Putnam, *Bowling Alone*, 107.

4. Putnam, *Bowling Alone*, 97–107.

5. Putnam, *Bowling Alone*, 121.

6. Putnam, *Bowling Alone*, 120. Emphasis original.

7. Bellah et al., *Habits of the Heart*, 163.

governments, churches, civic organizations, or activist groups. People are expected to choose for themselves how they will be a part of such communities.[8] Focusing on how people engaged in their local communities, Bellah and his colleagues found that people expressed "genuine concern" for their immediate neighbors and the betterment of their communities. This was done with an eye to the protection of the individual interests of those getting involved as well. "The civic-minded professional and the professional activist are often motivated by community concern, but they see the community largely in terms of a variety of self-interested individuals and groups."[9]

While people do, in fact, become part of a larger movement they do so with personal interests in mind as well. This is important to the discussion of STM because the parallels in the relationship between the goals of the individual participant and the group's mission can influence how the mission is designed, implemented, and evaluated. My follow-up survey revealed that participants joined a team of people, but not always to accomplish the team's goals. About half did not place an emphasis on team goals over their personal goals.

How Americans build relationships and what they do in those relationships changed dramatically in the latter half of the twentieth century. What they can contribute to a greater cause sometimes drives their involvement in groups and organizations. However, involvement is sometimes driven by the value they perceive they can gain for themselves by their participation. Such connections occur not just in the marketplace or in the civic halls or in secular charitable organizations. They also take place in churches.[10] By design, many churches implement small groups to build a community of relationships for the benefit of the group and the individual.[11] We now turn to a discussion of such groups and their role in the STM movement.

THE SMALL-GROUP MOVEMENT

It is possible that the STM movement has been influenced by the rise of small group ministries in American churches. There are some interesting parallels to consider. First, the connection to a small group leads to an increase in participation in organized efforts to help others. Many of the STM participants in my study reported a feeling that God called them to serve others. What was it that led them to participate in an international

8. Bellah et al., *Habits of the Heart*, 163–67.

9. Bellah et al., *Habits of the Heart*, 191.

10. Clark, "Rethinking the Decline," 588. Bellah et al., *Habits of the Heart*, 156–58.

11. Wuthnow, *Sharing the Journey*, 4, 64–76.

short-term service project? That question is a little harder to answer, but Robert Wuthnow's work, *Sharing the Journey*, may provide some clues. The power of a group of similars to work towards a common goal is a strong motivator. Wuthnow says that, "having had some kind of profound religious experience or spiritual awakening is a major reason why people in small groups become involved in community service."[12] Wuthnow further suggests that the spiritual awakening often led them to get involved in the needs and concerns of others. However, their participation in small groups was an indicator of their involvement in organized efforts to do so. "In other words, individual religious awakenings lead to individual caring activities; group participation leads to more organized efforts."[13] While working together with other members of the small group, individuals were seeking personal growth while responding to the perceived needs of others.[14]

The growth of the support/small group movement in the latter half of the twentieth century was a significant influence on American church culture. Many churches began and continue to offer small group[15] opportunities that can include Bible study groups, and groups designed to meet the specified needs of a variety of demographics. Wuthnow suggests that the surge in small groups in recent years was a reaction to the decline in social interactions mentioned by Putnam and others, as illustrated above. An important aim for small groups is to provide a sense of community relationships for their members. This is because of a perceived change in the structures of American families and communities.[16] The small group "movement as a whole is deeply populist."[17] The growth of small groups in churches was seen by many as a response to declining involvement in religious activities. The movement began to take hold in the late 1960s, grew in the 1970s, expanded rapidly in the 1980s, and remains an important part of many churches. Many such groups were initiated by clergy leaders to help members of their congregations grow individually, while getting them connected with a smaller number of people than one might find in a regular worship service. Such a dynamic was seen to foster self-expression, provide

12. Wuthnow, *Sharing the Journey*, 329.

13. Wuthnow, *Sharing the Journey*, 329

14. Wuthnow, *Sharing the Journey*, 330.

15. For the sake of clarity, I will usually refer to them as "small groups" rather than "support groups." Because I am engaging the role of small groups with the role of STM teams, I will use the term more common to many church communities in this context: small groups.

16. Wuthnow, *Sharing the Journey*, 345–46. Bellah et al., *Habits of the Heart*, 329–32. Putnam, *Bowling Alone*, 65–79.

17. Wuthnow, *Sharing the Journey*, 4–5.

an opportunity for further instruction and/or activities, and meet the personal growth needs of their congregants.[18]

A Variety of Offerings Designed to Meet the Needs of the Individual

More Americans can be involved in small groups than ever before. One reason for this is that

> these groups come in all shapes, colors, and sizes. They are much like breakfast cereals: Big boxes of all-purpose cereal are there for the whole family, but smaller boxes are available for people eating alone. . . . Support groups can be found to meet virtually everyone's taste.[19]

Churches routinely offer groups for special ages and stations in life like groups for women, men, youth, children, young adults, older adults, couples, singles, and the like. Groups are designed to fit the needs of the individual members, but in a collective spirit and environment. Typical groups are Sunday School classes, weekend or weekday Bible studies, self-help groups, and special interest groups. These groups meet at times and locations that are attractive to current and prospective members. Much in the same way that the groups come in various "tastes," the packaging and presentation too is designed to meet specific and broad appeals alike.[20] Similarities to these sorts of offerings can be seen in STM teams. I will point out several of these later in this chapter.

Small Groups and Methodism

However, this is not the first time that the church, let alone the American church, has seen an emphasis on the power of a small group of devoted people for spiritual development. John and Charles Wesley built upon the strong *collegia pietatis*[21] developments of the century before, which in turn developed from a tradition leading back to the early church. Between their days at Oxford University and their early days of the Methodist revival in

18. Wuthnow, *Sharing the Journey*, 43–44. See also Dougherty and Whitehead, "A Place to Belong."

19. Wuthnow, *Sharing the Journey*, 64.

20. Wuthnow, *Sharing the Journey*, 65, 145–54.

21. Literally: school of piety. These small groups were designed to strengthen personal devotion to God.

the Fetter Lane Society, the Wesley brothers relied heavily upon the benefits of small groups for personal growth and the growth of those under their teaching.[21] Although the Methodists are not the only ones to employ such a technique, the Methodist movement finds its roots in the network of small groups connected to a larger group. By the twentieth century, American churches utilized Sunday School programs to divide the congregations into smaller groups. These groups were often more homogeneous, designing classes for demographics profiles such as children, youth, young adults, and older adults. Classes divided by age and gender were the primary offerings for small group activities until the resurgence of small groups in the 1950s and 1960s. Sometimes encouraged by national church leadership, the re-birth of the small group movement was usually driven at the local church level.[22]

Goals of Small Groups: Strengthen Churches and Personal Growth

These groups are often designed to be supportive small groups. In Wuthnow's study, members of supportive small groups reported "that their lives have been deeply enriched by the experience. They have found friends, received warm emotional support, and grown in their spirituality."[23] Most members of small groups reported joining to strengthen their own faith. Members of small groups come together for a purpose: to participate together in the work of individual spiritual growth.

Most of Wuthnow's participants who were active in small groups reported deepening their relationships with others in the group. They felt a deeper connection to others because of their participation in small groups and had a better feeling about themselves.[24] The increase in connectivity, or building relationships, was even higher than the "[c]onsequences framed in specifically religious language."[25] Most participants in his study reported an increased depth of biblical understanding, faith-sharing abilities, and sensed an answer to prayer. Many of his respondents said, that because of their participation in a small group, they had grown closer to God and to one another. Because of the strong emphasis on interpersonal work, along with Bible study, "[p]erhaps small groups are encouraging an experiential

21. Heitzenrater, *People Called Methodists*, 113–37; Runyon, *New Creation*, 122–23; Collins, *John Wesley*, 120–23.

22. Wuthnow, *Sharing the Journey*, 41–45.

23. Wuthnow, *Sharing the Journey*, 4.

24. Wuthnow, *Sharing the Journey*, 6, 228–29.

25. Wuthnow, *Sharing the Journey*, 228.

form of spirituality."[26] Because of these reasons, and others, clergy members develop small group opportunities to extend the ministries of their churches and grow their congregations: both numerically and spiritually.

Goals of STM: Strengthen Churches and Personal Growth

Much like a STM team, small groups seek to limit their number for optimization of the goal of personal growth for the individual members while working with others. Recall that Rev. Wallace described the mission team of around twelve people as the "sweet spot." While some team leaders did describe an effort to keep their teams within a certain size range for logistical considerations of transport and housing, there are interpersonal considerations when selecting a team size. Rev. Wallace described the need to design a group's size to maximize the interpersonal connection among team members for their individual benefit. If the team is too large, the group loses cohesion. If the group is too small, the experience is awkward for the participants. Team design was about the group's collective and individual benefit.

Small group involvement strengthens the attachments between members of the group and the broader community, rather than a focus on self. Additionally, small groups are an effective way for people who are already members of a church to become more active and to serve the wider community. In other words, they build relationships among the group members themselves and make team members more aware of the needs of others in the broader world. Such were the stated goals of many of the STM leaders and participants.

At times, the offerings of STM team opportunities and small group opportunities look very similar. Visit the websites of some large membership churches that are involved in STM and it is likely that the listing of upcoming service trip opportunities will look much like the list of Sunday School and small group Bible study offerings. Groups designed exclusively for men, women, singles, couples, youth, college students, older adults and the like are normative for both mission and small-group programs. How people join these groups are also similar. Wuthnow's study revealed that many participants in small groups join because of what they have in common with others in the group. Additionally, people who join small groups often do so because they were invited by a friend.[27] STM team leaders reported that

---

26. Wuthnow, *Sharing the Journey,* 228.

27. Wuthnow, *Sharing the Journey,* 4–7, 330.

people who joined a STM frequently did so because of a one-on-one invitation from a friend who had participated in such a trip before.

Given the culture of small groups in many churches it may be a natural transition for many to move their small group Bible study meeting into more of a service-oriented meeting. Given the increased globalization and ease of travel, many in the group are likely to be aware of the needs of the Other overseas. When that same group has a leader whom they trust to help them safely navigate the travel logistics and participate in relief efforts, it may seem quite natural that they would participate together in a project like a week-long effort to help another while gaining some benefit themselves. Just as an increased participation in small groups is seen to grow the church in number and in maturity, many see STM as a way to grow the church in service, in maturity, and in number as well.[28]

As we have seen, Methodism has a rich history of small group ministries and using the individual and group dynamics to grow both. Methodism also touts active participation in mission projects. By design, United Methodism uses small groups to work in ministry and mission to both those inside the church and those seen as yet outside the church. Groups such as United Methodist Men, United Methodist Women, United Methodist Young Adults and others exist, in part, to participate in mission and the enrichment of the individual and collective spiritual lives of the members.[29] These groups operate at the local church level and up to national and international levels. They function as small groups as well as being organized with greater structure at the higher levels.

A Variety of Short-Term Mission Offerings Designed to Meet the Needs of the Individual

Small groups and STM teams also share common ground in their development. Likewise, other parallels between small groups and teams in the dataset could be found. One such area is the type and variety of STM trips offered by churches and organizations. Much like the variety of cereals available in Wuthnow's example above, many churches offer a variety of STM teams to suit a variety of tastes. Christian Campus Fellowship was made up of college students. City Central UMC's team was comprised of couples of retirement age who were already familiar with one another. The team from Clear River UMC was comprised of individuals who were, largely, already

28. See, for example Dearborn, *Short-Term Missions Workbook*; Lupton, *Toxic Charity*.

29. United Methodist Church, ¶2302, ¶1319, ¶202.

known to one another and were of similar age and station in life. Ramen UMC specifically designed a team for older adults. Richard designed his trip specifically for that age range when several older adults came to him seeking to participate in a STM trip. He began by looking around for a site where they could serve. After finding a site approved by the denomination's mission group, he contacted the mission leader about the need for accommodations and work projects suited to the special needs of his team. The mission leader in Central America agreed. Richard said: "[While on the mission trip, i]f somebody gets tired they can sit down. . . . Not a problem. They've got a variety of different ministries and that's just been wonderful in terms of accommodating the older adult crowd. . . . But they've been really good in terms of gearing the trip to a little bit slower pace."

STM trips designed for specific populations were also found in other congregations that were not a part of the formal research focus groups. While certain skills were sometimes listed as helpful, expertise such as medical training or construction experience was mentioned less often than a particular desired demographic. E-mail and website solicitations from churches, denominational leadership, and unaffiliated groups that broker STM teams frequently include social and demographic guidelines over spiritual guidelines or professional requirements. Websites that broker STM trips include options to browse the selections not only by region but also by the participant's demographic. One such site gives interested parties the chance to peruse through thousands of trips, from hundreds of organizations, that are billed to be suitable for categories that include individuals, groups, married couples, or families. In visiting websites of churches and brokers that were active in STM opportunities, I found that teams were often designed around demographic profiles that included women only, men only, single adults only, college students only, and couples only.[30]

Short-Term Mission as Yet Another Small Group Offering

In many ways, the design of STM teams and small groups overlapped. This may be because they share similar functions and traits. According to Wuthnow's survey, the top three reasons group members became involved in small groups were: 1."The desire to grow as a person," 2. "Being invited by someone you know," and 3. "Wanting to become more disciplined in your spiritual life."[31] Members of the focus groups described similar reasons for

30. For example: "Adventures in Mission," https://www.adventures.org. "2018 Mission Trips," http://www.shorttermmissions.com.

31. Wuthnow, *Sharing the Journey,* 84.

participating in STM groups. Their motivations discussed in the previous chapter included personal growth, a desire to become a more spiritual person, and the personal invitation of other team members.

It could be said that STM teams are yet another small group offering among many churches. Like many small groups, many STM teams are designed with a specific size in mind, sometimes to maximize the experience for the individual group members. Like many small groups, many STM teams are often designed to meet the needs of the team members by their demographic design. Like small groups, many STM teams are designed to provide an environment where individuals are afforded the opportunity for personal growth among a group of their peers. Especially in larger churches, ministries of small groups and STM opportunities are often expected as standard offerings.[32] In many ways, the small group movement in the American church has shaped how people engage in service to others. STM are often designed to serve the function of a small group that is engaged in a common service project.

I want to suggest that the goals, functions, and design of small group ministries have influenced the development of STM. This is important to consider when seeking to understand the larger role of STM in the mission of the broader church. Small group ministries exist to serve the individual participant's needs first, while doing so among a group. Those who participate in either/both are on "collective quests for the sacred."[33] The clear majority of those who participated in my dataset reported having previously participated in small group ministries of some sort, many of whom participated in a variety of opportunities. Therefore, they were already familiar with, and likely brought expectations of, the role and functions of a small group of people coming together for a spiritual purpose. Small groups and STM teams are lauded for their structure and organization.[34] This is likely due to more than just their commonality of the group dynamic. Both seek to use this group dynamic to meet personal and collective goals.

Small group ministries and STM opportunities both seek to meet personal and group goals through a variety of offerings through which participants may shop around as they see fit. Small groups are designed to be open to others, but often lack a long-term commitment for their participants. If small group members bcome dissatisfied, they will often drop out of a group and seek another one to join that better fits their needs.[35] While STM team

---

32. Priest, "U.S. Megachurches," 98; Wuthnow, *Sharing the Journey,* 342.

33. Wuthnow, *Sharing the Journey,* 57.

34. Wuthnow, *Sharing the Journey,* 131.

35. Wuthnow, *Sharing the Journey,* 141, 320.

members are committed for the duration of their trip, their commitment to the ongoing work of that particular project or to those particular team members may not be as strong. This is demonstrated by the fact that many STM participants in the dataset had served in a variety of contexts and with a variety of team members. Just as some shop around for a small group ministry that fits them, participants in short-term international service work may shop around until everything fits just right: the type of trip, location of the trip, who is going, how long will they be gone, does it fit into their schedule and do they like the people with whom they will serve? Consider that many STM trips are designed to fit into the schedules of the people who are traveling and that may not always be the best time for the hosts.[36] However, in STM the needs of the mission hosts must also be considered. If those needs/desires should collide, brokering a resolution can be difficult, as in the example of the cutting bamboo at the wrong time of the moon.[37]

These factors point to the idea that STM work, at least in part, is an outgrowth of small group ministries. Adopting a similar format and culture, STM teams came together because of the work already going on in some small group ministries. Of the seven STM teams in the field research, six were a product of existing small group activities. "The support-group movement is. . .successful on the whole because of the sweeping forces in American society—the tradition of interest in spirituality, the erosion of more established forms of community, and the availability of facilities, leaders, models, and other resources through churches."[38] As shown above, it is much the same in the STM movement. The success of the small-group movement has influenced the design, goals, and understanding of the STM movement. For many, their STM teams were functioning like another small group. They were seeking a deeply spiritual personal encounter while participating in a journey with a group of people for a short, intense period that may be repeated.

The way this spiritual and personal encounter was often described in the field data was with the term "experience." The experience was an important trait of the small group dynamic of the STM team. The sharing of the experience was seen to be enhanced by the participation of the other members of the small group, ergo the team. The team members were seen to enrich the experience with their contributions not just of labor or skills they would provide. Rather they enriched the experience with the fellowship

36. Priest et al., "They See Everything," 433. Priest illustrates how trips are often scheduled during school breaks like spring break, Christmas holidays, and summer vacations.

37. See chapter 5.

38. Wuthnow, *Sharing the Journey*, 130.

and community they provided by participating together. The members of the dataset placed a high value on experience as a goal for their STM trip. Much like the small group ministry movement, the desire for experience influences short-term service activities. We now turn our attention to the experience lodged within small groups and STM teams.

THE EXPERIENCE ECONOMY

It is difficult to fully express the influence that the notion of an "experience" had on the members of the dataset. "Experience" was a significant part of the discussion in each of the seven teams in the focus groups. This was expressed both implicitly and explicitly. In chapter 5, I reported the desire of team members to partake in an experience. This desire was keenly expressed in the conversation about keeping the STM team members at home and sending the money instead. Recall that Dr. Lyons rejected the idea because his team members would not have the satisfaction of the experience they were expecting while serving in South America. Other team leaders stressed the importance of the personal experience so that "you come back a changed person." It may have been suggested that the person who has experienced this will make a greater long-term impact. However, the experience is the key component for change in the STM participants.

Veteran STM participants recalled their previous encounters to discuss their desire to recapture the feelings of previous experiences. Paula Davis spoke of her need to remember the sights, smells, and sounds of the countries where she served previously. She wanted again to be immersed in the richness of all that the trip had to offer. Maureen Whitehall wanted to recapture a "mountain top" feeling that she had last time. Kenneth Frye wanted the experience in order to feel like he was "getting everything back for us" and to gain the "spiritual strength for us." Nancy Denson felt like she needed to recapture the feeling that "God's stretching me a little bit" through the experience she anticipated on her trip. The idea of "you get back more than you give" was influential in the dataset. Many times, the notions of experience influenced that sentiment.

These trips are often advertised as "life-changing" and "adventurous" for the participants.[39] Some brokering agencies emphasize the "adventure" to recruit STM participants. Some agencies clearly place the terms "adventure" and "mission" side-by-side in their advertising emphases or even organization names and brandings. This focus upon self seems to be attracting people to the practice. Subsequently, there is ambiguity in the role these trips play

39. Howell, *Short-Term Mission*, 21.

in mission. The participants in this present survey overwhelmingly affirmed the value of the trips for them personally, yet often struggled to define their role in the larger mission. Were they missionaries, evangelists, friends, servants, or something else? Remember Cecilia, who insisted that she and her teammates "are not evangelists." Rather, she offered, "'The Church Work Trip' would be better if you're trying to label it." Such a notion is a strong departure from the traditional way missional service has been described. If not mission and evangelism first, as the name suggests, what then is the purpose? When asked why she wanted to participate in this project, Cecilia's answer was like many others in the dataset, "To experience the people, etc. of a foreign country."

The Price to Pay

As I mentioned, I asked each group about their motivations to commit such a large contribution of time, service, and finances. These three were often seen as a price to pay for something else that they craved: the experience. The term "experience" was used to express the sights and sounds of a new country; the encounters with people from other cultures; the act of traveling to a new place; the sights, sounds and smells they associated with poverty; and the feelings they got from challenging themselves to do something new. The idea of experience was a significant contributing influence in the motivation of participants. Recall that the notion of "You gain so much more than you give on a mission trip" was influential for many. This gain was frequently seen as a primary motivator for several participants. Such transactional language is not native to much of mission theology. Yet, scholars like Brian Howell affirm that such an idea was prevalent in a larger body of research related to STM participants.[40] Concurrent with the rise in STM, new economic forces were developing in the United States that may have influenced the way short-term international service is practiced. It is important to further examine the idea of experience as a part of a transaction to help inform our understanding of current practices of STM.

Four Stages of American Economics

Joseph Pine and James Gilmore point out that much of the American economy is driven by what they describe as the "experience economy." The economy, they say, has seen four stages: commodity, goods, service, and

40. Howell, *Short-Term Mission*, 19–21.

now experience.[41] They illustrate the principle with the example of a childhood birthday party and the center of the celebration: the birthday cake. In the commodities economy, and as late as, say, the 1930s or 1940s, many mothers would have baked a cake in a home kitchen. She "actually *touched* such commodities as butter, sugar, eggs, flour, milk, and cocoa."[42] The cost of these ingredients would have cost just twenty or thirty cents.

In the goods economy, large corporations put many of these ingredients in a box. By the 1960s or 1970s a family in the goods economy would have purchased the pre-packaged goods, seeking time savings, a perceived improved flavor, and/or convenience. This increased value was reflected in the price paid for these qualities. Boxes of mix cost a dollar or two. Still not much, but considerably higher than the cake cost in a commodities economy.

The 1980s saw the rise of the service economy. Instead of baking at all, a mother or father would order a cake from a bakery or supermarket. This provided an increase in options so that customers could specify flavors, colors, exact pick up time, and designs and messages on top. Such a cake would cost between ten and twenty dollars, ten times the cost of the cake in the goods economy for the ingredients that cost less than a dollar. Consumers did so, as Pine and Gilmore point out, so that parents could focus their attention on the party.[43]

In the current experience economy, companies have taken advantage of such a focus. Families frequently outsource the party, and the cake, to a family entertainment company, such as Chuck E. Cheese's or "this Zone or that Plex of one kind or another. The companies stage a birthday experience for family and friends for $100 or $250 or more."[44] Pine and Gilmore point out that the "Progression of Economic Value" is reflected in the simple example of a birthday cake. Each stage: commodities, goods, services, and experience, is reflected in the offerings. These offerings: pure ingredients, packaged mix, professional cake, and staged party increase in cost because the buyers find each one more in alignment with their desires. Therefore, companies stage a variety experiences to differentiate themselves from their competition and may "charge a premium price based on the distinctive value provided, and not the market price of the competition."[45] This also means that consumers expect the opportunity to purchase an experience

41. Pine and Gilmore, "Experience Economy," 97.

42. Pine and Gilmore, *Experience Economy*, 32. Emphasis original.

43. Pine and Gilmore, *Experience Economy*, 32–33.

44. Pine and Gilmore, *Experience Economy*, 33.

45. Pine and Gilmore, *Experience Economy*, 34–35.

from a variety of options, and they expect to pay a premium price for new and unique experiences.

The experience economy, according to Pine and Gilmore, can be traced to Walt Disney and the advent of experiential film encounters. This was taken to new levels with the opening of Disneyland and Disney World, the first theme parks. The guests (intentionally not called customers) are invited to involve themselves in the experience of the sights, sounds, tastes, and aromas that create a unique experience for each. While Disney pioneered the experience offering, they are not alone in the market. Theme restaurants like Hard Rock Cafe, Medieval Times, and Bubba Gump Shrimp Co. use food as but a small part of the staging of an experience.[46] Bernd Schmitt suggested that providing holistic involvement in the consumption experience was a key to successful marketing in such an economy.[47] Do-it-yourself stores offer workshops and tours to raise the experience of buying tools and supplies. The travel industry has engaged the move from commodity to experience by easing the burden of travel, not just moving people at the lowest possible price in the shortest amount of time.

The logistics of moving from point A to point B is not the only way the travel industry has engaged the experience economy. New offerings are ever-emerging, some engaging old practices, some providing new ones: yacht chartering, mountain biking, cattle driving, rock climbing, puffin birding, whale kissing, and glacier walking.[48] An internet search for adventure travel provides scores of options for "Active Adventure" or "Comfort Adventure" to heighten the experience of the "Family Vacation." These offerings include diving the Great Barrier Reef, up-close safari experiences, or traveling to the Earth's poles. The offerings, and enticement, of the experience economy are pervasive. These experiences can be highly emotive for those who participate.

> While prior economic offerings—commodities, goods, and services are external to the buyer, experiences are inherently personal, existing only in the mind of an individual who has been engaged on an emotional, physical, intellectual, or even spiritual level. Thus, no two people can have the same experience, because each experience derives from the interaction between the staged event (like a theatrical play) and the individual's state of mind.[49]

---

46. Pine and Gilmore, *Experience Economy*, 98.

47. Schmitt, "Experiential Marketing."

48. Pine and Gilmore, *Experience Economy*, 3–39.

49. Pine and Gilmore, "Experience Economy," 99.

In the Economy of Experience, the sellers are seen not just as sellers, but as "stagers" and the buyers not just as buyers, but as "guests." Pine and Gilmore point out that the key to the experience economy transactions is that they are memorable, personal, revealed over a duration, and engage the senses.[50] It is important to point out that both the parties have an active role in the transaction. As C.K. Prahalad and Venkat Ramaswamy point out, "[h]igh-quality interactions that enable an individual to co-create unique experiences with the company are the key" to such transactions.[51] As shown in my data, some STMers spend months preparing for the interactions with their mission hosts. Such interactions, though brief, are emotionally intense for many. By their very nature, STM trips require the co-creation of the experience by all parties. STM leaders seemed to strive to provide "high-quality interactions" for the transaction.

Short-Term Mission Participants as Consumers in the Experience Economy

These same attributes were found in the STMers' narratives. Those with whom I spoke often discussed the goals of such an "experience" in the mission activities. Viewing the narratives of the focus group participants alongside Pine and Gilmore's work proves helpful in understanding the transactional language used by many. Wayne Kennedy typified the desire "to experience. . .Jesus in the culture and geography" and while doing so "to make new friends, to experience a type of humbling freedom from the spiritual experience and the nature and culture." According to the participants, the efficacy of the mission could often be measured by the experience the team members had while on their trip. Their measures of success often included things like personal spiritual growth, growing closer to team members, making new friends in their host countries, and experiencing other cultures and peoples. Recollect the importance Will and Sally Manning placed on the expressed goal for their team members to have a sense of purpose and accomplishment when participating in a STM trip. Gregory Booth needed to go on his STM because "it's almost like an addiction. . ." that he needs to satisfy for himself, personally. Gregory did say that he was going to work for and with his mission hosts, but he was going primarily because this was what he needed in his life right now.

50. Pine and Gilmore, "Experience Economy," 98; Pine and Gilmore, *Experience Economy*, 9.

51. Prahalad and Ramaswamy, "Co-Creation Experiences," 7.

Paula has participated in STM for several years. When I asked her why take the time, effort, and resources to participate in a trip like this, she was quick to reply,

> I think, one thing that I saw early on was that. . .you hear it over and over again. . .that you benefit more than you ever would imagine. So, from a personal standpoint, it is that opportunity to get beyond what we are here. When you go someplace and you smell and you see it opens up your eyes in such a way. Anytime that you see a news story or anything about somewhere that you've been. Like the people of Bolivia, or the people of Panama. . .the indigenous groups that we got to know there. Your ear always hears them. It's just a continual thing. And you just leave part of yourself wherever you go. There's no way that you can come back and not have been impacted by it.

Statements such as these expressed well what many of the team members wanted to convey: the experience is of utmost importance to them. The STMers were willing to give of themselves, their time, their resources, and their comforts. In return, they expected a particular experience. That experience was not universally expressed as a single, consistent idea across all of the team members interviewed. Such a finding gives credence to the idea that the economic transaction of an experience is highly personal and unique for each person because of the set of circumstances that each brings to the transaction, as Pine and Gilmore emphasized.

Most of the teams reported that the efficacy of the mission could be measured by the experience that the team members had while on their trip. Their measures of success included things like personal spiritual growth, growing closer to team members, making new friends in their host countries, and experiencing other cultures and peoples. Some teams did mention that the building project they had before them was a desired goal. The leaders, however, put the completion of the project as a secondary goal to the interaction with the people. These interactions were to be seen as opportunities not to just strengthen the experience, but to build relationships with the nationals in the destination countries.

Conversely, a bad experience on the part of the STMer was seen as the proof that the mission trip was a failure. What was largely absent in the discussions of efficacy of the mission trip was discussion of evangelism or other historical ideas of Christian Mission mentioned in the above material on mission, kingdom, and church. The expressed priority for many was instead the experience of the team members while working and serving to meet a perceived need in another cultural context.

Team Leaders as Stagers

Certainly, the team leaders should be affirmed for the great concern that they expressed to exercise all due diligence with the monies and people entrusted to them. However, the role of the team leader as more of a "stager" bears further discussion. Providing such an experience for the teams was certainly a goal for the team leaders. They worked hard, in the language of Pine and Gilmore, to stage the experience in such a way to bring about the desired transaction. If the STM trip is a transaction in the economy of experience, then the team leaders are among those who set the stage for the experience. Like those who design and execute the plan to engage the guests in the business world, so too the team leaders plan their work and work their plan.

The team leaders with whom I spoke worked on a variety of projects, but they all seemed to have one thing in common: putting forth a particular experience for their team. While all of them were "experience stagers," each seemed to take a somewhat different role. Some team leaders assumed the role of an educator, some more as a wilderness guide, some more as a travel agent.

Team Leader Richard Davis is a retired educator, and he used his STM opportunities to continue to teach. Experiential learning was key in his mind when he encouraged his team members to experience the culture, to learn the culture, and learn about the struggles of the people they would encounter. Just like other experiential transactions, experiential learning works best when the senses are engaged. He says, "[E]xperiential learning means that you're experiencing, you got your hands dirty, you're feeling, you're smelling, you're hearing, you're tasting the things in that culture. You can't do that. . .unless you're there in the middle of it." These sensory experiences are a part of his overall design for his team to return home deeply affected by the people and the culture where they served.

Dr. and Mrs. Lyons act more as experience brokers than as teachers. Their teams come not only from their local community, but from connections they have made all over the Southeastern United States. It is not unusual for their teams to include those who live hours away from the Lyons' local church. Because of the broad proximity, they do not have meetings to prepare the team for the upcoming experience other than a logistics meeting shortly before the departure date. Dr. Lyons said it was important that his trips were spiritually satisfying for those who participate. However, rather than work on preparing the team members spiritually, Dr. and Mrs. Lyons spend a great deal of time doing logistical arrangements months in advance: securing airline tickets, making hotel reservations, and coordinating with ministry contacts in South America. It takes a large part of their time because of the sometimes fickle nature of the team participants. When expressing his goals for their trip, medical care was certainly emphasized. The accompanying Bible School for children who were waiting to see doctors was important. But the experience of the mission participants was just as high a priority. He told me that he views their trips as successful when, alongside the good done for the pediatric patients, the team members felt satisfied and that they had a worthwhile experience. In some ways, it was akin to a travel agent making sure that the customers enjoyed their trip.

Veteran team leader Philip O' Connor concentrates his time on a few projects in order to make sure that they are thoroughly completed in a timely manner. He is well-educated and holds a good job that allows him to travel on his vacation days. He discovered his affinity for the Central American culture while taking his undergraduate coursework for a minor in Spanish. A classmate invited him on a STM trip, and he has been participating ever since. Decades later, his work in STM is thoughtful, deliberate, and focused upon the needs of the host nation as well as the STM participants. He has dedicated his time to improving his Spanish language skills and is one of the few interview participants who expressed a proficiency in the language of the host nations. However, Philip in many ways, leads his STM teams like a guide on an expedition getting people from point A to point B safely and on time.

Philip does not involve himself much in the pre-trip preparations for the team. He is only concerned that each person finds a way to present the needed funds, to follow his checklist of logistical considerations, and to show up when expected to do so. The prerequisite to participating in his teams? "You've got to be able to take care of yourself financially. And then [demonstrate] the desire to go." Though it was said by a member of another team, the idea expressed well the way Philip put together his trips: "The only way I'd be able to go is if someone else put this together. It'd be kinda like going off to the Rocky Mountains on an elk hunt. If you didn't have some idea where to go, you'd just be lost in the Rocky Mountains. So, we have a purpose." Another affirmed, "This is a convenient way to serve our purpose, isn't it? All we've got to do is pay our money and show up." Philip, and the other team leaders, provided the means by making the connections for the people. They provided a way for a transaction of an experience to take place: the STM participants paid with their money, their service, and their time. In return they got a particular experience around which they had framed a set of expectations.

In examples such as these, we can also see the emerging paradigms of mission at work. The hierarchical leadership is not deploying missionaries with specific goals and objectives for the broader church, as was the emphasis of mission at one point. Rather, when local leadership is utilized such leadership determines the priorities for mission. Often this is done amongst a group of peers. At least in these cases, similarities to an ECM church culture can be found where STM blossoms. The experience available in small-group relationships with peer leadership determines mission at a local level and is the fertile soil for STM.

To summarize what we have seen in the previous chapter and in this one, I have shown how my data indicated that experience is a strong motivator for STM participants, at times even more so than biblical mandates for service, evangelism, or the proclamation that the Kingdom of God is, in fact, near. I have shown that, in the absence of biblical mission instruction, cultural secular influences have dictated much of how mission is practiced. We also saw that STMers place a high value on the relationships they expect to build while overseas for brief, yet intensely personal, periods of time. This expressed quest for relationships occurs with a backdrop of an American culture that has reprioritized activities to put an increasing focus on the individual. Additionally, my data showed the power that the American small group movement has on a practice of mission. Certainly, for centuries before, missionaries served with co-workers in the field. Yet, STM is unique in that it brings together a group of people for a particular purpose: to travel to another place in the name of service. STM teams are designed by many churches to function like any other Christian education group, like a Bible study, Sunday School class, or support group.

Statements such as these expressed well what many of the team members regularly conveyed: the experience is of great importance to them. Their narratives often coincided with the idea that the economic transaction of an experience is highly personal and unique and can be described on a spiritual level, as Pine and Gilmore asserted above.[52] The STM trip was viewed by many as a part of an exchange. The STMers were giving of their time, money, and resources in exchange for an experience that they expected to be highly memorable, distinctly personal, revealed over the duration of the trip, and by the immersion of the international travel they would fully engage the senses. They were buyers in the Economy of Experience. What exactly were they seeking to buy? Critics of STM have labeled the practice as tourism disguised as a service trip.[53] I suggest that it is more than a mere holiday. The STM participants were looking for some sort of transformation from their experience. They expect their travels to an idealized place to be

---

52. Pine and Gilmore, "Experience Economy," 99.
53. Root, "Youth Ministry," 317.

transformative. The narratives in the dataset suggest that participants were seeking to pay for something akin to a pilgrimage. "Pilgrimage is a journey to a special or holy place as a way of making an impact on one's life with the revelation of God associated with that place."[54] Considering this definition of pilgrimage used by Craig Bartholomew and Robert Llewelyn, pilgrimage and STM have many parallels. In the following chapter, we will examine these parallels in further detail.

54. Bartholomew and Llewelyn, "Introduction," xii-xvi.

7

Pilgrimage, Tourism, and Mission

As I pointed out earlier in this project, scholars have suggested that, in many ways, STM functions like a pilgrimage. Recall that both Howell and Priest called for academic research that examines STM in light of the model of pilgrimage put forth by Victor and Edith Turner and the influences of tourism.[1] In this chapter, I will synthesize the academic studies of STM discussed in chapter 4, the data from my unique ethnographic work, and research related to the classic Turnerian model of pilgrimage. After a discussion of the relationship between STM and pilgrimage, we will turn our attention to another trans-cultural phenomenon that relates to STM: tourism. As Howell pointed out, "Given that STM is not exactly tourism, pilgrimage, or mission but a hybrid of all three and a thing unto itself, theologies around any one of these are inadequate for shaping our thought and practice."[2] First, we will examine pilgrimage.

The expectation that the teams would encounter something new for the transformation of the STM participant was a common narrative in the dataset. Remember that, when asked to describe some of the benefits of his STM trips with college students, Rev. Wallace pointed to this benefit to the students, "There is something very transformative, often, with mission trips. So, we. . .try to go to a place that will completely put the students out of their comfort zone. To help them try to understand and experience something that they have never experienced before. A lot of times, those conditions do a lot of good in students' lives." The notion of a designed experience,

1. Priest and Howell, "Introduction," 127; Howell, *Short-Term Mission*, 48–57, 229–31.

2. Howell, *Short-Term Mission*, 229.

to guide someone through new and marginally uncomfortable encounters, for the benefit of the participant, is not something new or limited to the STM phenomenon. Much the same could be said for a family trip across the United States, a ride on a roller coaster at an amusement park, or a religious pilgrimage to a holy site. Research into the STM phenomenon pointed out important similarities to modern and historic pilgrimage. Additionally, such research has suggested parallels to a model of pilgrimage described by Victor and Edith Turner. STM journeys are often "structured around phases of separation, liminality and reincorporation for the purposes of heightening religious awareness"[3] and, as such, bear examination for their agency as pilgrimage. As Priest correctly points out about STM trips:

> Like pilgrimages, these trips are rituals of intensification, where one temporarily leaves the ordinary, compulsory, workaday life 'at home' and experiences an extraordinary, voluntary, sacred experience 'away from home' in a liminal space where sacred goals are pursued, physical and spiritual tests are faced, normal structures are dissolved, *communitas* is experienced, and personal transformation occurs.[4]

Many of the STM participants in the dataset were like pilgrims in that they expected their travels and experiences to bring about a change in personal faith development. Of those who responded to the follow-up survey (n=30), only a few (n=6) disagreed with the statement: "Mission trips are more beneficial for those who go than for the people they seek to serve." I also asked participants to indicate the most important priorities for a STM trip. While "Contributing to the hosts mission" (n=18) and "Developing relationships with mission hosts" (n=16) were considered most important, more respondents prioritized "Developing my personal faith" (n=15) above "Serving the Poor" (n=11) and "Challenging myself to do something new (n=9) above "Preaching the Word of God" (n=8).[5]

Howell points out important parallels to STM and the Turners' studies in pilgrimage. The Turners' description of pilgrimage as an elliptical movement in three phases: separation, liminality, and aggregation is a helpful dialogue partner for STM narratives. He goes on to call for more work in the development of a theology of mission that engages STM with traits of tourism and pilgrimage.[6] Characteristics of tourism were found in the

3. Howell, *Short-Term Mission*, 55.

4. Priest et al., "Short-Term Mission," 433–34.

5. Participants were asked to rank the three most important priorities from a given list.

6. Howell, *Short-Term Mission*, 55–56, 229.

narratives of my dataset, but to a lesser degree than pilgrimage. Given the strong influences of traits of pilgrimage in my dataset, it is appropriate to consider issues of pilgrimage in STM service. To do so, I will address the Turnerian model in relation to STM, as Howell and Priest have mentioned. I will provide a brief history of pilgrimage to inform the discussion of the relationship between STM and pilgrimage. I then turn to a treatment of the Turnerian theory of pilgrimage and its traits that move towards a theology of mission that engages STM and pilgrimage. It is beyond the scope of our discussion to provide a full critical analysis of the Turnerian understanding of pilgrimage and the later developments in pilgrimage studies. Rather, my purpose is to answer the call from previous scholarship of STM to engage the theory that the Turners put forth.

PILGRIMAGE

Arnold van Gennep illustrates a view of pilgrimage that embraces the separation, margin, and aggregation in *The Rites of Passage* (1960). Victor Turner further developed the view in *The Ritual Process* (1969) and later expanded it in a work with his wife Edith in *Image and Pilgrimage in Christian Culture* (1979). Each of these phases, and the similar traits found in tourism, are discussed below. I will first turn to historical Christian pilgrimage to frame the discussion.

James Preston notes that "until recently pilgrimage has been neglected as a topic of inquiry by social scientists and historians of religions."[7] Such is the case, even though pilgrimage is manifested in nearly all world religions. Scholars have noted evidence of pilgrimage in shrines, historical documents, and pilgrim guides from several contexts. Perhaps one reason for the lack of previous work in the area of pilgrimage is the difficulty of studying a practice that is unbounded as it transcends geographical, religious, or ethnic delineations. This ubiquitous phenomenon is intertwined with religious, cultural, and social complexities that are difficult to contain in spatial or theoretical brackets often used to try to contain a subject for study.[8]

The Turners point out that "pilgrimage may be thought of as extroverted mysticism, just as mysticism is introverted pilgrimage."[9] This mystic property, Preston says, is one of the reasons why scholars stayed away from a study of pilgrimage. Only more recently were the more subjective aspects of human behavior deemed worthy of anthropological study. This legitimi-

7. Preston, "Spiritual Magnetism," 31.
8. Preston, "Spiritual Magnetism," 31–32.
9. Turner and Turner, *Image and Pilgrimage*, 33.

zation allowed a growing interest in the study of pilgrimage. The study of pilgrimage remains difficult. It is a "sprawling, processual" phenomenon.[10] Compartmentalized, fragmented methodologies are ill-equipped to engage it properly. A multi-disciplinary approach is required.[11] I seek to move toward a further understanding of STM and the complexities of mission, tourism, and pilgrimage that surround it. My intention is to consider (among the other fields mentioned in chapter 6) pilgrimage, a theology of mission, and the current practice of millions of Americans going overseas for a week or two in the name of Christian service. In earlier chapters, I discussed a theology of mission and STM. Now my intention is to focus upon what may very well be a modern day, and underestimated, practice of pilgrimage under the name of "mission" and how this might move the discussion towards a theology of STM.

It is impossible to address completely the practice of pilgrimage in this work. My intention is to address some of the complexities around Christian pilgrimage, which in itself is a daunting task.[12] When I began collecting field data from the focus groups, I expected to hear their implicit theologies of missional service. What I noticed instead in their accounts were aspects attributed to pilgrimage, such as communitas, liminality, and re-aggregation. Therefore, I narrow the discussion to Christian pilgrimage and some of the complexities therein. As the subjects of this ethnographic study are Christians, so the examination of pilgrimage focuses upon Christian expressions thereof. I do so not to discount other expressions of pilgrimage, but to focus the discussion in a relevant context.

PILGRIMAGE AND TURNERIAN THEORY

The Turners' understanding of pilgrimage is not about any specific place. For them, the focus of pilgrimage is upon the liminal state. It is this state of liminality, in both spatial and emotional location, that is central to pilgrimage. The Turners formed their analysis of pilgrimage based upon the earlier work of Arnold van Gennep whose research in tribal and ancient settings focused upon rites of transition. It is here that the Turners found the basis for the three phases of pilgrimage that they described as elliptical movement: separation, limen, and aggregation. The first phase, separation, "comprises symbolic behavior signifying the detachment of the individual or group, either from an earlier fixed point in the social structure or from a relatively

---

10. Preston, "Spiritual Magnetism," 32.

11. Preston, "Spiritual Magnetism," 31–32.

12. Turner and Turner, *Image and Pilgrimage*, xxv.

stable set of cultural conditions."[13] Van Gennep describes the second phase as liminal, a state in which the pilgrim is in an environment devoid of all familiar classifications. The "liminar" is in a state absent of traits of the previous or future states. Pilgrimage, the Turners say, is not truly liminal, but maintains some traits and they instead adopted the term "liminoid" to describe this middle phase. Last, the pilgrims seek to re-aggregate to the society from which they came while finding themselves somewhat different than before they departed.[14]

The Liminoid Phenomenon

Van Gennep insists that important passages in life involve "a special series of separation, a transition, and an incorporation" into the new state.[15] He labels each of these in reference to their place in the ever-important liminal state: separation: preliminal, transition: liminal, and incorporation: post-liminal. Van Gennep emphasizes that each of these are emphasized and elaborated at different levels.[16] The Turners take Van Gennep's work further by asserting that the spatiotemporal processes cannot be limited only to traditional rites of passage. These processes should be viewed as applicable to "all phases of decisive cultural change."[17]

Liminality embraces not merely the transition, but also the potentiality that is otherwise unavailable through the mundane. Such potentiality is available through more common liminal phases associated with ceremonies like a regular worship service, or a special service of baptism, ordination, funeral rites. The Turners assert that greater spatial liminality is frequently desired by people of various religious and ethnic backgrounds. They go on to argue that because Christianity did not have innate profound liminal rites and European societies were usually highly localized, "Christianity generated its own mode of liminality for the laity. This mode was best represented by the pilgrimage to a sacred site or holy shrine located at some distance away from the pilgrim's place of residence and daily labor."[18] However, they have missed the important fact that Christianity is a faith whose teachings require liminality. Given that when discussing the development of pilgrimage in Christian tradition, the Turners focus on Western Europe from the

13. Turner and Turner, *Image and Pilgrimage*, 2.
14. Turner and Turner, *Image and Pilgrimage*, 2, 35.
15. Van Gennep, *Rites of Passage*, 11.
16. Van Gennep, *Rites of Passage*, 11.
17. Turner and Turner, *Image and Pilgrimage*, 2.
18. Turner and Turner, *Image and Pilgrimage*, 4.

second century through the fifteenth century,[19] a time firmly entrenched in Christendom (this would be better stated, "*Christendom* generated its own mode of liminality for the laity"). Christianity requires one to move from self to another place, spiritually first and perhaps physically second. From the view of the Israelites as pilgrims to Jesus' instructions to leave all and "Follow Me" (e.g. Luke 18:21) to the command "Go into all the world" (Mark 16:15) to later New Testament allusions to Christians as "aliens and exiles" (1 Pet 2:11), Christianity is a religion intricately connected with liminality. Christendom asked the laity to encounter the liminal in the form of an earthly rite of passage.

Sites of pilgrimage have a key trait in common: "They are believed to be places where miracles once happened, still happen, and may happen again."[20] Pilgrims embrace the liminal state for, among other things, the potential blessings they expect to secure through their experience at the pilgrimage site. These blessings would include the expectation to witness or partake in such miracles. While mystics celebrate an interior pilgrimage, this sort of pilgrimage is a mysticism of the exterior.

The Turners further assert that while Christian pilgrimage has many of the liminal attributes of universal rites of passage, it is a voluntary and not a demanded societal obligation. Since it maintains the passage of an individual or group from one status to another within the mundane world, it is still movement through something liminal. Therefore, they deemed the practice as "quasi-liminal" or "liminoid."[21] The liminoid state is one of anti-structure and chaos, though not completely. Mathias Zahniser says that pilgrims, at their own request, enter the liminal state that "initiates return to the chaotic state of non-being in order to be reborn into a new and unknown reality."[22] This chaos, maybe it is better described as "disequilibrium," is where pilgrims seek new meanings and understandings in an effort to regain stability. Such a process is expected to bring about transformation. It is the expected transformation in this liminal state that pilgrims seek. Zahniser compares pilgrims, while in a liminoid state, to newborn babies and notes that the participants are ripe for bonding.[23] It is here that communitas is formed.

19. Turner and Turner, *Image and Pilgrimage*, 5, 18–19.
20. Turner and Turner, *Image and Pilgrimage*, 6.
21. Turner and Turner, *Image and Pilgrimage*, 34–35.
22. Zahniser, "Ritual Process," 7.
23. Zahniser, "Ritual Process," 7.

Communitas

Communitas is "social antistructure" and defined as "full, unmediated communication, even communion, between definite and determinate identities, which arises spontaneously in all kinds of groups, situations, and circumstances."[24] The Turners felt so strongly about communitas that they hold it as "an essential and generic human bond"[25] and placed it solidly within the framework of liminality. Communitas emerges as a recognizable characteristic of the liminal period when members of the liminal group submit to one another as equals and hierarchy is largely removed. They do so, even though, in a time before the liminal state, these individuals would have assumed the roles of their society that accepted a "structured, differentiated, and often hierarchical system of politico-legal-economic positions with many types of evaluation, [which separated them] in terms of 'more' or 'less.'"[26] It is important to note that communitas is not merely a move from the "secular" to the "sacred" but it is a recognition of certain human bonds that transcend position and status. "Liminality implies that the high could not be high unless the low existed, and the one who is high must experience what it is like to be low."[27] Because communitas presents itself in different forms, Victor Turner makes the distinctions between 1) existential or spontaneous communitas, 2) normative communitas, and 3) ideological communitas.

Existential or spontaneous communitas is a seamless movement that rejects "status" or "contract." This is an idealized community in which social structure is largely discarded and the needs of the others in the community come before the needs of the individual. The group is made up of innocents who know no need for crime, weapons, or conflict. Power is shared equally as there is no need for power over another. This sort of communitas is free from social structural forms and usually not brought about by design, but rather tends to rise unpredictably. Turner thought that these were brought about by a mystical power. He alluded to communitas as the ideal presented by the hippies of his day. This sort of communitas is not sustainable as the group will soon begin to seek structural norms. Normative communitas occurs when, over a period of time, the members of the group begin to normalize relationships as they deem necessary for the pursuit of the common

---

24. Turner, "Variations," 46.
25. Turner and Turner, *Image and Pilgrimage,* 250.
26. Turner, *The Ritual Process,* 96.
27. Turner, *The Ritual Process,* 97.

goals.[28] Ideological communitas is used "to describe the external and visible effects. . .of an inward experience"[29] of the participants. It is "the formulation of remembered attributes of the communitas experience in the form of a utopian blueprint for the reform of society."[30] It is ideological communitas that we can identify in many STM teams.

The Turners' study of liminality was originally in field research with African tribal rituals. They saw parallels to those rites of passage in Christian pilgrimage. Their areas of emphasis that relate to the study of STM, in particular, include the

> release from mundane structure; homogenization of status; simplicity of dress and behavior; communitas; ordeal; reflection on the meaning of basic religious and cultural values. . .movement from the mundane center to a sacred periphery which suddenly, transiently, becomes central for the individual, an *axis mundi* of his faith; movement itself, a symbol of communitas, which changes with time, as against stasis, which represents structure.[31]

The Turners go on to point out that pilgrimage is a voluntary activity. Therefore, it is better described as "quasi-liminal" or "liminoid" rather than a fully liminal state that Van Gennep describes.

Re-aggregation

The expectation for safe return is a key component to the liminoid state. The pilgrims do sometimes undergo great physical hardships (of their own volition) as they make their way to the pilgrimage site, but they expect to return safely.[32] Such safe return is the last of the Turners' three phases: re-aggregation. During the ritual process the liminars have been stripped of secular power and experience a new, sacred power. They have experienced a deep sense of community with their fellow pilgrims. They have moved to the margin and that has allowed them a new critical perspective of the normative structures. All the while, an expectation to remain in the liminal state for a fixed period of time has allowed them to remain entrenched in a liminoid state. Upon return from the liminal state, the re-aggregation phase

28. Turner, *The Ritual Process*, 132–39.

29. Turner, *The Ritual Process*, 132.

30. Turner and Turner, *Image and Pilgrimage*, 252.

31. Turner and Turner, *Image and Pilgrimage*, 34.

32. Turner and Turner, *Image and Pilgrimage*, 35, 197.

"installs them, inwardly transformed and outwardly changed, in a new place in society."[33] If those changes are permanent is hard to discern. In her study of pilgrimages to Lourdes, Andrea Dahlberg found that pilgrims engage in the journey several times over, hoping to recapture something that they had experienced before. "They said the Lourdes pilgrimage was 'addictive', 'you just get hooked and keep coming back.'"[34]

Fairs and Carnivals

Before this re-aggregation takes place, however, one more rite is frequently practiced amongst pilgrims. As early as medieval times, Christian-themed fairs at pilgrimage centers were commonplace at important sites like Chartres, Cologne, and others. In the twentieth century, such celebrations continued. The Turners describe one such carnival at a modern pilgrimage site outside of Mexico City: "a full-blown fair was taking place, with Ferris wheels, shooting galleries, and bumper cars, beside peddlers selling a wide range of goods."[35] They go on to make the important connection between the work of devotional pilgrimage and the play of recreational activities in the joyful portions of communitas. "Those who journey to pray together also play together in secular interludes between religious activities; sightseeing to places of secular interest is one common form of 'play' associated with pilgrimage."[36] These ludic activities provide as important a part of the ritual of pilgrimage as the solemn ones do.[37]

PILGRIMAGE, TOURISM, AND SHORT-TERM MISSION

The Turners also see tourism principles in the study of pilgrimage: "A tourist is half a pilgrim, if a pilgrim is half a tourist."[38] In many ways the role of tourist and pilgrim are complimentary to one another. Therefore, it is necessary to discuss these two together, at least to some extent.[39] Like pilgrimage, tourism has, thus far, garnered an inadequate amount of academic research. However, work in both of these fields is growing. As an academic field of

---

33. Turner and Turner, *Image and Pilgrimage*, 249.

34. Dahlberg, "Three Pilgrimages to Lourdes," 36.

35. Turner and Turner, *Image and Pilgrimage*, 36.

36. Turner and Turner, *Image and Pilgrimage*, 37.

37. Turner and Turner, *Image and Pilgrimage*, 35.

38. Turner and Turner, *Image and Pilgrimage*, 20.

39. Turner and Turner, *Image and Pilgrimage*, 20.

study, tourism gained attention in the 1970s. Though tourism, as a practice, was growing, many academics did not regard its study as a worthy field. Scholars such as Erik Cohen, Valene Smith, Nelson Graburn, and Sharon Bohn Gmelch have made important contributions to the field and helped it to become a respected academic area of study.[40] I will first consider the dialogue points of STM with pilgrimage before moving to the dialogue points of STM with tourism. Key to this discussion will be the important traits of pilgrimage that I pointed out in the previous section: communitas, liminality, and re-aggregation in an elliptical movement. In regards to tourism, I will particularly engage the role of recreation and spectacle as they will be relevant to our discussion of STM. While it is beyond the scope of this work to fully engage the scholarship of tourism, there are some important areas of overlap that may help shed light on the relationship between pilgrimage and STM. The lines of distinction between the three are not hard and fixed, but somewhat fuzzy and permeable. If the relationship between the pilgrim and the tourist is interchangeable, I want to suggest that such a relationship can be expressed about those who participate in trans-national STM service projects. They are not just a "missioner" or "pilgrim" or "tourist" but something akin to all of those and something else all to its own.

AS A PILGRIM

Upon launching this research project, it was not my intent to seek to define STMers in any particular manner, let alone consider them in the light of pilgrimage. Under the compulsion of the evidence of the qualitative data I began to explore the field of pilgrimage and found some compelling points of discussion. Consider Laurie Occhipinti's assessment of STM as a pilgrimage ritual:

> Short-term missions clearly act as a form of ritual, bringing the participant through a stage of liminality to a new sense of self. While they echo religious pilgrimage in this transformative journey, they contrast in some ways to more traditional pilgrimages, which often entail a visit to a site that is itself sacred. In the short-term mission, the destination is 'the poor,' and the experience of the sacred lies not in the site but in the act of service.[41]

We now turn to consideration of the facets of Turnerian pilgrimage in relation to STM: Communitas, Liminality, Re-aggregation, and Free Days.

40. Gmelch, "Why Tourism Matters," 6.
41. Occhipinti, "Religious Idealism," 15.

Communitas

Brian Howell and Rachel Dorr affirm the pervasive nature of communitas in their study of college students participating in STM in their essay, "Evangelical Pilgrimage: The Language of Short-Term Missions." Howell and Dorr note that "[t]he communitas is built into the fiber of the trip many months prior to the journey itself. But regardless of how a team member experiences these events—or the trip itself—rhetorically there was a profound emphasis on the expectation that, in the liminal state, communitas would result."[42] The most apparent example of communitas is the influence that the concept of "building relationships" had in the pre-trip narratives and post-trip survey. The desire to build relationships seemed pervasive. As I discussed in chapter 6, the vehicle for the relationship building was the model and example of small-group ministries. The deeper connection associated with communitas was the desired waypoint in the journey. All the focus groups used the language and functions of "team." A key implicit function of the team was to provide the participants small group growth opportunities in order to grow personally and to do so amongst a group of others. In other words, the small group was the team and one of the benefits, and expectations, of the team was communitas.

The expectation of the homogenization of status and dress and behavior codes are important points for an understanding of STM and its relationship to pilgrimage. Such principles are important for communitas. During mission trips, people who would assume roles of position and status in their normal settings often remove themselves from such status positions to become equals with team members. They do so with the expectation that such abasement is an essential trait to make the trip function well. Many times, people who at home are high-paid professionals may be relegated to moving cinder blocks up the hill in the name of the mission project. They are not allowed to lay the cinder blocks because they are unskilled and untrained in the masonry techniques to lay them correctly. Instead, they hand the blocks to nationals who may work as day laborers. It is the nationals who are skilled at the manual labor enough to complete the job satisfactorily. The nationals cannot leave the job to the American STMers. That would mean too much time and money in UN-doing the work they were unable to do. So, the STMers assume a homogenization of status amongst themselves and, at times, below the nationals with whom they work.

Similarly, the unskilled and untrained are assigned roles they would normally seek professional assistance for in the United States. Medical

42. Howell and Dorr, "Evangelical Pilgrimage," 14.

teams reported that members with no medical background received a quick training session on simple tasks normally given to nurses or other health-care workers. Tasks like triaging ailments and measuring blood pressure were assigned to people who were willing and available. Laypeople assumed the role of pharmacists, as long as they carefully followed the doctors' instructions. Nurses acted as physicians, if a doctor was nearby and available for questions. The homogenization of relationships meant movements in both vertical directions to find horizontal equality. Philip O'Connor illustrated such homogenization. Philip put forth the notion that the "theme of mission is humility." Such humility is demonstrated when mixing the large amounts of concrete needed for construction projects on his trips. "We mix it by hand, on the ground, with shovels. College professors, school teachers, pastors grab the shovel alongside the Nicaraguans and mix the concrete until they are physically exhausted. That's humility." In the liminoid state of their STM, team members and their hosts embraced the communitas "as they create[d] their own alternative social mode within the confines of the journey and its destination."[43]

Simplicity of dress is also an important pilgrimage-like trait for STM and another way of demonstrating communitas. Earlier we heard teams describe their fundraising dinners and the fact that they often wore matching aprons and/or t-shirts.[44] Communitas begins in the activities before the trip itself. It is common for teams to travel in matching shirts in bold colors and inspiring logos. A simple internet search for "mission trip t-shirts" calls up scores of online stores. Some promise to sell a "great way to show your team unity."[45] Groups both large and small move through airport hubs in matching t-shirts. This homogenization of dress not only shows team unity but removes the hierarchies of roles and status as the group members enter the liminal state.[46]

Team leaders in my dataset also frequently provided guidelines on appropriate dress for their team members. These guidelines often consider the cultural expectations of the host nation. For example, in some cultures, women are expected to wear dresses, pants, or skirts but wearing shorts is taboo. Simplicity of dress for all team members is also often encouraged. At times, STMers felt as though the simplicity of dress provided solidarity with the members of the community in which they worked. Racial, ethnic, language or other differences were nominalized through a dress code that

43. Howell and Dorr, "Evangelical Pilgrimage," 13.

44. See chapter 5.

45. Ministry Gear, http://ministrygear.com/mission-trip-t-shirts/.

46. See Priest, "Peruvian Churches." Howell and Dorr, "Evangelical Pilgrimage."

demonstrated unity among team members and nationals alike.[47] The homogeneity of dress and status is an important trait for many STM activities.

Liminality

The participants in these STM teams willingly entered a liminoid state for the purpose of an expected spiritual growth. Considering the differences between home and their places of service and the new roles they expected to embrace, STMers were looking for separation from their workaday world, a transition to a new environment, and incorporation into new roles and experiences (to use Van Gennep's terms). In the words of Naomi Shaw from Elmville UMC, team members gave up the routines of family, work, and church responsibilities to seek "spiritual fulfillment."

Separation. Team leaders and members expressed a desire for separation. Members of the dataset expected to go without their cellphones, access to the internet, or other such modern conveniences. Rev. Wallace described his upcoming trip as a "retreat" or a place where one can expect to encounter opportunities for spiritual growth. One of the ways that his team members can encounter such an opportunity is by entering a liminoid state where team members "intentionally put [everyday conveniences] down and only pick up the things that are going to draw *us* closer to Christ and others to well-being and to Christ."[48] Such a separation was not deemed appropriate for everyone. One pastor in the focus groups did not feel that all his congregants could cope with the lack of creature comforts or navigate the difficulties of the language barrier.

Transition. Entering a transition stage to a liminal state was visible and obvious for many who participate in transnational service trips. Many teams held a "commissioning" service in their home churches on a Sunday leading up to their departure. A typical commissioning would be held during the regular worship service, would be conducted by the pastor, and would include a special time of prayer for the team. However, an even more defined transition occurs: the international travel itself. All the teams in the data set traveled by airline to reach their countries of service. This defined transition had an impact upon some. They described the sensory inputs of the immersive experience of their arrival in the new environments and the stark contrast to their home nation. Similarly, the return transition is just as quick and just as stark.

47. Hancock, "Short-Term Youth Mission," 171.
48. Emphasis original.

Incorporation. At the pre-trip interviews, those who had previously participated in STM trips recalled the roles they assumed when seeking to incorporate into the new environment on those earlier trips. Many ate the foods of the host nation, attempted the local language, and sought to embrace the customs of their mission hosts. At the same time, they sought to be incorporated as an equal by many of the national hosts. Experienced STMers and new ones alike expressed a desire to: attempt to speak the local language, play with the children they would encounter (as an adult caregiver or another child might do), work under the supervision of national leaders, and do other things to show solidarity with the people they encountered. They seemed undaunted by the lack of a working knowledge of the language or in-depth study of the culture.

Just as the "liminar" maintains some traits of home when traveling, STM participants in the dataset maintained some of the familiarity of home when traveling overseas. Yet many expressed a desire to encounter difficulties, sacrifices, and hardships, at least to a certain degree. They were seeking to enter a liminoid state. STMers identified their hardships as going without the availability of communication by mobile telephone for a week and being forced to take cold showers. Remember the assertions made by Kate Powell of her "gift to herself." She expressed a desire to enter a liminoid state to provide some gain for herself. "I hate it. I do. It's the only thing I really hate. But it's my gift to myself. Now that's something I can give up. I hate cold showers." Her gift to herself, she went on, "Is to say that I can do this, that I can give up something. I can give up having ice [in my soft drink]."

This is only done to certain degree in that teams are often housed in separate facilities from their hosts. Sometimes this is in a hotel or a special dormitory built for STM teams. STM teams eat the local food only insofar as it is feasible for them. National hosts often must install special water filtration systems, for example, that eliminate bacteria that the American team members cannot tolerate. These systems may be used in kitchens used to prepare the food for the American teams. Such systems may not always be available to the nationals in the churches where they serve. STM participants often seek to serve those in their host communities, but they cannot and do not "live at the level of the people" they encounter during their short-term service.

American John Hull studied the role of liminality and short-term cross-cultural encounters in his research on the efficacy of STM to increase the participants' faith level. Studying seven short-term international teams from the United States, he concluded that liminality was an integral component to the personal faith development of those who served on STM projects. His study showed a combination of biblical instruction, cross-cultural interactions, and a liminal experience led to appreciable growth as measured by a faith maturity scale instrument.[49] Given the influence of the expressed desire to grow in their own faith by those in my research dataset, the desire to experience liminality for themselves seems quite natural. Hull goes on to describe the STM experience as a phenomenon that can be couched in an understanding of pilgrimage.[50]

And what do the STM pilgrims expect to see and/or experience during their liminoid encounters? First, recall the Turnerian description of the objects of pilgrimage: "They are believed to be places where miracles once happened, still happen, and may happen again."[51] Historically, objects of pilgrimage were chapels, cathedrals, grottos, temples, and the like. In the pilgrimage of STM, the objects of pilgrimage are more nebulous. They are anywhere and everywhere that the STM participants project their spectacle of idealization. Recall that members of the dataset expressed amazement at the joy they perceived because of (and in spite of) the poverty they perceived amongst those whom they encountered while in their host nation. The idealized images of strong family ties, spiritual vitality, or other such traits among their hosts became the objects of pilgrimage.

Pilgrims embrace the liminal state for, among other things, the potential blessings they expect to secure through their experience at the pilgrimage site.[52] STM participants often replaced the sacred sites with the people they encountered and their shared experiences. Larry Harris, who has led trips to the Caribbean, typified the feelings many STM members expressed:

> I firmly feel like STM trips are very beneficial to whoever goes. You're exposed to a world totally different from your own. Makes you so thankful for what God has given us in this country. And you realize the poverty that's out there. Because without so many material possessions, they have a stronger relationship with God. Because they depend on Him for their daily bread. And they're not hampered by all this stuff that we have.

Larry's feelings, and the feelings of those who expressed similar ideas, could be summed up by something like: "they have so much physical poverty, but spiritual wealth. And I have so much physical wealth, but spiritual poverty." The idealized Other, the poverty and the people in poverty, were prevalent in my conversations. STM participants engaged in the liminoid state to experience a perceived poverty in the destination country and the

49. Hull, "Faith Development," 310–12.
50. Hull, "Faith Development," 341.
51. Turner and Turner, *Image and Pilgrimage*, 6.
52. Turner and Turner, *Image and Pilgrimage*, 6–7.

people in that poverty, expecting personal transformation. The cathedrals and shrines of historical Christian pilgrimage perceived as sites of the miraculous are replaced with what is perceived as substandard housing and malnourished children. The STMers behave as pilgrims in that they then re-aggregate in the society they left while hoping to find themselves somewhat different than what they were before they departed.[53]

Re-aggregation

Re-aggregation as an inwardly transformed and outwardly changed person is a key component of the allure of STM. Though team leaders dedicated a great deal of time and effort to preparing the teams to enter the liminal stage, there was little evidence of efforts to help teams re-aggregate, at least formally. Most of my subject teams reported meeting for several months, even up to a year, before their trip. They discussed logistics, travel specifics, tips on exchanging money, packing pointers, and other such practical issues. However, very few took the time to reflect upon and/or analyze the journey in the same manner upon their return to the United States.

However, it is possible that more informal processing of issues of re-aggregation does, in fact, occur among team members. As I noted earlier, many teams were formed from among existing small groups or among individuals who were already acquainted with one another. It is reasonable to presume that such groups continued to meet informally after the STM trip. Such continued proximity to one another would allow those who experienced a STM pilgrimage to process issues of re-aggregation in informal settings. It is likely that such opportunities occurred in Sunday School settings, small group meetings, or other places of connection team members shared.

Free Days and Fun Time

Free days, carnival/adventure activities, and the like provide some opportunities to examine STM and pilgrimage in relation to tourism. Much like historical pilgrimages featured fairs and carnivals, STM has a similar manifestation of these. One regular feature of STM trip itineraries is the "Free Day." Such a day is usually built into the end of the trip, before heading back to the United States. Teams participate in activities that include, but are not limited to, shopping for native goods in a local market, sightseeing at culturally significant places, visiting a park or the beach, and recreational

---

53. Turner and Turner, *Image and Pilgrimage*, 2.

activities. Adventure activities like participating in a zip-line course, exploring the rain forest, or going white water rafting are commonplace. Team leaders emphasized these activities as team building, (or, we could say, communitas) exercises. They also said that they plan these days as a chance to "decompress" from the trip, to give the team members a chance to begin to deal with the reverse culture shock that would happen to them when they returned to the United States. Though they seemed aware of the reverse culture shock coming, it is problematic that the team leaders did not develop a strategy to deal with such issues after they returned home. Instead, leaders deemed a carnival-like day in the host nation as the more appropriate activity. Other team leaders reported the need to have a Free Day, or even free time throughout the week, to visit cultural sites, a national park, or something similar. They felt this would provide an even deeper appreciation for their mission hosts and the country.

STM teams also demonstrated a point that the Turners made: "One finds that play and solemnity are equally present."[54] Focus group teams often spoke of the importance of a daily debrief, each night, when back at their hotel or host dorm. During this time, the team members are encouraged to talk about the good and bad parts of the day. A devotional message is often given, reportedly one that includes a biblical message about mission related to their activities. During this time, the team is usually isolated from the national hosts and given time to ask questions about things they saw that day that may have been troubling or interesting. This time away from the work and activities of the day was often reported as a highlight of the trip for those who had been before. In fact, the college students told me that they were looking forward to this part of the day as much as the work they were expecting to do. They were planning on staying up late into the night, and thereby getting only a minimum amount of sleep, so that they could make the most of their time in the dorm with their friends. Peter Browning, of Elmville UMC, echoed the college students' desires to mix the solemnity of each evening's reflexive periods with a chance to play with his teammates: "[D]own there. . .we didn't have TV's. . .[In the evenings] we just kick back. We sat around. We talked. We joked. We play around. Don't worry about nothing. Time is. . .irrelevant."

Pilgrimage and STM have strong parallels. Both seek to escape the mundane to encounter the Other for the potentiality of a significant personal encounter for self-edification. Both embrace the communitas that occurs amongst fellow travelers and those encountered along the way. Participants in both re-aggregate to their home, and the mundane, more quickly than

---

54. Turner and Turner, *Image and Pilgrimage*, 37.

they embarked on their journeys. They make such journeys to experience the intensity of the state of separation to intensify one's attachment to one's own faith.[55] Just as STM participants are volunteers in their service, "pilgrimage may be said to represent the quintessence of voluntary liminality."[56] Americans who participate in short-term transnational service projects in the name of mission may be said to represent the same such quintessence.

As a Tourist

As noted, academic study of tourism is relatively young. One important early work on tourism was *Hosts and Guests: The Anthropology of Tourism* wherein editor Valene L. Smith defines the tourist as "a temporarily leisured person who voluntarily visits a place away from home for the purpose of experiencing a change."[57] Several scholars have engaged this definition for a discussion of various aspects of tourism. However, Nelson Graburn maintains that "tourism is best understood as a *kind of ritual*, one in which the special occasions of leisure and travel stand in opposition to everyday life at home and work."[58] The emphasis of tourism as a secular ritual for Graburn is important. He maintains that tourists travel because there is something at home that they want to leave behind and there is something about the place visited that they want to experience because of a perception that it cannot easily be experienced at home. He calls this a "ritual inversion" of a part of life the tourist desires to change, at least for a time. People who live in cold climates vacation in warmer climates. Lower-middle-class travelers seek to "live it up" in Las Vegas with a lavish lifestyle for a time. Those who live in the country want to visit the city. City dwellers seek the peace and quiet of the countryside.[59]

Graburn is correct to point out that the "inversion" is limited. For example, the educated do not want to become ignorant, though they do want to "get away from it all." Even the "all" is limited. Though the tourist may value certain parts of the place they will see, they are likely to want familiar food and amenities to which they are accustomed at home. The inversion "is

---

55. Turner and Turner, *Image and Pilgrimage*, 1–9.

56. Turner and Turner, *Image and Pilgrimage*, 9.

57. Smith, *Hosts and Guests*, 1.

58. Graburn, "Secular Ritual," 25. Emphasis original.

59. Graburn, "Secular Ritual," 26.

rarely an antithesis of. . .values."[60] He insists that the tourist does not expect to be "an entirely different kind of person."[61]

Smith provides some helpful guidelines for different types of tourism that directly relate to our discussion. The first is ethnic tourism which is "marketed to the public in terms of the 'quaint' customs of indigenous and often exotic peoples."[62] These tourists have an interest in seeing indigenous customs like dress, housing, food, rituals, and value the opportunity to shop for "primitive wares and curiosities."[63] Cultural tourism engages the local fare of a particular culture. The cultural tourist wants to see the remnants of a lifestyle that is fading away from the way it has been imagined by the tourist or the collective tourist ideal. Recreational tourism provides activities that would otherwise be unavailable at home.[64] Ethnic, cultural, and recreational tourism all have overlapping principles in the discussion of mission and pilgrimage alike. Some narratives of the focus groups illustrate explicit and implicit desires to experience the offerings of the indigenous peoples of the host nations. As mentioned above, teams visited local markets on Free Days to shop for things like "primitive wares and curiosities." STMers often wanted to try local foods. To some extent, they wanted the "authentic" experience. This desire overlapped with the expectation to behold a culture unlike the one back home. Many of the activities of Free Days mentioned above could fit into the category of recreational tourism.

Erik Cohen presents a definition of tourism that engaged several different roles that one may assume when traveling internationally: "businessman, travelling salesman, international representatives, [and] missionaries."[65] Though they are travelers, he excluded anyone in these categories in his definition of a tourist. Rather, he says, "A 'tourist' is a voluntary, temporary traveler, travelling in the expectation of pleasure from the novelty and change experienced on a relatively long and non-recurrent round-trip."[66] However, Cohen defined it as such in 1974, before the steep climb in the STM movement. When he says missionary, he most certainly would have meant one who traveled for an extended period of time and was not expected to return to their country of origin on a regular basis. Yet, when one considers the motivations of many STMers in the dataset to seek the plea-

---

60. Graburn, "Secular Ritual," 26.
61. Graburn, "Secular Ritual," 26.
62. Smith, "The Quest in Guest," 4.
63. Smith, "The Quest in Guest," 4.
64. Smith, "The Quest in Guest," 4–5.
65. Cohen, "Who Is a Tourist?," 532.
66. Cohen, "Who Is a Tourist?," 532.

sure of the experience, the novelty and the change, such travels resemble tourism in many ways.

Cohen also attempts to make distinctions between the pilgrim and the tourist in later work. He says that the pilgrim's goal is the Center. The goal of the tourist is the Other. Pilgrimage is usually institutionalized while tourism is voluntary and more driven by social desires.[67] A pilgrim looks for the Center in his or her own culture, in our case Christian discipleship. The pilgrim's role is functional: to recreate and revitalize the individual to those values at the Center. The tourist's role is also to be recreated and revitalized but each tourist has an "elective center" to pursue.[68] While these delineations are plausible when considering only tourism and pilgrimage, these lines become blurred when adding short-term transnational service to the discussion. The Other and the Center often become one and the same. Thus, the roles of this type of traveler become much less defined.

Gmelch offers definitions of tourism like those mentioned above. However, she points out the misunderstanding many have regarding tourism's economic impact in the Global South, among other locations. She admits that there are many complex factors to consider in regards to tourism and economic transactions like local and national profit controls, business influences in local communities and on a global scale, and the direct work of local populations who receive international visitors. Despite this, she maintains that very few of the tourism dollars spent in a particular country go to the residents of that community and/or nation. In an age of increased globalization, a great deal of tourism money goes offshore to the businesses and workers who came from other countries to build resorts, hotels, and recreational facilities. She offers that "the Caribbean as a whole loses from 70 to 90 percent of every dollar earned from tourism."[69] This is even more pronounced in the cases of all-inclusive resorts and cruise ships where the guests have little reason to leave the confines of the specified boundaries established by the tour operators.[70]

This may be one of the most significant ways that tourism and STM differ. There is no known research to quantify the monetary transactions between STM teams and their hosts, but it is important to note that money flows much differently in a STM team/national host transaction than the one between tourist and tour operator. While the tour operator or resort

67. Cohen's work embraces a larger field of pilgrimage than what I have proposed; he also engages non-Christian pilgrimage such as the Muslim *hajj*. I include his contribution here because of the overlap in the discussion as relevant to Christian pilgrimage.

68. Cohen, "Pilgrimage and Tourism," 58–60.

69. Gmelch, "Why Tourism Matters," 9.

70. Gmelch, "Why Tourism Matters," 9–10.

owner may send the money received from the tourists to a home office in another country, STM seems to put the money more directly into the hands of the local populations. Those in the dataset reported paying members of the local churches to serve as cooks, guides, translators, laborers, and a variety of other roles to support the needs of the STM teams. Most, if not all, the teams made direct financial contributions to the host churches. Because STMers send billions of dollars annually in cash transactions, STM could be providing more economic benefit to local populations than tourism.

As we can see the areas of tourism and pilgrimage have some clear distinctions. However, in many ways they overlap and one can move back and forth between them. When one considers STM and its current practice, similar distinctions and overlaps can be seen. It would seem that some who participate in STM take on both these roles at one time or another. Others may travel under the name of mission, but function in a much different way. The parallels with the Economy of Experience are present in pilgrimage, tourism, and STM. The pilgrim, the tourist, and the STMer all expect to exchange something of value for an anticipated experience.

As a Missioner

While Howell's participants in *Short-Term Mission: An Ethnography of Christian Travel Narrative and Experience* were adamant that they were not acting like tourists in their travel and efforts towards service work, this sentiment is not always clear across the practice of STM.[71] For many, the lines between tourism (and the adventure that can often be a part of visiting a new place) and STM are blurred. This happens not only on the part of the participants, but also on those who design short-term service opportunities. For example, in February 2015, a denominational organization that facilitates short-term service trips posted a particularly attractive advertisement for adventure seekers on its Facebook page. The advertisement read:

> Are you an accountant with an adventure-seeking heart for service? Our friends [in] Guatemala are looking for an 'adventurous accountant' to serve with them in-country for 2–4 weeks. You will have the chance to live and work short term with a dynamic mission team in a beautiful location.

The ad goes on to list financial requirements and contact details. Prominently placed with the ad are two photos of Harrison Ford as Indiana Jones,

---

71. Howell, *Short-Term Mission*, 48.

one as a bespectacled, bow-tie-wearing professor and the other as the rugged-looking treasure seeker.

A major travel company that provides travel services for Christian pilgrimages and cultural and historic tours advertised a special opportunity for "service." In February 2016, in the cold of winter, the company advertised its annual "Missions Cruise." The brochure touted a trip led by a husband and wife team with pastoral and medical experience and training from their denomination's mission organization. The cruise itinerary listed stops in Jamaica, Aruba, the Dominican Republic, and the Bahamas. Participants would have up to eight hours on each island for their "mission opportunities." Such opportunities included a chance to "Bring Love Offerings & needed supplies to local Methodist churches," "Connect with leaders on 4 islands," "Learn about the work that is needed," and to "Worship & Fellowship with a local Methodist congregation." This would be done while visiting with those from "very poor" families and touring a church that is "worshipping in a tent." Catered lunches on the islands would be offered as well.

On the opposite page from the description of the mission touring and visiting, the cruise ship is described as one of "timeless elegance in modern comfort." Participants in the Mission Cruise return each night to the "elegance and glamour" of the ship that includes an "opulent casino," "Broadway-sized theater," "Swarovski crystal staircases," a "gorgeous Infinity Pool," and plenty of "slow-food delicacies" to savor.

This is not to cast aspersions on such visits. I have affirmed the benefits of tourism elsewhere in this chapter. I have also affirmed the role of mission above. However, the confluence, and thereby confusion, of these two areas is exactly the sort of thing that national pastors lamented in chapter 4. It seems likewise problematic to advertise a tour to visit the poor, while sleeping each night in opulence. For whose benefit is this trip? For whom is the experience? Is there much difference between this trip and others billed as mission? Does this ad merely remove some of the veneer and instead honestly disclose what is underneath? Or does this push the STM movement in a new direction? Further research is required to answer such questions.

Further examples demonstrate the conflation of pilgrim, tourist, and missioner. STM sending agencies distribute advertisements for openings on STM teams regularly. These can include openings for an entire team or one or two individuals to complete a team or, perhaps, to fulfill a more specialized role. Consider one such request for a team leader. The successful candidate would lead medical teams to Honduras. "Medical training is not required for the team leader; organizational skills are a plus. Assistance in all aspects of planning for a mission team will be provided." There was no mention in the advertisement for spiritual leadership skills or experience, missional understanding, or other such traits. Rather "organizational skills" were required, much like one who would lead a tour group rather than those working to proclaim a kingdom message.

It is just as problematic when one operates under the name of mission for personal gain first and the needs of the recipients of mission service second. Such is the case when pilgrimage becomes the focus of the international travel done in the name of mission. Consider this assessment from American John Hull: "Because it fits our understanding of a pilgrimage, one of our primary goals should be to utilize short-term mission experiences to draw believing Christians closer to God and as a result, deepen their faith in him."[72] In much the same way that an as-yet spiritually immature John Wesley wanted to travel to Georgia in hopes of "saving his own soul," many of his modern-day followers are hoping to do something similar. I will expound upon the problems with such an expression of the activities done in the name of "mission" in the next chapter.

Let me summarize this chapter with a clear assertion: my data indicated that short-term mission was being used by some to purchase an experience. The time, money, and service of the STM project was a part of a transaction in which participants sought to experience a pilgrimage, to a place where miracles were believed to have happened and could happen again, for personal edification. While previous literature offered suggestions for considering STM in relation to pilgrimage and to tourism, my original ethnographic and academic literature research offers concrete examples of confluences in these areas.

In this chapter, I elucidated the areas in which my data coincided with notions of pilgrimage and tourism. In my data, a STM team functioned as a group of individuals who came together for a specified, finite period, to go to a place where many believe God has worked before and will work again. The idea that the group would work together for, among other things, the personal and spiritual fulfillment of the individual was a significant influence in my data. Those in my dataset used language akin to pilgrimage to describe their activities done in the name of mission. We have seen STMers demonstrate touristic behaviors during their activities. It is important to note, however, that often times STM, pilgrimage, and tourism operate in a dynamic, fluid relationship. As Howell pointed out at the beginning of the chapter, "STM is not exactly tourism, pilgrimage, or mission but a hybrid of all three and a thing unto itself."[73]

72. Hull, "Faith Development," 341.
73. Howell, *Short-Term Mission*, 229.

Yet, my research answers Howell's call for a more robust theology that engages STM and these other issues. Though Howell and Priest thought STM was lost in the sea of issues around Turnerian pilgrimage and tourism in both confluence and peculiarity, my research indicates that some are submerging STM into pilgrimage. I demonstrated how STM was heavily influenced by the small group movement, the dynamics of which are key for the communitas of pilgrimage. In Wuthnow's work, such small groups joined together on a spiritual quest. I demonstrated that the small groups that are STM teams assume the characteristics of pilgrimage when they make not only a spiritual quest, but also a physical one. My original data showed that the deep bonds that many STMers reported feeling occurred in the liminoid spaces when, using Zahniser's analogy, the team members were ripe for bonding in much the same a newborn baby is. My data indicated that STMers re-aggregated into the mundane and soon pined for the next opportunity, just as a pilgrim frequently does. Here we see a parallel with Dahlberg's account of the Lourdes pilgrims feeling "addicted" to the trip and my focus-group interview when Gregory Booth said, "It's almost like an addiction. . . . I feel like I am at a point in my life where I need to go on one. . . . I need one for myself personally."

While STM is being submerged into pilgrimage, there seems to be a bit of tourism mixed in the water as well. While Cohen distinguishes the Other as the goal of the tourist and the Center as the goal of the pilgrim, I have shown that the STM participants in my data often made this one and the same. The participants in my research desired to experience the Other. They were willing to pay a price for the opportunity to do so. The Other they sought was the perceived physical poverty that also exhibited a deep spirituality that they themselves could not seem to find otherwise. When experiencing the Other, they expected to find the Center in a way that they could not find in the mundane. In the case of STM from the those in my dataset, this Center was a deeper relationship with God that the Other seemed to possess.

8

Consuming Mission

Towards a Theology of Short-Term Mission and Pilgrimage

M y research has revealed that there was significant evidence that STM participants used their time, money and service to purchase an experience of pilgrimage. Those who had participated in STM previously wanted to do so again in hopes of recapturing something they had lost since the last experience. First-timers were seeking to experience what they had seen in the veterans. All of them seemed to be ready to consume mission activities for personal growth. I suggest, however, that rather than consuming mission activities for personal edification, those seeking to serve should submit to the consuming mission of God.

Admittedly, a discussion of the motivations for mission must be done with great care. People have served in mission, historically, for a variety of reasons, some of which were influenced by popular sentiment or world events. Often, such motivations overlapped with the biblical impetus for mission. "Rarely are motives for mission entirely pure; 'throughout the history of the Christian mission pure and impure motives have been as mixed through each other as the clean and unclean animals on the ark.'"[1] Throughout the church's history untold numbers of missionaries answered the call to serve no matter where that call may have taken them. Countless individuals left house and home knowing that they would likely die on the mission field. We must be careful with our judgments if we are not willing to

---

1. Ott et al., *Encountering Theology of Mission*, 166, quoting Verkuyl.

make the same sacrifice.[2] Through STM has no direct precedent in historical mission, some do serve in STM opportunities at personal risk and with great sacrifice. It is with some caution that I approach a critical study of any practice of mission. There are deep needs in the world. There are those who have the resources to meet those needs. The two should be joined together. Indeed, in some cases, STM work has led to long-term change in communities without previous access to proper food, clothing, shelter, education, and healthcare.[3] Additionally, it is important to remember that mission hosts remain open to STM. Nearly 70 percent of national pastors saw STMs as a benefit to their church and ministry. Only 10 percent of respondents said they would not want to receive a STM team.[4]

However, the practice has grown as a program of churches and parachurch ministries without the careful theological examination required for subsequent healthy practices. My interpretation of the narratives collected points to the conclusion that several ministries, in part or in whole, have developed STM programs with the primary goal of consuming an experience for the implicit, and sometimes explicit, benefit of the participants. STM leaders and practitioners must apply robust theological reflection to their efforts towards the realization that, as Bosch puts it so well, "mission is *missio Dei*, which seeks to subsume into itself the. . .missionary programs of the church."[5] Done correctly, Christian service is the cruciform participation in the liberating mission of Jesus[6] who came "to bring good news to the poor. . .to proclaim release to the captives and recovery of sight to the blind, to let the oppressed go free, to proclaim the year of the Lord's favor."[7] The *missio Dei* demonstrates a self-abasing stance towards the proclamation of Christian love. A theology of STM that confronts these principles of experience and pilgrimage must be developed and subsumed by a broader theological understanding of the *missio Dei*.[8]

This is not the first time the church has struggled with how to serve in mission. Historically, improperly placed motivations for mission have often resulted in problematic practices that required corrective action. For example, efforts to exert ecclesial power or influence on another culture is

---

2. Ott et al., *Encountering Theology of Mission*, 165–66.

3. Priest, "Short-Term Missions," 91.

4. See Eitzen, "Short-Term Missions." While others expressed similar feelings, Eitzen seems to be summative.

5. Bosch, *Transforming Mission*, 531.

6. Bosch, *Transforming Mission*, 531–32.

7. See Luke 4:18–19.

8. Howell, *Short-Term Mission*, 230.

a reoccurring issue.[9] At times, "[a]scetic motivation for mission is present 'when missionary service is sought for a means to come nearer to God along the road of self-denial, penance and sacrifice.'"[10] In the eighteenth century, the widespread reports from Captain James Cook and missionary William Carey of the "noble savages" they encountered led to problems when new missioners sometimes signed up for service under romantic ideals first, and biblical service later.[11] As shown above, these notions are still, at times, mixed with a quest for self-realization and edification. When the personal experience becomes primary, the central goal of Christian mission is hidden from view. Mission must be grounded in a biblical theology. Granted, the Apostle Paul does speak of receiving "the prize."[12] However, New Testament teaching is replete with instructions for the willingness to sacrifice and suffer, if necessary, for the sake of the gospel of Jesus Christ.[13] This message seems lost on many who are participating in STM. In this closing chapter, I offer some correctives to bring the practice in line with the missiological framework I have outlined.

A CALL TO ENGAGE THEOLOGICAL REFLECTION

Since STM grew as a practice without proper theological underpinning, it should not come as a complete surprise that these issues should arise. The fact that it is a populist movement further complicates how corrective action can be taken. It will not be enough to provide revamped missiological education in seminaries, colleges, and universities. Rather, such a reworking of missiological reflection must be conducted in the local church context as well. As I indicated in our discussion of Wesleyan missiology in chapter 3, we must heed Randy Maddox's warning: "We face a dire need for reintegrating the practice of theological reflection and activity into the life of the community of believers if we are to foster authentically Christian responses to the urgent problems of our times, including the problems of poverty and economic injustice."[14]

Similarly, Joerg Rieger is right to call for church revitalization as a key component for a grassroots retraining in theological discourse. His premise was that academic theologians have sought to be much too lofty to be

9. Ott et al., *Encountering Theology of Mission*, 169–71.

10. Ott et al., *Encountering Theology of Mission*, 171, quoting Van den Berg.

11. Ott et al., *Encountering Theology of Mission*, 174.

12. 1 Cor 9:23–25.

13. Ott et al., *Encountering Theology of Mission*, 175.

14. Maddox, "Wesleyan Resources," 44.

useful. Instead, he called for a bottom up education in theological discourse. Speaking of theological discourse between the clergy and the laity, he says, "The biggest hurdle to thinking theologically is neither the complexity of the issues nor the irrelevance of theological thought; rather, it is that people assume they already know all they need to know about God, including Jesus Christ, the Holy Spirit, and the church."[15] They often do not see the need to ask theological questions until "our doctrines are tested and shaped in the context of new encounters with God in our everyday lives, where the pressure is greatest."[16] This is one of the dangers of the prioritization of the "sacralized self" mentioned by Marti and Ganiel in their work on the Emerging Church. Outcomes of mission are decided by individuals and small groups who may not have the requisite theological tools to engage in proper reflections of mission, evangelism, pilgrimage, and cultural influences.[17] To illustrate, I again turn to Rieger:

> When people return from mission trips (whether to faraway places or close to home) many portray their encounters with suffering and pain as a life-changing experience. What usually goes unnoticed, however, is that in the midst of this experience serious theological questions are raised. What does this experience say about me and my humanity? Who am I, before God and other human beings? Where is God in all of this? Is God primarily where we think God is—in things ecclesial? What if God is in places where we have never even looked? Theological discourse can hardly be more vital than this. Unfortunately, however, such questions are hardly ever pursued further.[18]

To reengage Christians in theological discourse, teachers, pastors, and theological leaders must engage the grassroots Christians in the theological situations that present themselves. Often times, as in the case of STM, the opportunity is missed.

To embrace the contemporary opportunities of mission will require work on several different levels. Missiologists and seminary leaders should provide training in preparation for ministry. Trends show that the STM movement is only likely to increase. As Dennis Horton's research shows, many of yesterday's STM participants are tomorrow's pastors.[19] Additionally, some unhelpful patterns are already developing. As I pointed out in chap-

15. Rieger, "The Word of God," 34.

16. Rieger, "The Word of God," 35.

17. Marti and Ganiel, *Deconstructed Church*, 184–87.

18. Rieger, "The Word of God," 36.

19. Horton, "Effects."

ter 4, theological instruction around STM is largely absent in seminaries and Christian colleges and universities. Robust theological reflection here is vital to shape the next church leaders. These same institutions should also provide ongoing resources for ministry leaders that will address the changing complexities of STM and issues like globalization. Pastors should provide proper training that reflects the cruciform mission of Jesus in all aspects of ministry, including STM. A cruciform attitude towards service displaces self-fulfillment as a primary motivator for activities done in the name of Christian mission. Seminary leaders and pastors alike should raise awareness among STM leaders of the influences of culture that can shape mission efforts. I have pointed out the difficulties in the ECM of the "sacralized self" that can drive many to decide for themselves what is best without engaging the resources of the broader church. Ministry leaders should also raise awareness amongst STMers of the ways that culture can influence mission, as in the examples of the Experience Economy, pilgrimage, and tourism. All such correctives can only take place when a biblical view of the role of the church, mission, and the Kingdom of God is applied to all ministry activities. Such biblical applications should apply to all aspects of training, implementation, practice, and reflection. Quite simply: if it is Christian mission, it should be rooted in Christ's message.

THE FIVE PRINCIPLES OF WESLEYAN MISSION THEOLOGY

In chapter 3, I elucidated five foundational principles, that Wesleyan Mission: 1) is rooted in Scripture, 2) embraces the role of the larger church, 3) affirms that Evangelism is mission, 4) insists that mission is not merely evangelism, and 5) expects ongoing discipleship in the lives of practitioners and recipients. Each of these bears further examination considering the data from the STMers and the discussion of the manner and extent to which STMers reflect upon their work. In some ways, those in dataset reflected a few of the robust theologies of mission discussed. However, many in the dataset seemed to reflect the misguided romanticism of mission articulated by the immature John Wesley as he departed for his service in the Georgian Colony. Wesley expected to encounter an idealized Other that would lead to a personal spiritual transformation. As we have seen above, this notion was a prominent feature in the narratives. Therefore, it is important to also examine the narratives considering a more developed Wesleyan theology of mission.

Rooted in Scripture. While some participants gave generalized answers to my questions about scriptural motivations, many had difficulty articulating a passage of the Bible that reflected a robust mission theology. When I posed the question, I expected it to be one of the easiest for team leaders and team members to answer. However, the lack of Scripture in explaining mission is very telling. Even seasoned veterans had trouble providing common passages associated with mission. This trickled down to their team members in terms of the lack of intentional Bible study for their mission teams. Consider again that the *UMVIM Team Leader Handbook* did not offer a section on biblical or theological reflection of mission, only a suggestion to download a twenty-five-page devotional guide from their website. In the list of "best practices" the recommendation of "Spiritual Formation" is listed last behind logistical considerations.[20] A comparable resource offered for volunteers was similarly problematic. *A Mission Journey: A Handbook for Volunteers* is the resource offered from The United Methodist Church's chief mission agency, the General Board of Global Ministry. This work should be commended for utilizing Scripture more so than the *Team Leader Handbook*. The material does attempt to articulate a theology of mission aimed at the level of the STM practitioner. Yet, problems remain. The biblical material seemed to point to the enticement for "Volunteer Mission Experiences and Spiritual Transformation."[21] For example,

> United Methodist Volunteers in Mission (UMVIM) Experiences offer a unique context for spiritual transformation. . . . [W]e often become so immersed in our busy schedules and the noisy demands of our daily lives that we neglect to care for our souls. The act of going to a different place and leaving our ordinary lives behind may open us to hear God speaking to us.[22]

Such sentiments are firmly couched in the idealization of STM as personal pilgrimage. It is interesting that no teams reported using these materials, but echoed these sentiments.

A Mission Journey should be affirmed for seeking to articulate a theology for all of mission, including STM, with the United Methodist General Board of Global Ministries' statement entitled: "The Mission Theology Statement Guides Global Ministries' Participation in the *Missio Dei*." Though this statement does include language that alludes to biblical messages, there is no explicit instruction to use Scripture as a directive for mission. Additionally, the "Best Practices for UMVIM/VIM (Sending and Hosting Teams)"

20. United Methodist Volunteers in Mission, 6–7; Lyons, *Preparing for the Journey.*

21. Jones and Blankenbake, *A Mission Journey*, 17.

22. Jones and Blankenbake, *A Mission Journey*, 19.

only lists logistical and cultural concerns, not a directive for scriptural engagement.[23] Even in The United Methodist Church's key mission agencies' statements of mission, biblical engagement was not primary.

Since the Bible is not the significant part of mission training for team leaders or their team members, it may be expected that STMers had difficulties discussing their work with biblical motivations. This can leave room for other considerations, like experience, to take a primary motivational role. As I mentioned in chapters 1 and 2, the danger of allowing cultural influences to shape ecclesial practice is that something other than Scripture becomes the driving force in these activities. A proper understanding of the role of church, mission, the Kingdom of God, and the *missio Dei* cannot be found outside of Scripture.

Embraces the role of the broader church. The teams in the study seemed to embrace their role as a congregation connected to another, even if it was a loose denominational connection. Because it is a relatively new movement, one can expect STM to be short-sighted in its role in historical world mission. However, this should not remain the case. I pointed out in the opening chapter that some in the ECM are seeking to reject historical ecclesial history. STM leaders should learn from the best parts, and mistakes, of mission and service. At the same time, STM leaders should be affirmed for their participation in the larger church. The STM teams I studied all connected with local church leaders in their host countries. They sought to see God at work outside of their local context, at least in some ways. However, more can be done to embrace the role of the broader church. STM teams should be challenged to see the role of the *missio Dei* in their hosts' contexts for the hosts' benefit first and foremost and not for their own. STM teams should be encouraged to participate with national hosts in intercultural Bible study where different perspectives are offered on the same passage. As much as possible, churches who send a STM team should offer to host a STM from the church that hosts them, at the expense of the American team. By placing themselves in the role of the host, American churches can learn of the ongoing work of the church around the world, while learning some of the issues their hosts face during STM trips. STM teams should invite missiological reflections from their host pastors before, during, and after the STM trip. This should be done not only with open and frank dialogue, but also through activities such as Bible studies for the STM team led by the national pastor. The key to such activities is that they be done with specific intentionality to embrace the role of the broader church.

23. Jones and Blankenbake, *A Mission Journey*, 145–49.

Affirms that evangelism is mission. As seen in this study, this is a key area in which the STM teams studied depart from Wesleyan mission. The propagation of the gospel has driven mission throughout history. The current dynamic does not necessarily lend itself to evangelism, however. As Will Manning pointed out about his host church: "Everyone's already a Christian." Will and other team leaders did not necessarily see evangelism as a priority. Remember that Richard Davis placed faith-sharing fourth in his list of priorities. His primary aim was for his team to engage in "experiential learning" about the people and places they were visiting. Recall Cecelia Chandler's insistence that she and the members of her team were "not evangelists."

Some have tried to delineate mission and evangelism with definitions like: "Evangelism is the spreading of the good news by proclamation, whereas mission is the outflow of the love of God in and through our life, word and deed."[24] Many times these flow one into another. The balance of "proclamation," "deed," and "word" was not always clear-cut in the narratives. Some team leaders said that there is a "right time" and "right way" to share one's faith with those whom the team members would encounter. However, none of the team leaders in the dataset, provided explicit pre-trip training for their teams in knowing when and how to engage in faith-sharing.

All the team leaders expressed a desire to submit to the ongoing mission of the host church, which knew the special needs and concerns of their immediate constituency. They should be commended for doing so. As William Abraham rightly points out, such careful consideration of the needs and concerns of the hearers of the message is vital in evangelistic efforts.[25] However, because these international service trips, done in the name of mission, were working in established church communities, the dataset seemed to suggest that some STM team members saw themselves as now free from the directive to engage in faith-sharing endeavors. Since many perceived a greater faith in their hosts than they themselves possessed, STMers no longer saw their hosts as those with whom faith could be shared, rather they saw their hosts as those from whom faith could be gained. At times, their hosts were nearly venerated as models of faith and practice. It is little wonder, then, that evangelism would not be a priority for such service pilgrimages. This issue should be addressed in future work on STM and its relationship to pilgrimage.

In chapter 2, I pointed out that Cobus van Wyngaard affirms Bosch's concern that "[t]he problem of contextualization in the West is that 'we still

---

24. Geevarghese Mar Osthathios, "Worship, Mission, Unity," 39.
25. Abraham, *The Logic of Evangelism*, 172.

believe that the gospel had already been properly indigenized and contextualized in the West."[26] Through my discussions with STMers, it was evident that many STMers felt that the Church was already present in their host contexts to the point where faith sharing was not appropriate or necessary. However, this is no more true than the notion that there is no need for faith-sharing in North America. Pastors and team leaders should provide training for STMers to engage in appropriate faith-sharing. As I said in that same chapter, mission is to be conducted as a harbinger of the Kingdom of God.

Insists that mission is not merely evangelism. As noted above, teams had little trouble engaging in the practices that should accompany evangelism such as service to mind, body, and soul. In much the same way as Methodists historically sought to meet very real needs, so too do today's United Methodist STMers. Much like their predecessors, those in my dataset sought to provide food, clothing, medical care, and education where they saw a need. However, the question remains as to what degree these service activities were mission or tools for personal growth.

Expects ongoing discipleship in the lives of practitioners and recipients. The effectiveness of the early Wesleyan movement was the use of small groups to keep new converts growing in their faith beyond their initial conversion experiences. This same expectation was used in the mission efforts in eighteenth-century England. The STM teams in my dataset were careful to work through existing church structures. There were no reports of "parachute" missions where evangelists dropped into a community to present an evangelistic message and leave without providing a means for long-term follow-up. Anecdotes from some participants in the dataset and from populist literature suggests that such a practice still occurs. However, teams in this project seemed to embrace the ongoing growth of both the STM worker and the host.

GLOBALIZATION AND UBERIZATION

Many have pointed to the changing global landscape as the contributing factor to the rise of STMs.[27] Abraham points out that national borders are no longer the controlling influence. Cultural identities and economies cast influence around the world. He says that issues like terrorism, communications, natural disasters, and globalizations force people to reexamine their role in the world and

---

26. van Wyngaard, "Emerging Church," 4.

27. As illustrated in chapter 3.

are systematically reordering the life of nations. The state continues to exist but its mode is that of the market: while it will still provide indispensable, institutionalized services, it has shifted to an ethos in which personal initiative and the provision of opportunity are given privileged status.[28]

United Methodist mission reflects the growth of lay missioners making decisions about how to participate in missional service. As a result of the growing ministry of the laity, contributions to the denomination's mission agencies dropped while designated giving to specific projects, selected by individuals and congregations, grew. This shift, according to Charles Zech, is due to the church members' growing mistrust in the structures of the denomination. "In brandishing their new-found freedom and responsibility, church members often found the denomination to be more of an obstacle than an asset."[29] Fifteen years after Zech's observation, it appears that similar feelings still exist. Recall that nearly 90 percent of those who participate in mission from United Methodist churches do so without using the resources of the denomination's mission infrastructure.[30]

As I demonstrated in the discussion of Third Wave Mission, the constraints of time and space are being lifted. An awareness of global issues can develop in almost real time. Issues of globalization around the ease of communication and travel can put those who want to help in touch with those who want to receive such help with little hindrance. To go on a STM, as one team member put it, "All you got to do is show up and pay your money." Team leaders demonstrated that they were acting as travel agents and tour guides more so than mission guides. They were providing a service for the experience of pilgrimage. It could be said that this is the "Uberization" of mission.[31]

The Uber rideshare model utilizes mobile communication technology for on-demand transportation services. Walker Smith asserts that the Uber business model will be a pervasive global influence. "No business category will be unaffected by companies operating with an Uber-like, on-demand business model."[32] The two elements Smith deems critical to this model are personal service and the "on-demand availability anywhere, anytime."[33] A

28. Abraham, "Methodism," 80.

29. Zech, "Determinants," 252.

30. See chapter 2.

31. I am indebted to Glory E. Dharmaraj for this: Dharmaraj, "From Salinization of Mission to Uberization of Mission."

32. Smith, "The Uber-All Economy," 384.

33. Smith, "The Uber-All Economy," 385.

simple internet search for a STM trip will provide countless options in destinations and projects and a myriad of agencies and leaders who will broker
the STM experience for you. The growth of STM pre-dates Uber, but some
of the principles are transferable. While such opportunities could be yet another way that technological advances serve the propagation of the gospel,
without the requisite theological work as to why one serves in mission, this
will become yet another way economic influences shape the practice of mission. Due to the populist and grassroots nature of such models, teaching
robust theologies will likely be a growing challenge for missiologists and
theologians. As I pointed out earlier, grassroots and populist movements of
the church are ever-increasing, as demonstrated in the growing Emerging
Church Movement (ECM). It is possible that their increasingly-flattened
structures, emphasis on individual actions in service to others, and affirmation of community are influencing how STM is practiced. These qualities
bear further examination as both ECM and STM continue to evolve.

SUGGESTIONS FOR FURTHER RESEARCH

As can be expected such findings also raise a series of new questions. I wish
to offer a few suggestions on how issues of STM, pilgrimage, and experience
can be explored further. First, a study of STM teams in United Methodist
churches from other parts of the United States would demonstrate whether
such feelings cross regional boundaries. A similar study should be made
in other denominational traditions. Several different denominations participate in STM. I suggest such a study include Catholic, Protestant, and
non-denominational churches from both inside practitioners and outside
academics. Each of these groups has distinct understandings of the role of
mission, church, and kingdom. Hearing from them would enrich the understanding of the theology of current mission practice.

Second, the movements of theology should be examined. Philip
Jenkins pointed out that there is evidence of a decreasing influence of the
church in the Global North, but an increase of vitality in the Global South.[34]
If STMers are, in fact, being transformed by their experiences overseas, the
effects of these transformations on the North American contexts should be
examined. Will a movement of theology come out of the Global South and,
if so, to what extent did STM provide a vehicle for such a movement?

Third, missiologists and theologians should continue important discussions around the ongoing issues of globalization in relation to STM.
Matters such as advances in travel and communication, migration, and

---

34. Jenkins, *Next Christendom*, 11–20.

cultural and religious diaspora are likely to remain an influence on issues of ethnocentrism, plurality, and awareness of global issues. The way in which these issues influence STM, and the way STM influences the issues, deserves further examination.

Fourth, and perhaps most importantly, the voices of the mission hosts must be heard. There is a deficiency of literature that amplifies the voices of the millions of people outside of the United States who are impacted by STM year after year. Their perceptions and motivations for STM engagement should be considered as well. What are the feelings of those whom STMers see as the idealized Other and as an object of pilgrimage? What potential problems could arise with continuation of such a practice? In what ways is the Third Wave of Mission positively impacting these contexts? Are STM teams being sent from the countries once seen as the "objects of mission"? If so, how do they express missiological understandings of their service activities? Such questions are not being asked enough.

Since STM transactions are grassroots movements, those at the grassroots level should be expected to engage in these questions and answers. Not only should this be done in formal learning situations, but also in the experiences they seek. One simple way to foster such a deeper understanding is for STM teams to participate in cooperative Bible studies from and with their mission hosts. Additionally, churches who go away on STM trips should consider bringing their mission hosts to the United States as well. The sending church could raise the money to bring them to America, find them housing, translators, work projects, and recreational activities. Before, during, and after, meaningful dialogue should be fostered to hear the implicit and explicit motivations I discussed above. Such a reverse exchange might provide new insights for both groups. Embedding qualified researchers and American/National scholars in such groups may be one way to gain a broader understanding.

THE FUTURE OF SHORT-TERM MISSION

The STM movement may very well be a new expression of the *missio Dei*. Wesleyan mission theology holds that the poor are not just those who lack material things. The sick are not just those who suffer in body, but also in mind and spirit. Biblical mission seeks to break down the barriers of class and race. There is an eschatological horizon when God will bring forth the new creation. In the meantime, the poor (in all manners of poverty) are in need of the reconciliation of the gospel.

At its best, STM seeks to address many of these issues. However, STM is not always living up to its best. Rather, STM is failing to realize its potential due to a lack of robust theological reflection by its leaders and participants. When the practice moves away from pilgrimage towards a more robust practice of mission, it can begin to embrace such possibilities. The STM movement can, and should, function as an instrument of the *missio Dei* to strengthen the church around the world.

I am not suggesting that people stop traveling, stop serving, or stop learning. Quite the opposite. An increased awareness of the work of God around the world can only lead to good things. A life-changing pilgrimage is wonderful and should be applauded. Coming to a deeper understanding of the cultures of other nations leads to a better worldview. Yet, tensions remain. Deep problems arise when those who participate in practices deemed "mission" do so with the primary aim of bettering themselves or experiencing something new and exciting. Unhealthy practices in the name of mission (e.g. ethnocentrism, paternalism, and developed dependencies) are brought forth, much as has been done in other efforts over the centuries. Colonialism, imperialism, and other such influences on mission needed correction. Current practices of mission also need the helpful correctives that previous mission efforts required. I would suggest such work begin to engage in the manner of John Wesley's directive in the General Rules to the Bands and Societies: "First, by doing no Harm. . .Secondly, By doing Good. . .Thirdly, By attending upon all the Ordinances of God."[35] This begins with embracing the suggestions I have made here to participate in the *missio Dei*, in a way that specifically utilizes the five principles of Wesleyan mission mentioned previously.

Because STM is a deeply populist movement, any such correctives should address the populace. Most popular writings thus far do not engage the deeper issues at hand. Only a limited amount of academic literature does so. I have attempted to take a step to remedy that. STM is likely to continue to grow for the foreseeable future as more and more churches continue to expect the practice as a part of their overall programming for their congregants. Teenagers who went on the youth mission trip or children who went on the family mission trip are becoming the leaders of families, churches, and businesses that will support and encourage more such trips. Now is the time to actively engage the accelerating practice with robust theological reflection. Looking at the data I have collected and the theological principles we have explored, one simple but important thing would be that leaders in seminaries train pastors to properly lead the ubiquitous STM movement.

35. Wesley, *General Rules*, 6–9.

Pastors should train their team leaders and team members to embrace biblical motivations for mission. For, as Ott and his co-authors pointed out, "[m]otivation reflects attitudes, and attitudes in turn impact relationships and methods in profound ways."[36]

I have titled the project "Consuming Mission" because the evidence indicated that churches and individuals are participating in a transactional exchange designed by their pastors and ministry leaders. When talking about their STM activities, participants often describe their time, money, sacrifice, and service, applied in the name of mission, as a way to purchase an experience akin to personal growth commonly sought by pilgrims. Many STMers are using service, time, and money to purchase an experience. They are consuming "mission," functioning as pilgrimage, for self-edification. However, I have shown that the *missio Dei* is to be the Consuming Mission. Mission, properly understood and practiced, takes place when every self-abasing desire of the individual Christian, every program of the church, and the orientation of her leaders is consumed by the Mission of God. When the *missio Dei* consumes all the aspects of the church it is able to faithfully serve in mission to proclaim the Kingdom of God that Jesus initiated in this life and the life to come.

36. Ott et al., *Encountering Theology of Mission*, 165.

Appendix
Participating churches/ministries

I have utilized pseudonyms for these ministries and, by giving approximate numbers, attempted to remove identifying information.

Name:	# of Participants	Church Membership
1. City Central UMC	8	6,500–7,000
2. Clear River UMC	7	2,500–3,000
3. Elmville UMC	7	100–250
4. Neartown UMC	2	1,000–1,500
5. Ramen UMC	18	4,000–4,500
6. Riverbend UMC	1	500–1,000
7. Campus Christian Ministry	# of Participants: 12	University Enrollment: 15,000–20,000

Bibliography

Abraham, William J. *The Logic of Evangelism*. Grand Rapids: Eerdmans, 1989.

———. "Methodism, Mission, and the Market State." *World Mission in the Wesleyan Spirit*. Edited by Darrell L. Whiteman and Gerald H. Anderson, 74–80. Franklin, TN: Providence House, 2009.

———. "Saving Souls in the Twenty-First Century: A Missiological Midrash on John Wesley." *Wesleyan Theological Journal* 38 (2003) 7–20.

Adeney, Miriam. "When the Elephant Dances, the Mouse May Die." *Short-Term Missions Today*, 86–89. Pasadena, CA: Into All the World Magazine, 2003.

Alegre Villón, Joaquín. "Short-Term Missions: Experiences and Perspectives from Callao, Peru." *Journal of Latin American Theology* 2 (2007) 119–38.

Archbishop's Council on Mission and Public Affairs. *Mission-Shaped Church: Church Planting and Fresh Expressions of Church in a Changing Context*. 2nd ed. London: Church House, 2009.

Bahamonde, Marcos Arroyo. "Contextualization of Mission: A Missiological Analysis of Short-Term Missions." *Journal of Latin American Theology* 2 (2007) 227–48.

Bailyes, Alan J. "Evangelical and Ecumenical Understandings of Mission." *International Review of Mission* 85 (October 1996) 485–503.

Bartholomew, Craig and Robert Llewelyn, eds. "Introduction." In *Explorations in a Christian Theology of Pilgrimage*, xii–xvi. Burlington, VT: Ashgate, 2003.

Bassham, Rodger C. "Seeking a Deeper Theological Basis for Mission." *International Review of Mission* 67 (July 1978) 329–37.

Bauer, Bruce L. "Bounded and Centered Sets: Possible Applications for Adventist Mission." *Journal of Adventist Mission Studies* 3 (2007) 59–78.

Beers, Stephen Thomas. "Faith Development of Christian College Students Engaged in a One-Month Study Abroad Mission Trip." EdD diss., Ball State University, 1999.

Bekele, Girma. "The Biblical Narrative of the Missio Dei: Analysis of the Interpretive Framework of David Bosch's Missional Hermeneutic." *International Bulletin of Missionary Research* 35 (July 2011) 153–56.

Bellah, Robert N., et al. *Habits of the Heart: Individualism and Commitment in American Life*. Los Angeles: University of California Press, 2007.

Berthoud, Alex L. "Church and Mission." *International Review of Mission* 39 (July 1950) 263–69.

Bevans, Stephen B. and Roger Schroeder. *Constants in Context: A Theology of Mission for Today*. Maryknoll, NY: Orbis, 2004.

Beyerlein, Kraig, Jenny Trinitapoli, and Gary Adler. "The Effect of Religious Short-Term Mission Trips on Youth Civic Engagement." *Journal for the Scientific Study of Religion* 50 (December 2011) 780–95.

Bielo, James S. *Emerging Evangelicals: Faith, Modernity, and the Desire for Authenticity.* New York: NYU Press, 2011.

Blezien, Paul. "The Impact of Summer International Short-Term Missions Experiences on the Cross-Cultural Sensitivity of Undergraduate College Student Participants." EdD diss., Azusa Pacific University, 2004. ProQuest Dissertations & Theses Full Text.

Bonino, Jose Miguez. "Wesley in Latin America: A Theological and Historical Reflection." In *Rethinking Wesley's Theology for Contemporary Methodism*, edited by Randy L. Maddox, 169–82. Nashville: Kingswood, 1998.

Bosch, David J. "Evangelism: Theological Currents and Cross-Currents Today." *International Bulletin of Missionary Research* 11 (July 1987) 98–103.

———. *Transforming Mission: Paradigm Shifts in Theology of Mission.* Maryknoll, NY: Orbis, 2011.

Brunner, Emil. *The Word and the World.* London: SCM, 1931.

Campbell, Clark, et al. "Reduction in Burnout May Be a Benefit for Short-Term Medical Mission Volunteers." *Mental Health Religion and Culture* 12 (November 2009) 627–37.

Chapman, Stephen B. and Laceye Warner. "Jonah and the Imitation of God: Rethinking Evangelism and the Old Testament." *Journal of Theological Interpretation* 2 (Spring 2008) 43–69.

Clark, A. K. "Rethinking the Decline in Social Capital." *American Politics Research* 43 (Jul 2015) 569–601.

Coenen, Lothar, et al., eds. "Church, Synagogue." In *The New International Dictionary of New Testament Theology: Volume 1*, edited by Colin Brown, 291–307. Grand Rapids: Zondervan, 1986.

Cohen, Erik. "Pilgrimage and Tourism: Convergence and Divergence." In *Sacred Journeys: The Anthropology of Pilgrimage*, edited by Alan Morinis, 47–61. Westport, CT: Greenwood, 1992.

———. "Who Is a Tourist?: A Conceptual Clarification." *Sociological Review* 22 (November 1974) 527–55.

Collins, Kenneth J. *John Wesley: A Theological Journey.* Nashville: Abingdon, 2003.

Conklin-Miller, Jeffrey A. "Leaning Both Ways at Once: Methodist Evangelistic Mission at the Intersection of Church and World." ThD diss., Duke University, 2012.

Cook, Charles A., and Joel Van Hoogen. "Towards a Missiologically and Morally Responsible Short-Term Ministry: Lessons Learned in the Development of Church Partnership Evangelism." *Journal of Latin American Theology* 2 (2007) 48–68.

Corbett, Steve, and Brian Fikkert. *When Helping Hurts: How to Alleviate Poverty without Hurting the Poor. . .And Yourself.* Chicago: Moody, 2012.

Cray, Graham. "A Theology of the Kingdom." In *Mission as Transformation: A Theology of the Whole Gospel*, edited by Vinay Samuel and Chris Sugden, 26–44. Oxford, UK: Regnum, 1999.

Dahlberg, Andrea. "The Body as a Principle of Holism: Three Pilgrimages to Lourdes." In *Contesting the Sacred: The Anthropology of Pilgrimage*, edited by John Eade and Michael J. Sallnow, 30–50. Urbana: University of Illinois Press, 1991.

Daniel, Harrison W. "The Young John Wesley as Cross-Cultural Witness: Investigations into Wesley's American Mission Experience and Implications for Today's Mission." *Missiology* 28 (2000) 443–57.

Davison, Andrew, and Alison Milbank. *For the Parish: A Critique of Fresh Expressions.* London: SCM, 2010.

De Souza, Luis Wesley. "The Challenges of John Wesley's Theology in Latin American Contexts." In *World Mission in the Wesleyan Spirit,* edited by Darrell L. Whiteman and Gerald H. Anderson, 81–92. Franklin, TN: Providence House, 2009.

Dearborn, Tim. *Short-Term Missions Workbook: From Mission Tourists to Global Citizens.* Downers Grove, IL: InterVarsity, 2003.

Dharmaraj, Glory E. "From Salinization of Mission to Uberization of Mission." *UM & Global* (blog), *UM&Global.org,* September 22, 2016, http://www.umglobal. org/2016/09/glory-dharmaraj-from-salinization-of.html.

Dougherty, Kevin D. and Andrew L. Whitehead. "A Place to Belong: Small Group Involvement in Religious Congregations." *Sociology of Religion* 72 (Spring 2011) 91–111.

Effa, Allan. "Missional Voices Down Under: A Canadian Response to the Missiology of Michael Frost and Alan Hirsch." *Missiology* 38 (January 2010) 61–73.

Eitzen, Martín. "Short-Term Missions: Latin American Perspective." *Journal of Latin American Theology* 2 (2007) 33–47.

Engelsviken, Tormod. "Missio Dei: The Understanding and Misunderstanding of a Theological Concept in European Churches and Missiology." *International Review of Mission* 92 (October 2003) 481–97.

Farrell, B. Hunter. "From Short-Term Mission to Global Discipleship: A Peruvian Case Study." *Missiology: An International Review* 41(April 2013) 163–78.

Feinberg, Ben. "What Students Don't Learn Abroad." The *Chronicle of Higher Education* 48 (May 2002) B20.

Fenrick, David E. "Missional Experiential Education for Developing Christian Global Citizens." PhD diss., Asbury Theological Seminary, 2007.

Ferguson, Charles. *Organizing to Beat the Devil: Methodists and the Making of America.* New York: Doubleday, 1971.

Freudenberg, Maren. "The Emerging Church as a Critical Response to the Neoliberalization of the American Religious Landscape." *Politikologija Religije* 9 (February 2015) 297–320.

Friesen, Randall. "Improving the Long-Term Impact of Short-Term Missions." MBMS International. http://www.mbmission.org/files/staff/rfriesen/friesen_stm_thesis_summary.pdf.

Frost, Michael, and Alan Hirsch. *The Faith of Leap.* Grand Rapids: Baker, 2011.

———. *ReJesus: A Wild Messiah for a Missional Church.* Grand Rapids: Baker, 2009.

———. *The Shaping of Things to Come.* Peabody, MA: Hendrickson, 2003.

Gable, Mike, and Mike Haasl. "Training for the Third Wave of Mission: A Catholic Perspective." *Papers* 65 (2016) 19–27. http://place.asburyseminary.edu/firstfruitspapers/65.

Gaines, Timothy R. "Politics, Participation, and the Missio Dei in the Thought of Miroslav Volf and the Wesleyan Tradition." *Wesleyan Theological Journal* 47 (Spring 2012) 72–89.

Geevarghese Mar Osthathios, Metr. "Worship, Mission, Unity—These Three: Response to B. P. Arias." *International Review of Mission* 65 (January 1976) 39–43.

Glasser, Arthur F., et al. *Announcing the Kingdom: The Story of God's Mission in the Bible*. Grand Rapids: Baker Academic, 2003.

Gmelch, Sharon Bohn. "Why Tourism Matters." In *Tourists and Tourism: A Reader*, edited by Sharon Bohn Gmelch, 3–24. Long Grove, IL: Waveland, 2010.

Goheen, Michael W. "'As the Father Has Sent Me, I Am Sending You': Lesslie Newbigin's Missionary Ecclesiology." *International Review of Mission* 91 (July 2002) 354–69.

———. "A Critical Examination of David Bosch's Missional Reading of Luke." In *Reading Luke: Interpretation, Reflection, Formation*, edited by Craig Bartholomew, et al., 229–64. Grand Rapids: Zondervan, 2005.

González, Ondina E., and Justo L. González. *Christianity in Latin America: A History*. Cambridge: Cambridge University Press, 2008.

Graburn, Nelson H. H. "Secular Ritual: A General Theory of Tourism." In *Tourists and Tourism: A Reader*, edited by Sharon Bohn Gmelch, 25–36. Long Grove, IL: Waveland, 2010.

Hancock, Mary. "Short-Term Youth Mission Practice and the Visualization of Global Christianity." *Material Religion: The Journal of Objects, Art and Belief* 10 (June 2014) 154–80.

Harris, Robert. *Mission in the Gospels*. London: Epworth, 2004.

Hazle, Dave. "Practical Theology Today and the Implications for Mission." *International Review of Mission* 92 (July 2003) 345–55.

Heitzenrater, Richard P. "The Poor and the People Called Methodists." In *The Poor and the People Called Methodists*, edited by Richard P. Heitzenrater, 15–38. Nashville: Abingdon, 2002.

———. *Wesley and the People Called Methodists*. Nashville: Abingdon, 1995.

Hiebert, Paul G. "The Category 'Christian' in the Mission Task." *International Review of Mission* 72 (July 1983) 421–27.

Hoekendijk, Johannes Christiaan. "The Church in Missionary Thinking." *International Review of Mission* 41, no. 163 (1952) 324–36.

Hogg, William. "The Rise of Protestant Missionary Concern, 1517–1914." In *The Theology of the Christian Mission*, edited by H. Gerald Anderson, 95–111. London: SCM, 1961.

Hopkins, Sarah Mott. "Effects of Short-Term Service Ministry Trips on the Development of Social Responsibility in College Students." PsyD diss., George Fox University, 2000. ProQuest Dissertations & Theses Full Text.

Horton, Dennis J. "The Effects of Short-Term Mission Trips on Mission Team Participants." American Society of Missiology Annual Meeting, St. Paul, MN, June 18, 2016.

Howell, Brian M. *Short-Term Mission: An Ethnography of Christian Travel Narrative and Experience*. Downers Grove, IL: InterVarsity, 2012.

———. "Short Term Mission as the Undiscovered Country: Anthropology and Missiology in the 21st Century." *Papers* Book 64 (2016) 5–17. http://place.asburyseminary.edu/firstfruitspapers/64.

Howell, Brian M., and Rachel Dorr. "Evangelical Pilgrimage: The Language of Short-Term Missions." *Journal of Communication & Religion* 30 (November 2007) 236–65.

Hull, John K. "Faith Development through Crosscultural Interaction and Liminality: Bonding to the Meaning of Scripture through the Short-Term Mission Experiences." DMiss, diss., Asbury Theological Seminary, 2004.

Jeffrey, Paul. "Short-Term Mission Trips: Beyond Good Intentions." *Christian Century* 118 (December 2001) 5–7.

Jenkins, Philip. *Next Christendom: The Coming of Global Christianity.* Oxford: Oxford University Press, 2011.

Jennings, Theodore W., Jr. "Wesley and the Poor: An Agenda for Wesleyans." In *The Portion of the Poor: Good News to the Poor in the Wesleyan Tradition*, edited by M. Douglas Meeks, 19–38. Nashville: Kingswood, 1995.

Jones, U., and J. Blankenbake. *A Mission Journey: A Handbook for Volunteers.* Nashville: Upper Room, 2014.

Kim, Kirsteen. "Missiology as Global Conversation of (Contextual) Theologies." *Mission Studies* 21 (2004) 39–53.

Kirk, J. Andrew. *What Is Mission?: Theological Explorations.* Minneapolis: Fortress, 1999.

Koll, Karla Ann. "Taking Wolves among Lambs: Some Thoughts on Training for Short-Term Mission Facilitation." *International Bulletin of Missionary Research* 34 (April 2010) 93–96.

Köstenberger, Andreas J. "The Place of Mission in New Testament Theology: An Attempt to Determine the Significance of Mission within the Scope of the New Testament's Message as a Whole." *Missiology* 27 (July 1999) 347–62.

Linhart, Terence D. "Planting Seeds: The Curricular Hope." *Christian Education Journal* 2 (September 2005) 257–72.

———. "They Were So Alive!: The Spectacle Self and Youth Group Short-Term Mission Trips." *Missiology: An International Review* 34 (October 2006) 451–62.

Lupton, Robert D. *Toxic Charity: How Churches and Charities Hurt Those They Help.* New York: HarperCollins, 2011.

Lyons, R. G. *Preparing for the Journey: A Devotional Guide for Teams*, 2015. http://umvim.org/send_a_team/usa/spiritual_formation.html.

Macquiban, Tim. "Work on Earth and Rest in Heaven: Toward a Theology of Vocation in the Writings of Charles Wesley." In *Our Calling to Fulfill: Wesleyan Views of the Church in Mission*, edited by M. Douglas Meeks, 47–70. Nashville: Abingdon, 2009.

Maddox, Randy L. "'Celebrating the Whole Wesley' a Legacy for Contemporary Wesleyans." *Methodist history* 43, no. 2 (January 2005) 74–89.

———. *Responsible Grace: John Wesley's Practical Theology.* Nashville: Kingswood, 1994.

———. "An Untapped Inheritance: American Methodism and Wesley's Practical Theology." In *Doctrines and Disciplines: Methodist Theology and Practice*, 19–52. Nashville: Abingdon, 1999.

———. "'Visit the Poor': John Wesley, the Poor, and the Sanctification of Believers." In *The Wesleys and the Poor: The Legacy and Development of Methodist Attitudes to Poverty, 1729–1999*, edited by Richard P. Heitzenrater. Nashville: Kingswood, 2002.

———. "Wesleyan Resources for a Contemporary Theology of the Poor?" *Asbury Theological Journal* 49, no. 1 (Spring 1994) 35–47.

———. "Wesley's Prescription for "Making Disciples of Jesus Christ" Insights for the 21st Century Church." *Quarterly Review* 23 (Spring 2003) 15–28.

Marquardt, Manfred. *John Wesley's Social Ethics: Praxis and Principles.* Translated by John E. Steely and W. Stephen Gunter. Nashville: Abingdon, 1992.

Marquardt, Manfred, and Walter Klaiber. *Living Grace: An Outline of United Methodist Theology*. Nashville: Abingdon, 2002.

Marti, Gerardo, and Gladys Ganiel. *The Deconstructed Church: Understanding Emerging Christianity*. New York: Oxford University Press, 2014.

Maslucán, Rodrigo. "Short-Term Missions: Analysis and Proposals." *Journal of Latin American Theology* 2 (2007) 139–58.

Meeks, M. Douglas. "A Home for the Homeless: Vocation, Mission, and Church in Wesleyan Perspective." In *Our Calling to Fulfill: Wesleyan Views of the Church in Mission*, edited by M. Douglas Meeks, 1–10. Nashville: Kingswood, 2009.

Meistad, Tore. "The Missiology of Charles Wesley and Its Links to the Eastern Church." In *Orthodox and Wesleyan Spirituality*, edited by S T Kimbrough, Jr., 205–32. Crestwood, NY: SVSPress, 2002.

Miles, Rebekah L. "Happiness, Holiness, and the Moral Life of John Wesley." In *The Cambridge Companion to John Wesley*, edited by Randy L. Maddox and Jason E. Vickers, 207–24. Cambridge: Cambridge University Press, 2010.

"Mission Trips Directory." Mission Data International. Accessed September 1, 2018. https://www.shorttermmissions.com/directory/.

Moltmann, Jürgen. *The Church in the Power of the Spirit: A Contribution to Messianic Ecclesiology*. Minneapolis: Fortress, 1977.

Montgomery, Laura M. "Short-Term Medical Missions: Enhancing or Eroding Health?" *Missiology* 21 (July 1993) 333–41.

Newbigin, Lesslie. *Lesslie Newbigin: Missionary Theologian: A Reader*. Edited by Paul Weston. Grand Rapids: Eerdmans, 2006.

—. *The Open Secret—Sketches for a Missionary Theology*. London: SPCK, 1978.

Norton, Bryce. "Changing Our Prayer Behaviors through Short-Term Missions." *Missiology* 40 (July 2012) 329–41.

Nussbaum, Stan. "A Future for Missiology as the Queen of Theology?" *Missiology: An International Review* 42 (January 2014) 57–66.

—. *A Reader's Guide to Transforming Mission*. Maryknoll, NY: Orbis, 2005.

Occhipinti, Laurie. "Religious Idealism: Serving Others in the Name of Faith." *Practical Matters* 2 (August 2009) 1–30.

Offutt, Stephen. "The Role of Short-Term Mission Teams in the New Centers of Global Christianity." *Journal for the Scientific Study of Religion* 50 (December 2011) 796–811.

Osmer, Richard R. "Practical Theology: A Current International Perspective." *Theological Studies* 67 (November 2011) 2.

Ott, Craig, et al. *Encountering Theology of Mission (Encountering Mission) Biblical Foundations, Historical Developments, and Contemporary Issues*. Grand Rapids: Baker, 2010.

Outler, Albert C. *Evangelism and Theology in the Wesleyan Spirit*. Nashville: Discipleship Resources, 1996.

Parades, Tito. "Short-Term Missions: What Can Be Rescued, What Can Be Criticized, and the Challenge of Contextualization." *Journal of Latin American Theology* 2 (2007) 249–59.

Park, Kyeong Sook. "Researching Short-Term Missions and Paternalism." In *Effective Engagement in Short-Term Missions*, edited by Robert J. Priest, 504–28. Pasadena, CA: William Carey Library, 2008.

Petersen, Jim. *Church without Walls*. Colorado Springs: NavPress, 1992.

Peterson, Roger P., et al. *Maximum Impact Short-Term Mission: The God-Commanded, Repetitive Deployment of Swift, Temporary, Non-Professional Missionaries.* Cordova, TN: STEMPress, 2003.

Pine, B. Joseph, and James H. Gilmore. "Welcome to the Experience Economy." *Harvard Business Review* 76 (Jul-Aug 1998) 97–105.

Pine, B. Joseph, and James H. Gilmore. *The Experience Economy.* Cambridge, MA: Harvard Business Press, 2011.

Prahalad, C. K. and Venkat Ramaswamy. "Co-Creation Experiences: The Next Practice in Value Creation." *Journal of Interactive Marketing* 18 (Summer 2004) 5–14.

Preston, James J. "Spiritual Magnetism: An Organizing Principle for the Study of Pilgrimage." In *Sacred Journeys: The Anthropology of Pilgrimage,* edited by Alan Morinis, 31–46. Westport, CT: Greenwood, 1992.

Priest, Robert J. *Effective Engagement in Short-Term Missions: Doing It Right!* Pasadena, CA: William Carey Library, 2008.

———. "Peruvian Churches Acquire 'Linking Social Capital' through STM Partnerships." *Journal of Latin American Theology* 2 (2007) 175–89.

———. "Short-Term Missions as a New Paradigm." In *Mission after Christendom: Emergent Themes in Contemporary Mission,* edited by Ogbu Uke Kalu, Peter Vethanayagamony, and Edmund Kee-Fook Chia, 84–99. Louisville: Westminster John Knox, 2010.

———. "U.S. Megachurches and New Patterns of Global Mission." *International Bulletin of Missionary Research* 34 (April 2010) 97–102.

Priest, Robert J., et al. "Researching the Short-Term Mission Movement." *Missiology* 34 (October 2006) 431–50.

Priest, Robert J., and Brian M. Howell. "Introduction: Theme Issue on Short-Term Missions." *Missiology: An International Review* 41 (April 2013) 124–29.

Priest, Robert J., and Joseph Paul Priest. "'They See Everything, and Understand Nothing': Short-Term Mission and Service Learning." *Missiology* 36 (January 2008) 53–73.

Priest, Robert J., and Kurt Ver Beek. "Are Short-Term Missions Good Stewardship?: A Conversation between Robert Priest and Kurt Ver Beek." *Christianity Today* (July 5 2005). http://www.christianitytoday.com/ct/2005/julyweb-only/22.0.html.

Putnam, Robert D. *Bowling Alone: The Collapse and Revival of American Community.* New York: Simon & Schuster, 2001.

Raines, Jeffrey A. "An International Perspective on Short-Term Missions." DMin diss., Princeton Theological Seminary, 2008.

Rankin, Stephen W. "A Perfect Church: Toward a Wesleyan Missional Ecclesiology." *Wesleyan Theological Journal* 38 (Spring 2003) 83–104.

Reisman, Kimberly D. "Restorative Witness: Evangelism and Reconciliation: A Wesleyan Theological Exploration." PhD diss., Durham University, 2012.

Richebächer, Wilhelm. "Missio Dei the Basis of Mission Theology or a Wrong Path?" *International Review of Mission* 92 (October 2003) 588–605.

Rickett, Daniel. "Short-Term Missions for Long-Term Partnership." *Evangelical Missions Quarterly (EMQ)* 44 (January 2008) 42–46.

Rieger, Joerg. "The Word of God and the People of God: Revitalizing Theological Discourse from the Bottom Up." *Quarterly Review* 21 (Spring 2001) 33–44.

Ritschl, Dietrich, "Ecumenism," In *Dictionary Of Mission: Theology, History, Perspectives,* edited by Karl Muller et al., 518. London: Orbis, 1999.

Root, Andrew. "The Youth Ministry Mission Trip as Global Tourism: Are We OK with This?" *Dialog* 47 (November 2008) 314–19.

Runyon, Theodore. *The New Creation: John Wesley's Theology Today.* Nashville: Abingdon, 1998.

———. "The New Creation: The Wesleyan Distinctive." *Wesleyan Theological Journal* 31 (Fall 1996) 5–19.

Sallandt, Ulrike. "Short-Term Mission: A Great Opportunity." *Journal of Latin American Theology* 2, no. 2 (2007) 190–207.

Schmidt, K. L. "Ekklesia." In *Theological Dictionary of the New Testament.* Grand Rapids: Eerdmans, 1965.

Schmitt, Bernd. "Experiential Marketing." *Journal of Marketing Management* 15 (January 1999) 53–67.

Schreiter, Robert J. "Third Wave Mission: Cultural, Missiological, and Theological Dimensions." *Missiology* 43 (January 2015) 5–16.

Senior, Donald, and Carroll Stuhlmueller. *The Biblical Foundations for Mission.* Maryknoll, NY: Orbis, 1983.

Slimbach, Richard. "The Mindful Missioner." In *Effective Engagement in Short-Term Missions,* edited by Robert J. Priest, 152–83. Pasadena, CA: William Carey Library, 2008.

Smith, Valene L. *Hosts and Guests.* Philadelphia: University of Pennsylvania Press, 1989.

———. "Introduction: The Quest in Guest." *Annals of Tourism Research* 19 (1992) 1–17.

Smith, J. Walker. "The Uber-All Economy of the Future." *Independent Review* 20 (2016) 383–90.

Snyder, Howard A. "The Missional Flavor of John Wesley's Theology." In *World Mission in the Wesleyan Spirit,* edited by Darrell L. Whiteman and Gerald H. Anderson, 62–73. Franklin, TN: Providence House, 2009.

———. "What's Unique About a Wesleyan Theology of Mission? A Wesleyan Perspective on Free Methodist Missions." *Free Methodist Missions Consultation* (2002) 20–28.

Trinitapoli, Jenny, and Stephen Vaisey. "The Transformative Role of Religious Experience: The Case of Short-Term Missions." *Social Forces* 88 (September 2009) 121–46.

Turner, Victor W. *The Ritual Process: Structure and Anti-Structure.* London: Routledge & Kegan Paul, 1970.

———. "Variations on a Theme of Liminality." In *Secular Ritual,* 36–52. Amsterdam: Van Gorcum, 1977.

Turner, Victor W., and Edith Turner. *Image and Pilgrimage in Christian Culture.* New York: Columbia University Press, 2011.

Tuttle, Robert G. "God at Work in the World." In *World Mission in the Wesleyan Spirit,* edited by Darrell L. Whiteman and Gerald H. Anderson, 112–22. Franklin, TN: Providence House, 2009.

United Methodist Church. *The Book of Discipline of The United Methodist Church.* Nashville: United Methodist Publishing, 2012.

United Methodist Volunteers in Mission. *Team Leader Handbook: United Methodist Volunteers in Mission, Southeastern Jurisdiction.* Birmingham, AL: United Methodist Volunteers in Mission, 2015.

Van Engen, Charles. "Church." In *Evangelical Dictionary Of World Missions*, edited by A. Scott Moreau, 192–95. Grand Rapids: Baker, 2000.

Van Engen, Jo Ann. "The Cost of Short-Term Missions." *The Other Side* 36 (January & February 2000) 20–23.

Van Gennep, Arnold. *The Rites of Passage*. Chicago: University of Chicago Press, 1960.

van Wyngaard, Cobus. "The Emerging Church as Contextualization of the Gospel in the West: Reading Brian McLaren through the Work of David Bosch." South African Missiological Society Meeting, 13–15 (January, 2010).

Ver Beek, Kurt Alan. "The Impact of Short-Term Missions: A Case Study of House Construction in Honduras after Hurricane Mitch." *Missiology: An International Review* 34 (October 2006) 477–95.

Walker Smith, J. "The Uber-All Economy of the Future." *Independent Review* 20 (Winter 2016) 383–90.

Walls, Andrew F. *The Missionary Movement in Christian History: Studies in the Transmission of Faith*. Maryknoll, NY: Orbis, 1996.

Ward, Pete. *Liquid Church*. Eugene, OR: Wipf and Stock, 2002.

Warner, Laceye. "Kingdom Witness and Helen Barrett Montgomery's Biblical Theology." *Review & Expositor* 101 (Summer 2004) 451–71.

———. "Spreading Scriptural Holiness: Theology and Practices of Early Methodism for the Contemporary Church." *The Asbury Journal* 63 (Spring 2008) 115–38.

Wesley, John. "The Character of a Methodist." In *The Methodist Societies: History, Nature, and Design*, edited by Rupert E. Davies. *The Bicentennial Edition of the Works of John Wesley* Vol. 9, edited by Richard P. Heitzenrater, 30–46. Nashville: Abingdon, 1984.

———. *Hymns and Sacred Poems*. London: William Strahan, 1739.

———. "The 'Large' Minutes, A and B (1753, 1763)." In *The Methodist Societies: The Minutes of Conference*, edited by Henry D. Rack. *The Bicentennial Edition of the Works of John Wesley* Vol. 10, edited by Richard P. Heitzenrater, 844–74. Nashville: Abingdon, 1984.

———. "The Marks of the New Birth." In *Sermons I*, edited by Albert C. Outler, 1-33. *The Bicentennial Edition of the Works of John Wesley* Vol. 1, edited by Richard P. Heitzenrater, 417–30. Nashville: Abingdon, 1984.

———. *The Nature, Design, and General Rules of the United Societies in London, Bristol, Kingswood and Newcastle Upon Tyne*. London, 1743.

———. "On Visiting the Sick." In *Sermons III*, edited by Albert C. Outler, 71–114. *The Bicentennial Edition of the Works of John Wesley* Vol. 3, edited by Richard P. Heitzenrater, 385–97. Nashville: Abingdon, 1984.

———. "Original Sin." In *Sermons II*, edited by Albert C. Outler, 34–70. *The Bicentennial Edition of the Works of John Wesley* Vol. 2, edited by Richard P. Heitzenrater, 170–85. Nashville: Abingdon, 1984.

———. "The Scripture Way of Salvation." In *Sermons II*, edited by Albert C. Outler, 34–70. *The Bicentennial Edition of the Works of John Wesley*, Vol. 2, edited by Richard P. Heitzenrater, 152–69. Nashville: Abingdon, 1984.

———. "To the Revd. John Burton." In *The Works of John Wesley* Vol. 25: *Letters I* (1721–1739), edited by Frank Baker, 439–42. Oxford: Clarendon, 1980.

———. "The Way to the Kingdom." In *Sermons I*, edited by Albert C. Outler, 1–33. *The Bicentennial Edition of the Works of John Wesley*, Vol. 1, edited by Richard P. Heitzenrater, 217–32. Nashville: Abingdon, 1984.

Wickeri, Philip L. "Mission from the Margins: The Missio Dei in the Crisis of World Christianity." *International Review of Mission* 93 (April 2004) 182–98.

Woolcock, M., and D. Narayan. "Social Capital: Implications for Development Theory, Research, and Policy." *World Bank Research Observer* 15 (August 2000) 225–49.

Wright, N. T. "Imagining the Kingdom: Mission and Theology in Early Christianity." *Scottish Journal of Theology* 65 (2012) 379–401.

Wuthnow, Robert. *Boundless Faith: The Global Outreach of American Churches*. Los Angeles: University of California Press, 2009.

———. "Religious Involvement and Status-Bridging Social Capital." *Journal for the Scientific Study of Religion* 41 (Dec 2002) 669–84.

———. *Sharing the Journey: Support Groups and America's New Quest for Community*. New York: Simon & Schuster, 1994.

Wuthnow, Robert, and Stephen Offutt. "Transnational Religious Connections." *Sociology of Religion* 69 (June 20, 2008) 209–32.

Zahniser, A. H. Mathias. "Ritual Process and Christian Discipling: Contextualizing a Buddhist Rite of Passage." *Missiology: An International Review* 19 (January 1991) 3–19.

Zech, Charles E. "Determinants of the Denominational Mission-Funding Crisis: An Evaluation of the Hypotheses." In *Connectionalism: Ecclesiology, Mission, and Identity*, Vol. 1, 245–64. Nashville: Abingdon, 1997.

Zehner, Edwin. "Short-Term Missions: Toward a More Field-Oriented Model." *Missiology: An International Review* 34 (October 2006) 509–21.

Zürcher, Ernst. "Plants and the Moon-Traditions and Phenomena." *HerbalEGram* 8, no. 4 (April 2011).

Index

Bosch, David, 3–14, 16–32, 39–43, 79, 153, 206

ekklesia, 12–14, 17, 33, 38, 43
Emerging Church Movement, 28, 31, 33–39, 45–46, 179, 209, 211, 215
evangelism, 7, 12
    Methodist missions and, 48, 53, 57–59, 212, 213
    mission and, 63, 154, 208, 212
    short-term missions and, 66–67, 109–10, 149–52, 172, 176, 179
Experience, Economy of, 171–79, 201, 209

Fresh Expressions, 28, 31–33, 38, 40, 45–46

globalization, 68–69, 82, 87, 167, 200, 209, 213–15

Howell, Brian, 10, 66–68, 74–75, 80–82, 86, 172, 181–83, 191–92, 201, 203–04, 206

lay ministry and mission, 27, 30, 46, 48, 59–64, 185–86, 208, 214

Methodist missional theology
    history of, 47–59
    five principles of, 62–64, 153–55, 209–13
missio Dei, 24–28, 32–33, 38–41, 44–46, 60–62, 77–81, 206–07, 210–11, 216–18

money
    fundraising, 99–100
    why not just send the, 140–46

Newbigin, Lesslie, 9–11, 24–26, 43

Operation Mobilization, 66–67, 71

pilgrimage
    communitas, 81, 182, 184, 186–93, 197–98, 204
    liminality, 81, 182, 184–88, 190, 193–96, 198
    re-aggregation, 182–84, 188–90, 196
poverty, 7–10, 26, 54–58, 62, 68, 79, 115, 118–19, 121–22, 124–26, 137, 138–40, 153, 172, 195–96, 204, 207, 216
Priest, Robert, 61, 65, 67, 69–70, 72, 74, 76, 79–82, 86–90, 93, 181–83, 204

relationships
    building of, 71, 76, 94, 103, 106, 109–11, 114–16, 118–20, 141–42, 159–66, 176, 179, 182, 187, 191–92
    with mission hosts, 133–40, 147–49, 153
    with team members, 129–33

short-term mission
    adventure and, 70, 75, 111–12, 168, 171, 174, 196–97, 201

short-term mission *(continued)*
  affirmations of, 71–72
  criticisms of, 69–71
  free days, 196–99
  future of, 216–18
  globalization and, 68, 82, 167, 209,
    214, 216
  goals of, 110–18
  motivation for, 100–18
  origins of, 66–67
  personal faith development and,
    66, 105–6, 117–18, 152, 159, 171,
    182, 195, 203
  theology of, 74–82, 100, 129, 133,
    152–55, 172, 182–84, 204–13,
    215, 217–18
short-term mission teams
  as a small group, 166–67
  cost of, 67, 140–41
  design, 92–94
  hosts, 70–74, 76, 79, 81, 88, 90–94,
    97, 103, 114–22, 125, 127–29,
    133–43, 145–52, 160, 170,
    175–76, 178, 182, 192, 194–95,
    197, 199–201, 206, 211–13, 216

  leaders, 95–96
  purposes of, 148–52
  recruitment, 91–96
  site selection, 96–97
  training of, 97–98

Third Wave of Mission, 66, 68, 214,
  216
tourism, 71, 81–82, 179, 182–84,
  189–90, 196, 198–204, 209
Turner, Victor and Edith, 181–85,
  187–89, 195–98

United Methodist Volunteers in Mission (UMVIM), 61, 150, 210

Van Gennep, Arnold, 183–85, 188, 193

Wesley, John, 12, 47–64, 154, 164–65,
  203, 209, 217
Wuthnow, Robert, 61, 74, 86–87, 92,
  163, 165–70, 204

Youth With A Mission (YWAM), 66

CPSIA information can be obtained
at www.ICGtesting.com
Printed in the USA
FFHW011315300719
53975060-59684FF